First Football Histories: The Arsenal FC story

Mark Rasdall

ISBN: 1537018116
ISBN-13: 978-1537018119

CONTENTS

ACKNOWLEDGMENTS

Text

No primary sources were used in the research for this book, only secondary sources already available in the public domain as listed in the Bibliography. The author would like to thank The Islington Local History Centre in particular for their time and welcoming approach as a user of their newspaper cuttings collections

Images

The publishers have made all reasonable efforts to ensure that only original images available in the public domain and indicated as cleared for free reuse by their copyright holders under Creative Commons Licenses, or paid-for images from image stock libraries, have been used and subsequently adapted to form new illustrations for this publication.

If you have any questions or concerns over these, please do not hesitate to contact the publishers of this book directly.

Original images we have used are listed below with appropriate photo credits:

1. "Greater London administrative area in England" by Rob984 - Derived from English metropolitan and non-metropolitan counties 2010.svg by Nilfanion.. Licensed under CC BY-SA 3.0 via Wikimedia Commons - https://commons.wikimedia.org/wiki/File:Greater_London_administrative_area_in_England.svg#/medi

a/File:Greater_London_administrative_area_in_England.svg

2. "Islington in Greater London" by TUBS - Own work. This vector graphics image was created with Adobe Illustrator.This file was uploaded with Commonist.This vector image includes elements that have been taken or adapted from this: Greater London UK location map 2.svg (by Nilfanion).. Licensed under CC BY-SA 3.0 via Wikimedia Commons - https://commons.wikimedia.org/wiki/File:Islington_in_Greater_London.svg#/media/File:Islington_in_Greater_London.svg

3. Arsenal's squad for the 1888-89 season by Unknown - here, Public Domain, https://commons.wikimedia.org/w/index.php?curid=706788

4. Image of Herbert Chapman by Por Desconhecido - book: Football And All That An Irreverent History, Norman Giller, ISBN 0340835885, Domínio público, https://commons.wikimedia.org/w/index.php?curid=7581127

5. Image of Bertie Mee by Peters, Hans / Anefo - Ajax tegen Go Ahead Eagles 3-0 om KNVB beker ; Jaap van Praag (links) en Bertie MeeDutch National Archives, The Hague, Fotocollectie Algemeen Nederlands Persbureau (ANeFo), 1945-1989,Auteursrechthebbende Nationaal Archief CC-BY-SA, Nummer toegang 2.24.01.05 Bestanddeelnummer 925-3969, CC BY-SA 3.0 nl, https://commons.wikimedia.org/w/index.php?curid=22811961

6. Image of Arsène Wenger by http://www.postproduktie.nl , CC BY 2.5, https://commons.wikimedia.org/w/index.php?curid=2881409

INTRODUCTION

This book is not intended to be a comprehensive history of Arsenal FC from training ground to the trophy cabinet. It is written as a story for the fans – a narrative of characters, scenes and events that provide an introduction to some key moments in the club's history; from their humble origins in Woolwich as 'Dial Square' in 1886 to the first publishing date of this book: August 2016.

It is hoped that, as the flow of history weaves its way in and out of times and places, readers will step off at different points and explore more about football clubs, competitions, countries and players for themselves - as well as the general social and political history providing the backdrop to each tale.

There is from the very beginning a distinctly Scottish theme running throughout this particular story and, in football history, there are numerous reports of club rivalries and key matches between them: some clubs just seem to cross each other's paths more than others.

In the Arsenal story local rivals such as Chelsea, Millwall and, of course, Tottenham Hotspur, feature a lot; but so do teams from the North such as Leeds United, Liverpool, Manchester United and Newcastle United.

In weaving together an overall picture of the history of football, the Arsenal story, therefore, becomes a key part of other clubs' records.

1, 2: Images showing location of London and position of Islington in Greater London boroughs

The club we now know simply as 'Arsenal' grew out of a set of unpromising conditions – geographically, politically and financially – and has always had to fight to survive, as well as being prepared to take risks.

Football history shows that a backbone of steel runs through the club – sheer determination not to be beaten on or off the pitch – in order to challenge the rules that others created.

The team that used to train on the stones and muddy craters of Plumstead Common has become known for its silky skills and stylish football as displayed on the lush pitch at the all-seater Emirates Stadium. However, there are many moments when the club could have lost its way altogether.

Arsenal were never content to just 'fit in.' Their pioneering approach to football is shown far more by the number of entries in the Records/Firsts section of this book than just in the number of trophies won.

Coupled with the insight and imagination of a few key individuals along the way, the club has made the long journey from an armaments factory in South-East London to the entertaining of millions of football fans worldwide: a truly global brand.

From 1919 Arsenal have played continuously in the top tier of English football (known as the 'football pyramid': The Football League First Division until 1992 and the Premier League from 1992/1993. The Records/Firsts and Club Honours sections refer to this structure throughout.

1919

From 1919 Arsenal have played continuously in the top tier of English football

We have amassed a great deal of information during the research for this book and striven for accuracy throughout but if any readers have spotted any errors or wish to ask us any further questions please don't hesitate to contact us on info@thefootballground.com and we'll do our best to help.

Revisions and updates will subsequently be made to reflect aspects of the most recent club history.

For links to latest breaking news and opinion and up-to-date club honours please go to the dedicated Arsenal Football Club page on our website: http://www.thefootballground.com/clubs/uk-ireland/england/arsenal-football-club

RECORDS/FIRSTS

1. At the club's Annual General Meeting (AGM) in 1891, the club decided to turn professional – the first club in the south of England to do so.

2. On 31st May 1893 Arsenal became the first southern team to join The Football League.

3. Arsenal met Chelsea at Stamford Bridge on 9th November 1907; with this being the first competitive match to be played by two London clubs in the First Division it is also the first major 'London derby.'

4. When relegated from the First Division in the 1912/13 season (the only time Arsenal have been relegated) they set a record for the worst ever top tier performance with just three wins - and only one win at home. The overall win 'record' was matched more than 70 years later by Stoke City in the 1984/85 season who played more matches but still only managed three wins all season.

5. From 1919, Arsenal hold the record for the longest, continuous period in the top tier of English football.

6. On January 22nd, 1927 Arsenal's match against Sheffield United at Highbury became the first English league match to be broadcast live on the radio: on the BBC's World Service. The match ended in a 1.1 draw with Arsenal's Charlie Buchan scoring the first goal ever to be heard live on the radio.

7. In 1927 Arsenal played in the first FA Cup Final at Wembley Stadium to be broadcast live on radio (again, by the BBC), with Cardiff City winning the match 1.0.

8. Arsenal's signing of David Jack from Bolton Wanderers in 1928 for £10,890 was the first time in the world that a footballer had been bought for a five-figure sum.

9. Arsenal, alongside Chelsea (at home to Swansea Town), began the 1928/29 season wearing numbers on the backs of their shirts. The Arsenal team played their first league match wearing shirt numbers at Sheffield Wednesday on August 25th, 1928, though they and others may have experimented with them in friendly matches prior to this. The Football League did not officially give permission for shirt numbers to be worn until 1939.

10. On 21st April 1930, Arsenal took part in the highest-scoring league draw in English football's top tier: 6.6 at Leicester City (this aggregate score was equalled in a Second Division game between Charlton Athletic and Middlesbrough on 22nd October 1960 – also finishing 6.6).

11. Arsenal hold the record for the most away goals scored in a season – 60 – in 1930/31

12. Arsenal became the first London (and southern) club to be crowned English League Champions in 1931

13. Arsenal became only the second club – behind Huddersfield Town in 1923/24, 1924/25, 1925/26 - to win three successive league titles: in 1932/33, 1933/34, 1934/35. (Liverpool have subsequently equalled this achievement as have Manchester United (twice))

14. On October 31st, 1932 the local London Underground station at Highbury – Gillespie Road – was renamed 'Arsenal (Highbury Hill).' This was the first and only tube station to be named after a football club. The 'Highbury Hill' suffix disappeared in the early 1960s when the station's name became, simply, Arsenal.

15. An Arsenal player – Ted Drake – holds the record for most goals scored in a top-tier match – 7 - at Aston Villa on 14th December 1935.

16. On 16th September 1937, an exhibition match between Arsenal's first team and the reserves became the first football match to be televised live on BBC TV, one year after the first television broadcast from Alexandra Palace, just over three miles from Highbury.

17. Arsenal took part in a match with Manchester United on 17th January 1948 where the Football League's highest ever attendance for a league match was recorded: 83,260. The match was played at Maine Road (home of Manchester City) because United's ground at Old

Trafford had been damaged in WWII and would not see football action again until 1949.

18. On January 12th, 1956 Arsenal won a Third Round FA Cup Replay 2.1 at Bedford Town. This was the first match to be covered for independent television by ITV which had been founded less than four months earlier

19. On 22nd August 1964, the highlights of the match between Liverpool and Arsenal at Anfield were the first to be featured on BBC 2's new 'Match of the Day' television programme. Arsenal lost 3.2.

20. In 1970/71 Arsenal became only the second team – after near neighbours, Tottenham Hotspur, in 1960/61 - in the Twentieth Century to do the League and Cup 'Double'

21. Arsenal became the first team to win the Football League Cup and FA Cup in the same season: 1993.

22. Arsenal hold the record for the highest number of consecutive games in which they have scored – 55 – between May 2001 and November 2002, thus including the entire 2001-02 season when they scored in every match.

23. Arsenal hold the record for the most consecutive league wins in the top tier – 14 – between February 2002 and August 2002.

24. Arsenal became the first team to achieve the feat of appearing in three consecutive FA Cup Finals twice: 1978,1979,1980, and 2001, 2002, 2003

25. Arsenal achieved the record for the most consecutive away games unbeaten – 27 – from April 2003 until September 2004

26. Arsenal went a record 49 consecutive league games unbeaten in English football's top tier, from May 2003 to October 2004.

27. Arsenal became only the second team in English football league history (after Preston North End in the inaugural league programme of 1888/89) to remain unbeaten throughout an entire season in the top tier - in 2003/04. That team, like Preston's before it, will be forever known as 'The Invincibles.'

28. Arsenal became the first team to win the FA Cup Final on penalties when they beat Manchester United 5.4 at the Millennium Stadium in May 2005.

29. Arsenal are the first English team to beat Real Madrid at Santiago Bernabeu, Bayern Munich at Allianz Arena, Borussia Dortmund at the Westfalenstadion, AC Milan and Inter Milan at San Siro and Juventus at Stadio Communale.

30. In facing Barcelona in the UEFA Champions League Final of 2006, Arsenal became the first London team to reach the Final.

31. Arsenal became the first club in European football history to field a team containing 11 different nationalities during the same Champions League game – a 2.1 win over Hamburg on 13th September 2006.

32. On 31st January 2010 Arsenal played Manchester United at the Emirates in the first match to be screened live

by Sky Sports in 3D format.

33. Arsenal hold the record for most consecutive away wins by a top tier club in all competitions - 12 – between March 2013 and October 2013.

34. Arsenal have won more league championship titles (First Division and Premier League combined) than any other London club.

35. Arsenal have won the FA Cup more times than any other club: 13.

LOCAL HISTORY

Arsenal Football Club was formed in Woolwich in South-East London but the club moved across the River Thames to Highbury in Islington in 1913.

93 years later they moved again: this time just 500 yards down the road to Ashburton Road in the Holloway district and still within the London Borough of Islington.

The area we now call the London Borough of Islington was only formed in 1965 but its origins go back much further than that.

In Anglo-Saxon times it was known as Giseldone and then Gislandune. formed from 'Gisla' – an old Saxon name – and 'dun' which means hill and so: Gisla's Hill.

Did you know?

Islington is one of the oldest parts of London, being first mentioned in Anglo-Saxon times

By the time it was recorded in the Domesday Book after William the Conqueror came to the English throne, its name had become Isendone and eventually, it became known as Islington.

One early observer described Islington as a savage forest ***"full of the lairs of wild beasts***" where bears and wild bulls roamed.

The small hamlet grew into a medieval village as drovers – on their way to Smithfield meat market in the City of London - sheltered their cattle there overnight while lodging in the numerous pubs that had been built along the High Street and Upper Street.

Did you know?

The King's Head Theatre and Pub was the first pub theatre to be founded in England and has existed since at least the time of the famous playwright William Shakespeare

Islington became an area known for its herds of dairy cattle which supplied much of London's butter, cream and milk but all of this began to change as a result of the Industrial Revolution which began in the middle of the eighteenth century.

Islington village grew quickly and, with the coming of the railways in the following century, much of the farming and grazing land was lost forever.

New factories and warehouses were built on a large scale. For those who had grown rich from this industrial development, there were elegant new houses, built around tree-lined squares. But many ordinary Islington residents who worked in the new factories came home to often squalid, overcrowded housing conditions in endless rows of 'back to back' streets.

Rebuilding after both World Wars and transport improvements – especially London Underground's new Victoria Line in 1968 – meant that Islington became fashionable again as a place to live in the late twentieth century. For those with money, Georgian terraces were restored and disused warehouses converted into luxury flats and creative studios.

Despite Islington being the third smallest London Borough, covering an area of just over six square miles, it is estimated that it now has a multicultural population of over 200,000.

Did you know?

The London Underground station at Angel – which, at one end of Upper Street once marked the boundary of the original Islington village – has the longest escalators on the London Underground network and third longest in Western Europe (behind stations in Stockholm and Helsinki)

Residents of Islington have been at the heart of wider political change over the years. Sir Walter Raleigh and Sir Francis Bacon lived here at one time, as did Lenin.

In 1994 a famous meeting between former British Prime Ministers Tony Blair and Gordon Brown was supposed to have taken place at the now defunct Granita restaurant in Upper Street.

The borough has an established tradition of entertainment too, pretty much from the early days of the King's Head onwards.

By the 19th century and especially around Islington Green, there were many theatres and music halls and one of London's if not the world's most famous dance venues – Sadler's Wells – still exists on Roseberry Avenue in the Clerkenwell district of Islington.

Did you know?

The name Sadler's Wells originates from Mr Sadler, who owned the land, and also the finding of springs – originally discovered by monks – who thought that the well water had medicinal properties

Arsenal Football Club attempted to add a new form of entertainment for the masses in Islington when it sought to move to Highbury in 1913, 27 years after the club was founded in very different circumstances and in a quite different part of London.

Famous Locals

The following are a selection of other famous people who have either lived, worked or were born in Islington, confirming its place in entertainment history:

- Douglas Adams, writer
- Adewale Akinnuoye-Agbaje, actor
- Lily Allen, singer
- Tash Aw, writer
- Nina Bawden, writer
- John Betjeman, poet laureate
- Jim Broadbent, actor
- Jonny Buckland, musician
- Alexandra Burke, singer
- Jimmy Carr, comedian
- Charlie Chaplin, actor
- Phil Daniels, actor
- Alan Davies, actor
- Dido, singer
- Pete Doherty, musician
- Colin Firth, actor
- Kate Greenaway, writer and illustrator
- Tony Hadley, singer
- Alfred Hitchcock, film director
- William Hogarth, artist
- Nick Hornby, writer (author of 'Fever Pitch' about being an Arsenal fan)
- Yusuf Islam (formerly Cat Stevens), musician
- Damian Lewis, actor
- Bob Hoskins, actor
- Edward Lear, writer and poet
- Heath Ledger, actor

- Leona Lewis, singer
- James McAvoy, actor
- Scott Mills, radio DJ
- Carey Mulligan, actress
- George Orwell, writer
- Stephen Poliakoff, playwright
- Jon Snow, television presenter
- Nicky Spesh, rapper
- Emma Watson, actor
- Charlie Watts, musician
- Evelyn Waugh, writer
- Samuel West, actor
- Kate Winslet, actress

ORIGINS

The football club we know as Arsenal began life within an armaments factory in the town of Woolwich, on the south bank of the River Thames in South-East London, now part of the London Borough of Greenwich. It is from here that the football club gets its name, its nickname – 'The Gunners' - and the cannon which is still part of the club's logo.

Woolwich Arsenal (on the outskirts of London but then, technically, in the county of Kent) was a collection of military weapons (including, eventually, torpedoes) factories, explosives testing areas and warehouses which were built for the British Armed Forces from 1671 onwards.

The main storehouse was used for gunpowder which could be quickly loaded onto ships moored on the nearby river. The manufacture of cannon and gun carriages began mainly out of the need for protection from the Dutch during the Anglo-Dutch wars of that period.

These armouries were known collectively as 'The Warren' as they were built on land originally used as a domestic warren - where rabbits were raised for meat – in the grounds of a large Tudor manor house: Tower Place.

Renamed 'Royal Arsenal' by King George III in 1805, it served the Army through many other overseas campaigns - including the Crimean War, Boer War and both World Wars - until it finally closed in 1994. At its busiest point, during World War I, it employed almost 80,000 people.

1805

Battle of Trafalgar took place in which Admiral Nelson led the Royal Navy to victory over combined French and Spanish fleets

At the beginning of our Arsenal story, an arms race was in progress as the military plans of countries on the other side of the English Channel were being viewed with suspicion by the British. France and Germany had been at war as recently as 1870 and the seeds of the European Wars which would become World Wars in the next century were being sown.

Britain needed to keep up with its potential enemies which meant that the armaments factory in Woolwich was busier than ever

Dial Square (1886)

When Queen Victoria had come to the throne in 1837 England was easily the richest country in the world with incomes twice as high as in France and some three times bigger than in Germany.

The Great Exhibition in Hyde Park in London in 1851 was held to illustrate Britain's superiority in the industrial world.

The world's first underground railway – The Metropolitan Line – opened 12 years later, in 1863, running from Paddington in West London to Farringdon in the east of the city.

1863

World's first underground railway opened in London

However, by the 1880s other countries' economies such as the USA's were beginning to catch up.

The British Empire was still expanding though and, at its peak, would control around one-quarter of the world's territories - giving rise to the well-known assertion that 'the sun never sets on the British empire' because at that time, somewhere on earth, it would be daytime in a British colony.

This global expansion had brought great wealth through overseas trade, much of it passing through new London docks such as Millwall, just across the river from Woolwich.

The Victorian era had produced industrialists, inventors and engineers who had prospered greatly as a result of continued industrialisation, while hundreds of thousands of men working in factories, at the coal faces and on the new railway tracks faced great hardship at work and in the dreadful housing conditions – as in Islington – they had to endure at home.

Shifts in the munitions factory at Woolwich were long and hard and the work was often dangerous. To try to relieve some of the strain men were encouraged to take up some kind of recreation or sport, and football offered an opportunity to get them outside to enjoy some fresh air and to play the game with their mates.

In 1885, at the age of 22, David Danskin, a mechanical engineer from the tough town of Burntisland in Fife, Scotland, had turned his back on the Ravenscraig shipyard where most of his friends worked and made the journey south to Woolwich instead. It is possible that he was forced out of his tiny home as his parents needed room for his sisters.

At around the same time another young man – John 'Jack' Humble – had left a poverty-stricken background in Durham in the north east of England and allegedly walked, with his brother Arthur, the 400 miles to Woolwich where he soon met up with Danskin.

1885

David Danskin and Jack Humble arrive in Woolwich

With friends Elijah Watkins and Richard Pearce, they worked in an area towards the centre of the factory, known as Dial Square - named after the 1764 sundial placed over its entrance – and quickly got together with other football-loving workers – of which there were many, often with football roots from Scotland.

In October 1886 Danskin organised a collection around the workshop to raise money to buy a football which they could kick around in their lunch breaks. Fifteen men allegedly paid sixpence each and Danskin contributed three shillings of his own money – significant amounts at the time.

Another worker named Joseph Smith is alleged to have gone on to ask the Woolwich Arsenal cricket team early in 1886 whether part of their pitch could be used by a football team called 'Woolwich Union' but was politely refused.

Eight years earlier a football club had been formed in Blackburn, Lancashire: Blackburn Olympic.

This club was started by workers from local factories and mills and, though they were in existence for barely ten years, became the first working class team and the first from the north of England to win the FA Cup, in 1883. Each of the previous Finals had been won by wealthy amateur teams.

Olympic's experience helped to persuade the Football Association (FA) to accept professionalism in 1885 which meant that men could now earn money from playing football, but the first professional league was still three years away.

1885

The Football Association accepted professionalism in football

Women also played football at the time and this became especially popular during the First World War which would break out some thirty years later.

With so many men away fighting at the Front, women were needed to work in factories to keep both the country's industrial output flowing but also to supply much-needed armaments for the war effort.

In remarkably similar fashion to their fellow workers just ten miles away in Blackburn, but particularly to the workers in Dial Square in Woolwich, a group of working-class women joined the Dick, Kerr & Co armaments factory in Preston, Lancashire to help produce ammunition for the war.

They too were persuaded to take up sport to boost morale and formed a works football team which played (and usually beat) other workers – mostly men – in lunch and tea breaks.

Becoming known as Dick, Kerr's Ladies F.C. they quickly became the most successful women's team of the period, playing a series of charity matches around the country to raise money for injured servicemen during and after the war.

However, women's football was frowned upon by The FA who eventually banned it in 1921 from being played on their members' grounds as it was viewed as ***"distasteful"*** and ***"ought not to be encouraged."***

The FA argued that women were not physically equipped to play football, but it may have been that they feared the popularity of women's football would affect the growth of the men's game.

The ban stood for 50 years and was only lifted in 1971, after which women's football could flourish once more.

Did you know?

Three classic novels were published in 1886:

'The Death of Ivan Ilyich' – Leo Tolstoy
'Kidnapped' – Robert Louis Stevenson
'The Mayor of Casterbridge' – Thomas Hardy

Back in Woolwich, Blackburn Olympic's experience must have been known about and inspired the workers at the Woolwich factory and, later that year, after considerable pressure by Humble and Danskin in particular, the first Arsenal team was formed and took its name from their workplace: Dial Square

Arsenal's first recorded (but unreported) match as Dial Square came on December 11th, 1886: a friendly against a team called

'Eastern Wanderers' across the River Thames on a swampy piece of scrap land in Millwall on the western side of the Isle of Dogs.

December 11, 1886

Arsenal's first recorded match as Dial Square

Wanderers had most likely been formed from one of the Engineering factories nearby. The only witness to this match was the Secretary of Dial Square, Elijah Watkins. Because the players had to bring their own kit they played in an assortment of different coloured shirts, trousers and boots with few having shin guards.

There were no cross bars or pitch markings and the ball had to be retrieved regularly from a stinking, open sewer nearby. History stories tell us that Dial Square won the match 6.0 and 'The Reds' or 'Woolwich Reds' were on their way.

PRE-WORLD WAR I (UP UNTIL 1914)

Royal Arsenal (1887-1893)

A few days after their first match, and possibly on Christmas Day, 1886, David Danskin called a meeting of their 15 players in the Royal Oak pub next to Woolwich Arsenal station.

Unhappy with the Dial Square name because they thought that nobody outside of Woolwich would ever have heard of it, the players decided to change it to 'Royal Arsenal.'

1886

Club's name changed to Royal Arsenal

This was done partly because of the name of the pub and area that they were drinking in - but also because the name of their factory had become famous all over the world. The club's original crest included three cannons to reflect their origins.

Another significant event in Arsenal's early history also took place at this time. Fred Beardsley, along with team-mates Joseph "Morris" Bates and Bill Parr, had all previously played for Nottingham Forest.

A goalkeeper, Beardsley wore his old Forest shirt which was so admired that he volunteered to ask his old club if they would donate a set of their dark red – 'redcurrant' - strips to his new team, which they promptly did (as well as another ball).

The team's first shirts were thus dark red with long sleeves and including a collar and three buttons on the front. Their shorts were white and knee length and the kit was finished off by woollen socks with blue and white hoops.

The goalkeeper's shirt was a hand-knitted cream polo neck jumper. In 1906 the President of Sparta Prague in Czechoslovakia (now the Czech Republic), Dr Petřík, visited Woolwich and was so impressed with the dark red jerseys that he took a set home with him: that team still wears deep red today.

Uninvited and unloved

Danskin and his fellow countrymen from Scotland who had made similarly long journeys south in search of work not only faced opposition from other workers within the factory, who planned to form their own football teams, but were viewed with suspicion by many in South-East England.

The working classes were generally seen by some as not just violent and largely 'uneducated' but also politically dangerous.

Karl Marx, the German philosopher who jointly wrote *The Communist Manifesto* had died only three years earlier and his revolutionary theories on workers rising up to take control of their own lives were feared in many parts of England – including in the quiet countryside towns and villages of Kent.

3: Early picture of the Arsenal squad 1888-89 (David Danskin is seated on the right-hand side of the bench; Fred Beardsley is standing at the back with his arms folded)

Others who had known only hardship all their lives were more easily persuaded. Jack Humble, for example, mixed with those who campaigned for better working, social and housing conditions which were being written about by social reformers such as Charles Dickens.

The Labour Party came into being at the turn of the century, formed out of protests such as these and encouraged by the trade unions which fought for more jobs and better working conditions up and down the country.

27 February 1900

The Labour Party was formed out of the trade union movement and late nineteenth-century socialist parties

Because of fears of the war in Europe, the country as a whole was on high alert for any suspicious activities and intentions of 'foreigners' but most local people in those days had barely travelled outside of Kent. Scottish accents were often mistaken for other, foreign, tongues and a number of instances of Scotsmen being mistaken for French spies and beaten up were reported at the time.

This new Arsenal team was packed with what some described as 'foreign mercenaries' – a theme that would come back to haunt English football in the Modern Era, just over a hundred years later.

Arsenal player and manager George Graham said then:

> *"It doesn't bother me that we're not well-liked. It's part of our history."*

That view was just as true in the 1880s and only added resolve to the players of Royal Arsenal who were intent on playing football in the South of England.

Association football was becoming more and more popular in the Midlands and North of England where it had begun but, though established public schools had been largely responsible for shaping and writing down the codes and rules of the game, and the FA had been formed around a standard version of them, it hadn't yet reached a large fanbase in the South and was consequently looked down on by the traditional, gentleman followers of Kent county cricket and rugby.

1850

Parliament passed the Factory Act which meant that all work now had to stop by 2.00 on a Saturday afternoon

Finally, Parliament had passed the Factory Act in 1850 which meant that all work had to stop by two o'clock on a Saturday afternoon, so allowing workers to have more time with their families and, in this case, for the Royal Arsenal team to play football on Saturdays and draw 'unwelcome crowds' to the county to watch them.

In short, late Victorian England was a country struggling to stay ahead of the rest of the world economically, politically and militarily through the strength of its armed forces. At home, it was a society of 'haves' and 'have nots,' with increased protests being made about the inequalities of wealth, living and working conditions and a growing determination to change things.

Whereas today we often hear of rich businessmen – many of them from overseas – buying football clubs and pouring money into new players and improved stadiums, the Arsenal club had no such start in life.

David Danskin, Jack Humble and their teammates came from poor, unpromising backgrounds and, not only that, they were seen as part of an unwelcome social revolution: uninvited and unloved by many.

Early days

Back in the 1880's Royal Arsenal played very much up to the image that their enemies had labelled them with: hard, aggressive young men from Scotland, fused with tough factory workers around a nucleus of former club players. The men from Forest were especially uncompromising. They had been used to hard training regimes as well as superior football tactics.

Morris Bates, a full-back, was known as the 'iron-headed man' because he was capable of heading a football (which weighed considerably more than they do now, especially when the leather became wet) half the length of the football pitch. Bates died of tuberculosis at the (even in those days) relatively young age of 41.

Programme Notes:

Morris Bates was known as the 'iron-headed man'

The whole team wore factory boots which had strips of iron fixed to the bottom. Taking out their frustrations from working twelve-hour shifts or more in the factory, they were prepared to effectively maim their opponents in order to win football matches.

Royal Arsenal - now nicknamed 'The Royals' as they were the only club in England ever to have the prefix 'Royal' - also had the advantage of playing their 'home' games on Plumstead Common, using the nearby Star Inn as a changing room.

This area of the Common not only had lots of stones on the surface that could cut players' legs really badly but had once been used for pig breeding. It was also used also for military exercises by the Royal Horse Artillery whose horses churned up great patches of mud and also left ruts and craters in the ground which could easily lead to footballers' ankles being twisted or broken.

Royal Arsenal played their first official match on the Common on 8th January 1887 – the year of Queen Victoria's Golden Jubilee, celebrating 50 years on the throne.

8 January 1887

Royal Arsenal played their first official match, beating Erith 6.1

The team beat Erith 6.1 and, in their first official season – 1886-87 – went on to win seven out of their ten home games, all of them 'friendlies.'

Their first ever defeat came in an away match at Millwall Rovers on 5th February 1887, a match they lost 4.0.

In spite of this success they remained largely shunned or even hated, not just by the landed gentry or middle classes of Kent but by every team that had to travel to play them on what was effectively a battlefield supplied by the Royal Arsenal.

In September 1887, as they began their second season, the club rented the Sportsman Ground on the Plumstead Marshes. Named after the local Sportsman pub (which is now a prison) it too was a former pig farm – with plenty of mud to prove it.

Programme Notes:

In September 1887 the club rented the Sportsman Ground in Plumstead

They also played Tottenham Hotspur for the first time just two months later but across the river on the Tottenham Marshes (now part of Lee Valley Park).

Their first match in what was to become one of football's great rivalries took place on 19th November 1887.

19 November 1887

Arsenal's first match against Tottenham Hotspur

Tottenham Hotspur had been established five years earlier, in 1882, in very different circumstances to those of the workers in Dial Square. They were formed by middle-class schoolboys as 'The Hotspur Football Club' supposedly because two of the pupils were fascinated by English Knight, Sir Henry Percy – who was also known as Harry Hotspur.

The Percy family estate also covered much of the Tottenham area as we now know it.

Spurs initially played on the marshes though – just like Dial Square and then Royal Arsenal – where fights would often break out between clubs wanting to use the best available public pitches.

This first match between the clubs was a friendly! The match finished 2.1 to Tottenham, although it finished 15 minutes early due to the Arsenal team getting lost on the way to the ground and therefore the light deteriorating before the match could be completed.

So, even their first football encounter was a controversial one. They would play seven more friendly matches in the eight years between 1888 and 1896 with Arsenal winning three of them and Tottenham victorious in four.

During the 1890's Tottenham Hotspur built a reputation for stylish football which was in direct contrast to the tougher, rougher approach of Arsenal teams with their fans labelling Tottenham 'Totts' and 'Marsh Dwellers' and Tottenham's own fans frequently hurling mud at them. Arsenal were also building a reputation back then of being uncompromising and increasingly hard to beat

In 1898, Spurs moved to Asplins Farm which stood next to the railway line at Northumberland Park. After another match against Arsenal one year later they had to move again – to White Hart Lane. The game was attended by some 14,000 fans and crowd chaos followed as they hadn't anticipated and nor could they cope with such huge football crowds.

The Royal Arsenal team played its home games at the Sportsman Ground for some six months before it flooded and they moved again in 1888 to another field nearby: The Manor Field.

Programme Notes:

In 1888 Royal Arsenal moved to the Manor Field

It was soon renamed the Manor Ground (almost certainly to make it sound more impressive or even more intimidating to visiting teams and their fans) where they stayed until the end of the 1889-90 season.

The pitch here was little better than at the Sportsman Ground and a sewer ran along its southern boundary. This was 'sewer bank' - the Southern Outfall Sewer Pipe - which was the main disposal point for liquid waste from most of South London.

It also cost the club in terms of match income as some people could watch for free from this high vantage point; it being effectively a massive covered earth mound. However, crowds were beginning to grow and, as a result, the pubs where team members originally changed – the Royal Oak still and also the Railway Tavern – were getting busier so they changed in a disused railway hut instead.

There was no terracing in place and only a rope separated supporters from the pitch, apart from those who had similarly climbed on to wagons borrowed from the nearby Army bases in order to see better what was happening during matches.

There was often a thick layer of mist around the Manor Ground which came from a nearby engineering company and this accompanied the rancid smell that greeted visitors to Royal Arsenal's new home ground

The sewer was not the only connection with that first match played by Dial Square just under two years previously.

30 March 1888

Royal Arsenal's first match at the Manor Ground – against Millwall Rovers

The opposition in their first match at the Manor Ground on 30th March 1888 was against Millwall Rovers – a team formed one year before Dial Square by workers at the local J.T. Morton canning and preserve factory

They were also known as Millwall Dockers due to their local fan base and would change their name to Millwall Athletic the following year.

Did you know?

Murderer "Jack the Ripper's" first victim was discovered in London on 31st August 1888

Royal Arsenal won this match 3.0 having lost for the first time in their brief history to the same opposition just over a year before.

First cup successes

As football had not yet really taken off in the South of England no leagues had yet been formed so Royal Arsenal continued to play only friendly matches but, in that one and only season at the Sportsman Ground they had taken part in their first cup competition – the London Senior Cup (or just 'The London Cup') – losing 4.0 early on to Barnes in the Second Round. In 1888-89, at their new ground, they got all the way to the Semi-final which they lost to the eventual winners Clapton at their Spotted Dog Ground.

The match was also significant in that David Danskin had been selected as the goalkeeper as he had been struggling with a knee injury. It proved to be his final match for the club. Arsenal lost the match 2-0, but it was a major collective step forward.

19 January 1889

David Danskin played his last match for Royal Arsenal

In that same season, they competed in the Kent Senior Cup but were expelled from the competition by the Kent Football Association after a Third Round tie at Gravesend.

As in Royal Arsenal's first friendly match away at Tottenham in 1887, Gravesend had turned up late for the match which finished 3.3 at the end of normal time. By now the temperature was falling and the light was fading so Royal Arsenal refused to play extra-time for fear of injury to their players, which was somewhat ironic given the toughness and near brutality generally shown on the pitch by the Arsenal team.

Danskin and Humble had their own network of contacts in other factories up and down the country. Effectively acting as spies, if these 'talent spotters' sent good reports on players they had seen, jobs were found for them in the Woolwich Arsenal purely so that could become part of the football team.

Royal Arsenal also recruited some quality players with league experience to play alongside the hard men of defence and midfield.

Programme Notes:

Some early Royal Arsenal recruits:

- **Richard Horsington**
- **Humphrey Barbour**
- **James Charteris**

Richard Horsington joined from Swindon Town and Humphrey Barbour – who had played for Airdrie in the Scottish League – scored 59 goals in his 71 matches for the club.

James Charteris from Kirkcaldy, just down the road from Danskin's birthplace and equally as tough and argumentative, scored 25 goals in 29 matches and also scored seven goals on two separate occasions for the new reserves team in the 1889-90 season.

Like Morris Bates, Charteris died young – from a suspected heart attack – at just 28 years old and in as impoverished and unpromising circumstances as during his childhood.

It was the Royal Arsenal reserves that won the club its first trophy which came on 1st March 1890 in the Kent Junior Cup Final against Chatham Excelsior.

Held at 'The Bat and Ball Ground' in Gravesend - a cricket ground whose owners allowed football to be played there during the winter months – the reserves won 6.0 with centre-forward Kime getting a hat-trick. Records are sketchy but it might also have been Kime's first match for the club.

The 1889-90 season was very much a breakthrough season for the senior team too.

Although they finally got to the Final of the London Senior Cup which they lost 1.0 to the Old Westminsters team, they did beat Thanet 3.0 to win the Kent Senior Cup.

They also won the London Charity Cup – organised by the London branch of the Football Association – beating Old Westminster's 3.1 in the Final on 5th March 1890 (and so avenging their defeat in that season's London Senior Cup).

Programme Notes:

In 1889-90 Royal Arsenal won a hat-trick of cups:

1. Kent Junior Cup
2. Kent Senior Cup
3. London Charity Cup

FA Cup

This was also the first season in which Royal Arsenal entered the FA Cup. Their first match in the competition was in the first qualifying round (equivalent to the Third Round today) and took place on 5th October 1889 against Lyndhurst.

There is some confusion over whether Lyndhurst was in Surrey at the time – some records list them as 'Champions of Surrey' – or Hampshire.

5 October 1889

Arsenal played their first FA Cup match, beating Lyndhurst 11.0

There is no doubt though that Royal Arsenal won their first ever FA Cup tie 11.0 with Humphrey Barbour and outside-left William Scott both scoring hat-tricks. It is thought that around 2,500 fans watched the match.

The club drew 2.2 away at Norwich Thorpe in the next round but there was to be no replay back at the Manor Ground in Plumstead as Thorpe apparently could not afford the travel fare.

So, Royal Arsenal progressed to the next round against a team from Leyton in Essex (now part of the East London Borough of Waltham Forest) called Crusaders. Crusaders had been one of the founder members of the FA in 1863 but it is thought that they did not survive beyond the 1890's.

Arsenal beat them 5.2, after extra time, with Hope Ramsay Robertson scoring twice for the Royals in front of a crowd almost double that of their first FA Cup match: 4,500.

They were not so lucky in the next round – the fourth qualifying round. Crowd numbers at the Manor Ground had increased again, to 6,000 – but the team lost 5.1 to fellow amateur team Swifts from Slough.

Swifts was a popular part of football clubs' names in those days (like 'United' or 'Rovers' today) and there were powerful Swifts teams in the North and Midlands such as Burton Swifts, Rotherham Swifts and Walsall Town Swifts.

The Swifts club that beat Royal Arsenal had got all the way to the Semi-final of the FA Cup on no less than three occasions already and eight of their players had been capped by the England national team. So, to lose to such a side was no disgrace and had also proved that a good FA cup run – as today – could swell match attendances.

In September 1890 - after their various cup successes and in order to accommodate regular supporters who, boosted by those same cup runs, now numbered around a thousand for each home match - the club moved to the Invicta Ground, named after the Kent county motto (Invicta means undefeated or unconquered).

Programme Notes:

In September 1890 Royal Arsenal moved to the Invicta Ground

They signed a lease with its owner - George Weaver, landlord of the local Green Man public house (where some of the players would change on match days) – to rent the ground for three years.

Situated on the south side of Plumstead High Street with proper concrete terracing and a corrugated iron stand as well as changing rooms, it also had a capacity of 12,000 which was practically reached on 30th March 1891 when the Heart of Midlothian team came down from Edinburgh for a friendly match. Hearts were Scottish Cup holders at the time and easily beat the Arsenal team 5.1.

Did you know?

In July 1890 Artist Vincent Van Gogh shot himself and died in France, aged just 37

In their first season at the Invicta Ground, as London Charity Cup holders, the club again took part in that competition and reached the Semi-finals where they were knocked out by Old Carthusians (but only after two replays).

The team did finally win the London Senior Cup that season though, beating St Bartholomew's Hospital 6.0 in the Final on

March 7th, 1891 at Kennington Oval in front of a crowd of 6,000. The Kentish Independent reported on the team being driven home:

in *"open carriages"* amid much *"shouting and singing."*

So, by 1891 significant progress had been made by Royal Arsenal as they won a treble of both Kent Cups and the London Charity Cup in 1889-90 and then the London Senior Cup in 1890-91.

In spite of these breakthrough successes, Royal Arsenal continued to be largely unloved by the football world outside of Woolwich. Long and tiring journeys from football strongholds in the North and Midlands undoubtedly contributed to this view.

The Liverpool Tribune described Royal Arsenal as:

"the team that played at the end of the earth"

and the Newcastle Echo would later describe a visit to Woolwich as:

"the annual visit to hell."

Their issues weren't just the long journeys to London itself but the fact that it still took a further forty minutes on packed steam trains from Cannon Street station in central London to Woolwich, out in what was effectively the geographical wilderness of North Kent.

The sports journalist, George Allison, who reported on Arsenal matches and became the editor of its match-day programme, added that:

"fans...could travel on the South Eastern and Chatham Railway from London Bridge, Cannon Street or Charing Cross. The trains stopped at every station. There were the same halts on the return journey with the added

difficulty that no-one knew where the trains were going."

Allison's continued association with the club would lead to him eventually becoming its second-longest serving manager.

Royal Arsenal's continued physical and sometimes ugly approach to the game, watched by factory workers and tough army squaddies who were often reported for rudeness and swearing, also helped to form this perception.

On 15th January 1891 the Derby Post, under the headline, 'Carnage in Kentish Fields', reported a local fan's view:

> *"A journey to the molten interior of the earth's core would be rather more pleasant and comfortable an experience than our forthcoming visit to the Royal Arsenal."*

Professionalism

In fact, it was in an FA Cup First Round match against Derby County – the first team from the Football League the team had ever faced - two days later on 17th January 1891 when post-match events were alleged to have taken place leading to Royal Arsenal showing once again that were unprepared to accept either defeat or football's status quo.

17 January 1891

Royal Arsenal played Derby County in the FA Cup: the first team from the Football League they had ever faced

They did lose the match at the Invicta Ground to Derby, 2.1, in front of 8,000 fans but, by all accounts, the team played one of its best matches to date and the score was 1.1 with just a few minutes to go and a replay looking likely until County got a late winner.

After the match, it is alleged that three of the Arsenal players – possibly including Peter Connolly – were offered professional contracts by Derby captain and acting secretary-manager, John Goodall.

Goodall, also a Scot, had previously played as centre-forward for Preston North End and England. He had been part of the Preston team that remained undefeated in the first season of the Football League in 1888-89, also winning the FA Cup, and becoming known as "The Invincibles."

By the time he played in the Derby team at Plumstead he was playing as a wing-half and would have had plenty of time to assess the quality as well as the undying spirit of the Arsenal players. If Connolly was approached, it didn't work as he continued in his job at Woolwich Arsenal and playing for the Royal Arsenal team on an amateur basis.

However, even the suspicion of such an approach (we would call it 'tapping up' players today) was a major concern to the Royal Arsenal club. In truth, professionalism had been a long time coming – to the game as well as this club.

As we have seen, the FA lifted its ban on players being paid in 1885, but even then only under 'certain restrictions' that specified that players had to have been born or had lived for a minimum of two years within a six-mile radius of their home ground.

The reality was that they only agreed to do this for fear of a breakaway British Football Association being formed and led by northern industrial teams such as Blackburn Olympic, Goodall's Preston North End and Newton Heath (later to become Manchester United) which had actually been paying their players small sums of money for years.

It attracted a label of 'shamateurism' as was neither really one thing nor the other, though the pressure for real change, endorsed by the FA, was growing. Indeed, the Preston chairman and manager – Major William Sudell – was a key supporter of professionalism, arguing that its introduction was inevitable and to continue to oppose it was like trying to stop the North American waterfall, Niagara, ***"with a three-legged stool."***

Arsenal's recent progress in cup competitions had led to a label of 'Champions of the South' being attached to them which in turn drew attention to their players from further afield.

Programme Notes:

Thanks to their recent progress in cup competitions, Royal Arsenal had been given the nickname: 'Champions of the South'

As we found earlier, the club had no rich benefactors and it was understandable that their players might begin to seek a decent wage for playing football. Fears of their best players being approached must have been very real and the Derby incident only served to highlight this. How much better might it be if Arsenal were the only professional club in the region and thus attract the best amateur players itself?

It was also the case that, though they had indeed progressed as a football club, it could be plainly seen that they were still behind top clubs of the day such as Swifts and Derby County when drawn against them in the FA Cup and having the opportunity of competing on the national stage.

David Danskin was less convinced by the argument and this turn of events may have hastened his move away from the club as he failed to gain re-election to the Arsenal Committee the following year. He went on to run a bicycle shop.

Jack Humble – also a member of the Committee - was desperate to preserve the club that he had helped to create and so embraced the idea of the club turning professional. However, he was equally determined to preserve its working-class roots.

Humble suggested that Royal Arsenal become a working man's collective and, further:

> *"The club has been carried on by working men and it is my ambition to see it carried on by them..."*

The Committee accepted this and, at an Extraordinary General Meeting (EGM) on 2nd May 1891 voted by 250 votes to 10 to turn professional - the first football team in the south of England to do so.

2 May 1891

The Committee of Royal Arsenal voted by 250 votes to 10 to turn professional

The club knew that the cup competitions it had previously played in and organised by the London or Kent Football Associations were only open to amateur teams and so resigned from both Associations.

Humble's role in this move was key and many of the early Arsenal documents that we football historians can work with today are thanks to him, as he later became the club's unofficial historian.

As with Elijah Watkins's account of that first match in 1886, much of this early Arsenal history in the late Victorian Age was based on personal memory that could become less accurate as time passed.

In the media world of the twenty-first century, where 'news' is reported, shared and more or less instantly verified on social media by many other sources, it is hard to imagine this being the case.

Jack Humble's involvement in preserving written documents was especially important in Royal Arsenal's case as many early records and club minutes were later destroyed by the club's centre-half Richard Price while drunk in the Lord Raglan pub.

This momentous decision by Royal Arsenal to turn professional caused shock – even outrage – in football circles. At its own special meeting on 5th June 1891 the London Football Association proposed to ban any of its members from playing against professional sides (apart from in FA Cup ties) and specifically any professional clubs based in the south of England.

If this was an attempt at scaremongering it didn't work as the proposal was defeated by 76 votes to 67. Interestingly the Woolwich Gazette reported London FA founder N.L Jackson's views during the debate when he asked if it was right that:

"professionals should govern a game of so much national importance (when they) had not had the advantages of the earlier education which amateurs had."

In short, he wanted the London members – and probably football in general – to remain under the control of the same gentleman amateurs that had been so horrified by the rise of the Dial Square football team in the leafy lanes of Kent in the first place.

Some of Royal Arsenal's own amateur players also rejected professionalism and later broke away to form an alternative side – Royal Ordnance Factories Football Club (ROFFC). Peter Connolly was one of these players but, following his death in 1895 and mounting financial problems, the club had ceased to exist by the end of 1896.

For Royal Arsenal though, professionalism marked a new beginning in its five-year history, if an unpromising one at first.

Although the London Football Association had done its best to ban any of its members from playing against Royal Arsenal or any other professional team, they had failed to do so. If they had hoped that teams in the south, jealous of Arsenal's 'Champions of the South' tag, would anyway now see professionalism as an excuse to avoid playing them then that proved to be a false hope too.

During the 1891-92 season, the team played friendlies against eight of the nine teams that had already committed to matches prior to the Royal Arsenal decision to turn professional.

In fighting once again for what they believed in – and known already in some quarters as 'the subversives' – this works team had shown that they were prepared to take on anyone.

However, no longer being allowed to play in local cup competitions and losing 5.1 away to Small Heath (later to become Birmingham City) in the First Round of the FA Cup on 16th January 1892, friendlies were the only matches that Royal Arsenal could play.

These were infrequent and the fixtures unreliable with other teams often pulling out at late notice – especially when faced with the long journey to Plumstead.

When games did take place they often only attracted small crowds. All of this meant no regular income coming into a club which was now committed to paying its players wages.

The club explored the possibility of setting up a new 'Southern

League' with Fred Beardsley – now vice chairman of Royal Arsenal – instrumental in contacting other clubs from the south and trying to generate interest in the idea.

It was proposed that the new league would be run along similar lines as The Football League in the North and Midlands. A famous Victorian sportsman and one of the first English football 'Greats,' Charles Bambridge, had first proposed this, two years earlier.

Bambridge (known as 'Charlie Bam') was a left-winger of exceptional pace and quality. He played for Corinthians and the same Swifts club that beat Royal Arsenal in the FA Cup. He appeared for England at just 17 years old, and two of his brothers also went on to play for their country.

However, even with this fine reputation behind him, his idea was rejected. The 'old boys' public school network that still dominated football in southern England saw it as a threat to the gentleman amateur.

The same N.I. Jackson who had spoken out against Royal Arsenal following their decision to turn professional, persuaded his fellow members at a meeting at the Salutation Tavern in Newgate Street, London that a Southern League

"would not really benefit London football."

His motion was carried by 47 votes to 46.

47:46

Royal Arsenal's attempt to form a 'Southern League' in 1892 was rejected by just one vote by the London FA

The attempt to form a Southern League in 1892 was probably as much to do with funding and finding enough backers to get it off the ground as the enduring opposition by the authorities to football (and especially the workers' team of Royal Arsenal) trying to change the way it was organised.

A 'Southern Alliance' of amateur clubs including Tottenham Hotspur and Erith – vanquished in that first Royal Arsenal game four years earlier - did run for one season from 1892 but neither the professional Royal Arsenal team nor Millwall Athletic were members.

In fact, it was Millwall who continued to press the case for a Southern League and they succeeded in 1894 with 16 founder members. In 1908 the first Charity Shield (now the Community Shield) match was played at Chelsea's new Stamford Bridge ground, between the champions of the Southern League (Queens Park Rangers) and the Football League's First Division champions, Manchester United (United won 4.0 after a replay – the only Charity Shield match to go to a replay).

Tottenham Hotspur only received one vote in Royal Arsenal's attempt to form a Southern League and only joined it after turning professional themselves in 1895. However, they went onto become Southern League champions in 1900 and won the FA Cup in 1901 – the only amateur club ever to do so and still the only team from below the second-tier of English football to lift the Cup.

1893

A number of events occurred in the spring of 1893 that would combine to effectively prevent the newly-formed professional Arsenal club from going out of business.

A good FA Cup qualifying run at the start of the season had seen them beat four teams including the Highland Light Infantry; City

Ramblers (a 10.1 win including hat-tricks from each of Charles Booth, Arthur Elliott and James Hendersen), and Millwall Athletic.

This last win came in front of a record home attendance of 12,000 at the Invicta Ground, many of who had crossed the river on the Woolwich Ferry. The crossing had become a free service in 1889, following the removal of tolls across London's bridges to the west.

The team then lost away to Sunderland at their Newcastle Road ground, 6.0, on 21st January 1893.

It was to be the club's last significant match as Royal Arsenal, though their final friendly took place against Stoke on 29th April 1893 which they lost 1.0.

21 January 1893

The club's last significant match as Royal Arsenal

Their season was effectively over bar the occasional friendly match the club might be able to arrange. This state of affairs could not continue with the club effectively relying on a good FA Cup run each season in order to stay afloat.

George Weaver – owner of the Invicta Ground - had also been talking about charging the club more for a further three years of its lease to play there, which was shortly due to run out.

With one eye on joining the Football League, the committee members decided to form a limited liability company of which they became company directors.

The Football League would only admit limited companies to its leagues but Companies' House rules meant that no company could be registered with a name that could be deemed to associate it with the Royal Family and so, in early May 1893, the new company officially took over Royal Arsenal under a new name: Woolwich Arsenal.

May 1893

The club officially changed its name to Woolwich Arsenal

Jack Humble had opposed the move to form a new company when the club turned professional two years earlier but realised now that, financially, they had little alternative.

The Football League had decided to extend its Second Division from 12 to 16 teams in time for the new season and, as Woolwich Arsenal, the club now applied to join.

They were successful, joining the league on 31st May 1893, at the same time as Newcastle United, Rotherham Town and Liverpool. Woolwich Arsenal thus became the first team south of Birmingham to join the Football League.

31 May 1893

Woolwich Arsenal joined the Football League – the first team south of Birmingham to do so

Two teams – Accrington and Bootle - subsequently had to withdraw from the league because of their own financial difficulties. Middlesbrough Ironopolis took Accrington's place but Bootle left it too late for a replacement to be found and so the 1893-94 season would begin with just 15 Second Division teams.

Seeing the likelihood of far greater success on the field, Weaver then proposed to raise the rent at the Invicta Ground by even more than expected: from £200 per year to £350 per year – a 75% increase that the club could not afford and, with typical Arsenal working class determination not to be taken advantage of by richer businessmen, would not afford.

Houses were eventually built on the Invicta Ground space but some of the original terracing can still be seen in the back gardens of some of those houses on Hector Street today.

When Weaver rejected the club's compromise rent offer of £300 Woolwich Arsenal decided to move back to the Manor Ground opposite Plumstead Station.

Instead of renting it as before though and running the same risk of that rent being unreasonably increased again, they decided to purchase it through the new limited liability company.

Shares were issued and some £4,000 was raised. A new main stand, tiny press box, and banks of terracing, separated from the pitch by iron fencing, were built - largely thanks to the volunteer efforts of the club's supporters - during the summer of 1893 in time for the new season.

£4,000

Amount of money raised to buy and refurbish the Manor Ground

Buying the ground meant that company directors such as Jack Humble and Fred Beardsley had to offer guarantees to their shareholders that they would pay back the cost of their shares if the company that they now owned the club had failed.

As members of the Football League, they were also committing to paying for long journeys to the likes of Liverpool and Nottingham. As individuals, they would have lost everything if the new company had failed but they were prepared to take the risk. Had they not done so, the club may not have been able to play its new league fixtures and may have folded altogether.

Instead, Arsenal had now become a national rather than local club, with the opportunity to play regularly against the leading clubs in the North and Midlands.

Their new name – Woolwich Arsenal - reflected both their location in London and that of the world-famous armaments factory. At the focal point of world trade and the heart of the British Empire and with a population of around seven million people at the end of the century, London dominated the country and beyond.

Associated with inventions such as gas lighting and underground railways, Woolwich Arsenal represented a forward-thinking and innovative club, yet run by local working men on behalf of local working men.

The new name enabled them to create a brand – one of the first in football – as the armed forces' favourite team and that of patriotic football fans across the globe.

As we saw, their original crest featured three cannons (which looked like chimneys but which could easily be applicable to their origins in factory life) and leopard's (lion's) heads.

With their club motto of 'Clamant nostra tela in Regis querela,' meaning 'Our weapons clash in the King's quarrel,' branding experts today would have approved of its forward-looking stance on football fields while celebrating its geographical roots and heritage of providing for action on the battlefields of the British Empire.

Woolwich Arsenal (1893-1913)

Wearing flannelette shirts costing 2s 5d each, shorts costing 3s 3d and russet calf boots at 8s 6d, Woolwich Arsenal's first official match, and the club's first Football League game, took place on 2nd September 1893 at home to fellow newcomers, Newcastle United.

2 September 1893

Woolwich Arsenal played their first game in the Football League

Walter James Shaw (after just eight minutes) scored Woolwich Arsenal's first league goal in a 2.2 draw.

The attendance for the club's first match back at the Manor Ground is recorded as 6,000 but the Kentish Mercury estimated it as being far higher:

> *"That the now-famous "Reds" have lost none of their popularity by their transference from the Invicta Recreation Ground to their new ground on the Manor Field, Plumstead was fully proven on Saturday when close upon 10,000 paid at the gate to witness the match with Newcastle United."*

Woolwich Arsenal secured their first league win on 11th September 1893 at home to Walsall Town Swifts, 4.0, with centre forward, Joseph Frederick Heath, scoring their first hat-trick.

They had to wait much longer for their first away win and just before the turn of the year – on 30th December 1893 when they beat Ardwick A.F.C. 1.0.

This was the club's first league 'double' having beaten Ardwick at home that November, also 1.0. At the end of that season, due to their own financial difficulties, Ardwick were reformed as Manchester City.

Did you know?

The first car number plates appeared in Paris, France on 10th October 1893

Eventually finishing ninth with 28 points from 28 matches, Woolwich Arsenal had to endure some heavy defeats in that first season, including a 6.0 loss in the away game at Newcastle United.

Their record home defeat in the league - 5.0 - came on 28th October 1893 in their first match against Liverpool (who would go on to win the Second Division - in this their first league season too - but come straight back down again the following season).

However, Woolwich Arsenal did run up some high scores of their own including six goals against Clapton, Northwich Victoria and Middlesbrough Ironopolis.

Most emphatically, on 14th October 1893, they beat Ashford United 12.0 in the first qualifying round of that season's FA Cup. This remains the club's biggest home win in the Cup and would equal their biggest ever home win, which came in the league seven years later.

Old rivals Millwall Rovers provided the FA Cup opposition two rounds later along with a huge following from the Isle of Dogs in a crowd estimated at 20,000 at the Manor Ground – by far the biggest attendance there to date.

Woolwich Arsenal won 2.0 and continued their cup run until the January of 1894 when they finally lost at home to The Wednesday (the third oldest professional club in the English league and later to become Sheffield Wednesday).

Did you know?

The Manchester Ship Canal – also known at the time as the 'Big Ditch' - opened in 1894, creating the world's first inland port

The club made steady progress in those early league seasons, finishing eighth the following season and then seventh in 1895-96.

The club had appointed a 'secretary-manager' – Sam Hollis – in 1894 to take over from the former club committee and handle all team affairs. He may have been little more than a trainer and after three years he was replaced by Thomas Brown Mitchell – a Scot from Dumfries who had held a similar role at Blackburn Rovers, winning four FA Cups.

30 March 1895

Woolwich Arsenal played Newton Heath (later to become Manchester United) for the first time and won 3.2

Mitchell is considered by many to be Woolwich Arsenal's first professional manager and the club came fifth under his management in 1897-98 – the only season he was in charge.

This was the highest league position they would reach in the nineteenth century. Mitchell's successor – William Elcoat - was at the helm for even fewer games (25) and was, himself, replaced by Harry Bradshaw who would transform the fortunes of the club on the field.

If league progress was evident and crowds were building, there was no obvious improvement in respect for the club, not just in Kent but now much further afield. The new Victorian network of railways enabled 'football excursions' to take place whereby large numbers of Woolwich Arsenal's mostly factory worker fans could travel to away games, though local transport links in their part of South London remained poor.

On 16th March 1896, the club played in their first floodlit match (the world's first ever floodlit football match had taken place at Bramall Lane, Sheffield almost 18 years earlier).

16 March 1896

Woolwich Arsenal played in their first floodlit match, against Thames Ironworks

This game, played under electric lights, was against Thames Ironworks (later to become West Ham United). Allegedly the lights went out each time Woolwich Arsenal came close to scoring but they had the last laugh, winning 5.3.

Did you know?

The first modern Olympic Games were held in Athens in Greece in 1896

Trips to the Manor Ground were as intimidating as ever for opposition teams and officials alike.

On 26th January 1895 Woolwich Arsenal were held to a 1.1 draw by Burton Wanderers at the Manor Ground in front of 7,000 fans. Upset over Burton's equalising goal, the referee was attacked and beaten up by some of those fans and, as a result, the Manor

Ground was closed for six weeks.

Woolwich Arsenal thus became the first league club in English football to have their ground closed by the authorities who cited 'unsportsmanlike behaviour' as the reason. In the meantime, they played their 'home' matches at nearby grounds including at New Brompton (later to be renamed Gillingham FC) and Leyton until the Manor Ground was re-opened.

Much more sinister acts of aggression were happening many miles away from London and would have a far more profound and lasting effect on the club's fortunes.

1899–1902

The Second Boer War took place in South Africa

The Second Boer War - or the 'South African War' - broke out in October 1899 and would last until May 1902. The First Boer War had taken place from 1880-81 and was fought between the British and descendants of Dutch settlers - The Boers - in the southern states of Africa.

After the first war, British Prime Minister William Gladstone had agreed that the Boers could govern themselves in the state of Transvaal but it was an uneasy peace. In 1899, the Boer leader - Paul Kruger - was concerned that the number of immigrants (known as 'uitlanders') - largely from Britain - would outnumber the native Boers and would seek to outvote them and regain control of the region and its rich gold reserves for the British Empire.

If Britain was unsure of the intentions of Germany to expand its own influence in Africa or its own relationship with the Germans, it became clearer when Germany provided Kruger and the Boers with military equipment which they used in raids on British army garrisons such as at Ladysmith, Mafeking and Kimberley.

The British quickly sent reinforcements, regaining control of the Boer capital - Pretoria - but the raids and attacks lasted for two more years.

Lord Kitchener, the new British Chief of Staff in South Africa, responded to this guerrilla warfare by destroying Boer farms under its 'Scorched Earth' policy, poisoning wells and salting fields so that the Boers could not be fed by civilians

Tens of thousands of women and children were forced into concentration camps which had previously been set up as refugee camps. This was the first time that concentration camps had been used against a whole nation.

Did you know?

The first time that concentration camps were used against a whole nation was when the British introduced them in the Second Boer War

The Boer War ended with the signing of the Treaty of Vereeniging in May 1902 under which the Transvaal and Orange Free State would no longer exist as Boer republics but the British would aim to restock and repair farmland.

For Woolwich Arsenal, the effects of the Boer War were alarming for financial reasons. The munitions factories had to be extended and men were forced to take compulsory overtime, often including Saturday afternoons, and working around the clock to supply the soldiers on the South African Front, thus preventing them from regularly attending football matches at the Manor Ground.

It is estimated that average attendances at the Manor Ground fell by around 40% in 1899. A significant number of Arsenal's fans were actually soldiers in the armed services so they too were absent fighting the Boers.

In the context of guerrilla warfare and its inevitable civilian casualties, and refugees being rounded up on foreign fields, it seems of little significance to talk about the financial hardship of a football club, but, for the record, the effect on the relatively new company's income was enormous, thanks directly to its origins and location at Woolwich Arsenal.

A series of loans kept the club afloat and other fundraising events were arranged including an 'archery contest' in 1902 which may, in fact, have been more of a lottery with arrows being fired at pieces of paper representing the 80,000 tickets bought by the public and stuck to a huge board at the Manor Ground.

The 'tournament' allegedly raised £1,200 for the club and three players were bought with the proceeds: Tommy Shanks, Percy Sands and goalkeeper James 'Jimmy' Ashcroft, all of whom would be instrumental in the club's promotion season in 1903-04.

Programme Notes:

The following players were bought with the proceeds of an 'archery contest' in 1902:

- **Tommy Shanks**
- **Percy Sands**
- **Jimmy Ashcroft**

In the space of 17 days in the autumn of 1899, Woolwich Arsenal met New Brompton five times in the FA Cup third qualifying-round tie and four replays, finally losing 1.0 after nine-and-a-half hours.

5

Number of times Woolwich Arsenal met New Brompton in the space of 17 days in the FA Cup

In March 1900 the club achieved its record home league win (and joint record home win with the FA Cup win over Ashford) but less than a thousand people turned up to watch it.

The club was facing mounting financial problems as were a number of others: Second Division rivals Darwen – once FA Cup semi-finalists - had left the Football League in the 1898-99 season after a record 18 consecutive defeats.

Burton Swifts – founder members of the Football League's Second Division, alongside Woolwich Arsenal – would be forced to merge with Burton Wanderers in 1900-01 to form Burton United.

The well-known names of late Victorian football league sides were disappearing and the future for Woolwich Arsenal, after such a bright start to their life as a professional league club, was not promising,

The new century

The twentieth century started well enough for Woolwich Arsenal. That record league win of 12.0 came on 12th March 1900 against Loughborough, with a hat-trick from Ralph Gaudie and including two goals each from James Tennant, Alexander Main, John Dick and Ernest Herbert Cottrell.

22 January 1901

Queen Victoria died, aged 81

The uncompromising Harry Bradshaw was beginning to mould together a successful team and the home crowds began to grow again.

On 7th February 1903 they played Sheffield United in the First Round of the FA Cup, losing the match 3.1. However, the crowd at the Manor Ground that day was recorded as 24,000 with gate receipts of £1,000 – the first time it had reached a four figure sum.

The following season Woolwich Arsenal were promoted to the Football League's First Division for the first time, winning the first eight matches of the season and finishing as runners-up behind Preston North End.

1903-04

Woolwich Arsenal were promoted to the First Division for the first time

They won 21 of their 34 matches in total, scoring a huge 91 goals in the process – easily the highest of any club in the League's two divisions that season. The Reds scored eight goals in matches against both Burton United and Leicester Fosse and six against Chesterfield Town and then Gainsborough Trinity.

Some of the proceeds earned by promotion were spent on improvements at the Manor Ground. The side of the ground in front of the old sewer pipe was replaced by a new steeply- banked terrace which would be named 'Spion Kop' by soldiers who had returned from the Boer War in South Africa.

With promotion to the top flight secured, Bradshaw left for Fulham before the team could play their first game in the First Division which came on 3rd September 1904 against Newcastle United - a 3.0 away defeat at St James Park.

3 September 1904

Woolwich Arsenal played their first match in the First Division

The club had to wait until their fourth game to secure their first win (and first goals) in the top tier of English football – on 24th September 1904 in a 2.0 win against Wolverhampton Wanderers, watched by a Manor Ground crowd of 20,000.

Charles 'Charlie' Satterthwaite had been bought from West Ham United, weighed 16-stone and was legendary for his shooting power. He scored Arsenal's first goal in the First Division. Tim Coleman, who had been a prolific scorer in the previous season's promotion campaign, added a second.

Programme Notes:

Charlie Satterthwaite scored Arsenal's first goal in the First Division

On December 5, 1904, Woolwich Arsenal hosted the 'Parisian XI'- a team made up of some of the best French players at the time and so could have been equally termed 'The French National Team.'

Details about the match are scarce but club records suggest that Woolwich Arsenal, playing in Division One for the first time that season, won 26.1.

On 31st March 1906, now under the management of Phil Kelso

(another tough Scot who had previously coached Hibernian) the club reached its first FA Cup Semi-final, losing to Newcastle United 2.0 at Stoke City's Victoria Ground.

The following year they got to the Semi-final again, this time at Birmingham's St Andrews ground, attended by 36,000 fans. They lost 3.1 to The Wednesday, in a match often shrouded in thick fog, despite Billy Garbutt giving them an early lead.

1906

An earthquake in San Francisco, Californian led to the deaths of over 3,000 people

On 9th November 1907 Woolwich Arsenal travelled to Stamford Bridge to play Chelsea for the first time. This was the first ever First Division match to be played by two London clubs and so is known as the first 'London derby.' It is thought that the 'local derby' description could have its origins from a game first played in the Middle Ages, over Shrove Tuesday and Ash Wednesday, in the town of Ashbourne in Derbyshire (and so also known as the 'Ashbourne Game').

9 November 1907

First ever 'London derby' match: Chelsea v Arsenal

The whole town takes part and forms two teams – the 'Up'ards' consisting of anyone born north of Henmore Brook (River Henmore) which flows through the middle of the town, and one from south of the river (Down'ards). Play starts in the town centre and the goalposts are three miles apart. The major difference with football as we know it today is that teams try to carry the ball back to their own goal to score.

Alternatively, the word 'derby' can refer to a type of bowler hat, worn by working men – who might more usually have worn cloth caps - on special occasions such as family weddings or funerals, especially in Victorian times. Matches between local clubs could well have been construed as similarly special occasions and thus become known as 'local derbies.'

Chelsea won that first London derby match 2.1 with both of their goals scored by the legendary George Hilsdon (the first player to score 100 goals for Chelsea) and Satterthwaite replying for Woolwich Arsenal. The match was watched by a then record crowd for England's top division: 65,000.

The attendance was boosted by a huge away following from Plumstead as it was the 66th birthday of King Edward VII and so the munitions factory was closed, enabling large numbers to attend the fixture in West London. Every league meeting to date between these two clubs has taken place in the top-tier of English football.

Satterthwaite would end his career with Woolwich Arsenal, retiring in 1910 but other 'star' players that had been brought in had to be sold to rival clubs to raise money.

Woolwich Arsenal had become a 'selling club.' Players moved on included Caesar Jenkyns, a typically rugged defender in the Arsenal mould who had started his professional career at Small Heath and would become Woolwich Arsenal's first international player when being capped for Wales against Scotland in March 1896. He was sold to Newton Heath.

Programme Notes:

Caesar Jenkins was the club's first international player

Jimmy Ashcroft set all kinds of goalkeeping records for the club and was their first full England international, but the club had to cash in and sold him to Blackburn Rovers in 1908. Tim Coleman went to Everton the same year as did another striker, Bert Freeman.

Woolwich Arsenal later refused to pay 11 shillings to cover the 17-year old Charlie Buchan's travel costs for a series of reserves games and training sessions with the club and, as a result, Buchan (born in Plumstead) vowed never to play for Woolwich Arsenal again.

Football was booming in the early part of the twentieth century but Woolwich Arsenal simply could not compete with the competitive wages being offered by top teams from the North and the Midlands and so would never be able to challenge for the league title itself.

The underlying – and immoveable - financial problem was still the location of the club. The sweep of the River Thames effectively cut in half what could have been Woolwich Arsenal's natural geographical fan base.

Moreover, Plumstead was little more than an outer suburb of London in those days – twenty minutes further out by train than 'The Valley' (home of Charlton Athletic from 1919) with much too small a population to support a local football club with national ambitions.

Good FA Cup runs as witnessed in the middle part of the decade were not sustained. They went out of the competition early in 1908 (at Hull), 1909 (to local rivals, Millwall) and 1910 (a 5.0 thrashing at Everton's Goodison Park).

Each of these defeats meant an end to cup matches and therefore any extra income from crowd attendances (clubs playing away were entitled to a percentage of the match takings as well as keeping most of the money from their gates at home).

They also suffered some heavy away defeats in the league, especially in the 1909-10 season when they conceded five goals at Aston Villa, Middlesbrough, Notts County and Liverpool; six at Sunderland and, on 2nd October, 1909 seven in a 7.0 defeat at Blackburn Rovers which was their worst away defeat in the league at the time and still equals their worst ever away league defeat.

As in the build-up to the Boer War, the club was very much dependent on the fortunes of the various munitions factories that made up the Woolwich Arsenal.

One of these was the Royal Navy Gun Factory where British torpedoes were being manufactured. In 1910 the government decided to centralise torpedo manufacturing – ironically given the history of the Arsenal football club – in Scotland. The Evening Citizen predicted that this move would have a dire effect on the local economy:

> *"Woolwich...is now greatly exercised by the forthcoming removal of the torpedo factory to the Scottish town of Greenock... in consequence of this decision by the Admiralty some 500 men will be leaving the town within the next few months..."*

Transport links to Plumstead hadn't really improved significantly over the twenty years of the club's existence. Indeed, even the local tram company did not put on extra trams on match days.

While football fans even then were prepared to travel long distances – however difficult those journeys were – there must have been some impact on attendances at the Manor Ground as nearby clubs such as Clapton, Millwall, Tottenham Hotspur and West Ham United, as well as clubs in West London such as Fulham and Chelsea, began to develop and attract their own sets of loyal fans.

Another factor behind the club's financial problems might well have been that the architect, Archibald 'Archie' Leitch, who was responsible for the rebuilding of the Manor Ground that Arsenal's new limited liability company had purchased in 1893, did not appear to have been paid and so the large debt stayed on the company's books.

Leitch was also from Scotland and had worked on Glasgow Rangers' Ibrox Park stadium.

5 April 1902

First Ibrox disaster in which 25 football fans died

During a Scotland v England match there on 5th April, 1902 the wooden West Tribune stand collapsed, after heavy rain during the previous night, killing 25 football supporters and injuring 517 so it may have been that the club wanted to satisfy themselves that their new ground was safe and fit for purpose before paying for the work.

However, payment was never made and, on paper at least, by 1910 the club did not have the assets to cover this and other debts.

The club had for years relied on donations and loans from key individuals such as those from George Leavey – owner of a gentleman's outfitters in Woolwich High Street and Chairman of the club since 1899 – which helped to pay players' wages and transfer fees.

In the end, Leavey saw that the financial position was hopeless and so took the club into voluntary liquidation with debts estimated at £3,000.

£3,000

Woolwich Arsenal's estimated debts as the club went into voluntary liquidation in 1910

Henry Norris

Henry Norris came to the club's rescue. Leading a consortium of businessmen including William Hall, who by 1913 was a member of the Football League's Management Committee, he invested enough money in the club to make it solvent once more and became the club's majority shareholder, effectively owning the club and becoming Chairman two years later.

The Kentish Independent trumpeted the move:

> *"Arsenal club saved. Fulham Gentlemen on the board. The Arsenal Football Club crisis has taken another and a sensational turn."*

Given the financial state of the club, before he arrived, the Woolwich Arsenal board welcomed Norris with open arms though subsequent history does not always judge him as simply the timely benefactor he was considered to be at the time.

One thing is certain: he had an enormous influence on the club and, just as at the end of the previous decade, without his investment and with another much larger military conflict – World War One - brewing, the club could easily have gone out of business permanently and its story would have ended in 1910.

Born in 1865, at the height of Victorian enterprise, Norris was a self-made man with a fortune from property development in south west London, his companies having built some 2,000 houses in

Fulham and Wimbledon alone.

He was also a leading political figure at the time, being Mayor of Fulham, and had a wide network of influential friends including leading politicians, businessmen and society figures such as the Archbishop of Canterbury – many of whom felt indebted to him in some way such that he could call in favours - seemingly at will.

Suspicions over his methods and a lack of transparency over his transactions often gave rise to suggestions of corruption though he dismissed such allegations out of hand and any evidence was slow to emerge.

His ancestor – Sir Henry Norris – was a similarly controversial figure in Tudor times. He was accused of 'intriguing' with Henry VIII's second wife, Anne Boleyn, and known for his 'raffish charm' but, again, nothing was ever proved.

The Victorian version was a ruthless, uncompromising figure standing at over six feet, and so, given their early history, potentially tailor-made for Woolwich Arsenal. Leslie Knighton, who would later serve as club manager under Norris described his debating skills:

> *"When I disagreed with him at board meetings and had to stand up for what I knew was best for the club, he used to flay me with words until I was reduced to fuming, helpless silence."*

Having said this, somewhat ironically, the club motto did evolve under Norris to 'Victoria Concordia Crescit' meaning 'Victory through Teamwork.'

Norris was also Chairman of Fulham Football Club at the time and, as a director, had overseen their progress from the Southern League to Division Two of the Football League. There were rumours at the time that money had changed hands to help Fulham's progress but no hard evidence was ever found.

Another Edwardian businessman called Henry – Henry Augustus Mears – had acquired Stamford Bridge in West London with a view to making it one of the finest venues for association football in London, if not the country.

Mears offered Norris the chance to move Fulham FC to the ground but Norris refused to pay the annual rent of £1,500. Mears created his own team instead – Chelsea FC – in 1905, which duly hosted Woolwich Arsenal in that first London derby match two years later.

Had Norris not been so careful with his money, there might not have been a Chelsea football club at all. Instead, Norris went on to oversee the development of Fulham's own home ground – Craven Cottage – into one of the best football stadiums in the country at that time.

Norris's cigars and brandy lifestyle may have been in stark contrast to the working-class backgrounds of the likes of Danskin and Humble but he was very much a hands-on chairman and similarly ferocious in his ambition.

He wanted a London team to quickly challenge the dominant football clubs from the Midlands and the North of England but had realised that Fulham was not the right vehicle to achieve this.

With Woolwich Arsenal's existing debts paid off, a new company was formed: Woolwich Arsenal Football and Athletic Company. However, Norris quickly saw that one of the major causes of the financial problems which had engulfed the original Woolwich Arsenal was its location in Plumstead.

Average attendances at the Manor Ground were between 10,000 and 11,000 when he arrived – far less than average home crowds enjoyed by London rivals Chelsea (who reportedly had an average of 28,000 supporters attending their home games) or Tottenham Hotspur, and half of what they had been in their promotion-winning season of 1904.

The ground itself was still described as a 'perfect quagmire' or 'mud revel' and frequently flooded during the worst days of winter.

With a foot in both football clubs, Norris attempted to deal with the financial problem in Woolwich by merging Woolwich Arsenal with Fulham to form a London super-club but the Football League blocked the move (possibly the first time they had looked after the long-term interests of Woolwich Arsenal).

Norris then suggested that Woolwich Arsenal at least play their home games at Fulham's Craven Cottage ground on alternate Saturdays. This move was also rejected and so Norris began to look at locations elsewhere in the capital which were closer to and more accessible from Central London.

These included possible sites in Battersea to the south of the River Thames and Harringay to the north.

Norris will also have been acutely aware of the recent history of old Arsenal rivals Millwall who had just dropped the 'Athletic' part of their name. They had hosted Woolwich Arsenal in an FA Cup Second Round tie on February 6th, 1909 – which ended in a 1.1 draw – in a match attracting some 32,000 spectators.

In 1910 Millwall moved from North Greenwich to a new ground – The Den (now known as the Old Den) – in Cold Blow Lane, New Cross and so were a fellow South London team.

Norris took in the fact that local football rivalry – even when the two teams had been separated by the River Thames – could generate huge crowds (and potential income). This concept of more than one city team in the Football League had begun in 1893 with The Wednesday and Sheffield United in Sheffield, and Ardwick and Newton Heath in Manchester.

Norris also saw that it had been possible for a team to move away from its historical and geographic origins – in this case, the Isle of Dogs – and move right away, across the river, and still thrive as a football club.

Had Norris not been so certain that his club needed to leave Woolwich, the Arsenal v Millwall rivalry could have become the key local football derby in South London.

While Norris continued his search and plans for the future of the club, the team's results on the pitch failed to improve.

Despite the cash injection that Norris and his consortium had provided, little money found its way into quality players on the pitch and the fact remained that Woolwich Arsenal had sold their best players such as Ashcroft, Coleman and Freeman.

The arrival of striker Alf Common for £250 – the first player to be transferred for a fee of £1,000 on his transfer to Middlesbrough from Sunderland in 1905 – in the twilight of his career could not stop the club's decline on the pitch.

They also sold centre-forward Andy Ducat to Aston Villa for £1,000. Ducat was only 26 and in his footballing prime but clearly, Norris saw him merely as a valuable asset that could be cashed in to help pay off the club's debts.

Ducat – who also played cricket for England – was in no hurry to leave the club either, telling Athletic News that:

> *"I'd stayed loyal to the club throughout many hard times. I was very much at home down in the south, but it was indicated to me that a move to Aston Villa would be in everyone's best interests."*

Woolwich Arsenal had only finished higher than tenth in the First Division on two of the seasons since their promotion in 1904 and just avoided relegation in the 1909/10 season in the final two matches, including an away draw at Tottenham Hotspur.

29 April 1912

Woolwich Arsenal played Tottenham Hotspur in a charity match to raise money for Titanic survivors

The club beat Tottenham 3.0 in a charity match at White City, West London on April 29th, 1912 to raise money for the survivors and families of the Titanic disaster but, while Tottenham were struggling to survive in the First Division, it was almost inevitable that Arsenal were relegated the following season - setting a record in the process for the worst ever top tier league performance with just three wins.

After a 3.1 win at Sheffield United on 21st September 1912 the team failed to win again in the league until a 1.0 win at Manchester City on 8th March 1913, followed by their only home win of the season – 1.0 - in the next match against West Bromwich Albion.

3

Lowest number of wins in a top- tier English league season

They did manage a 2.1 win against Croydon Common at the Manor Ground in a First Round FA Cup replay in January 1913 but lost in the next round at home to Liverpool 4.1.

Chelsea's 2.1 league win at Liverpool confirmed Woolwich

Arsenal's relegation from the First Division with Norris – possibly still seething from their FA Cup thrashing - practically accusing Liverpool of throwing the match.

The Football League investigated and found Liverpool 'spineless' but not corrupt. Chelsea (and Tottenham Hotspur) would themselves occupy the First Division relegation positions two years later.

Under manager George Morrell Woolwich Arsenal finished bottom of the table with only 18 points and supposedly just £20 to their name. Their last game in the pre-war First Division ended in a 1.1 home draw against Middlesbrough in front of just 6,000 fans.

This was the club's worst ever league season and is the first and last time the club has ever been relegated. Morrell very nearly resigned to join Leeds City at this point but Norris persuaded him to stay and a different football manager – Herbert Chapman – got the Leeds job instead.

Woolwich Arsenal lost 23 of their 38 league games that year and, again, critics suggested that Norris had deliberately underfunded the team, making their decline that much more certain.

It certainly provided the impetus for a change and in early 1913 the Kentish Independent, which had frequently reported on the club's fortunes through its 'Redshirt' cartoon character (a man dressed in a cannon) had printed an article under the headline:

"Arsenal to move to the other side of London."

The article went on to accuse Norris of being prepared to sell the club's soul and effectively removing the very people who had played such key roles in the club's past from being part of its future.

On the other hand, success on the football field itself under their guidance had hardly yielded any meaningful success in the 27 years of its existence apart from that 1904 promotion season and the two FA Cup Semi-finals.

A letter from Paul Donaldson to the Kentish Gazette at the time summed up the shock felt by Woolwich Arsenal fans:

> *"Mr Norris has decided that financial gain is more important than protecting our local club...you cannot 'franchise' a football club..."*

There are obvious parallels here with the experience of Wimbledon fans in the Modern Era when their club was uprooted from south west London and ended up in Milton Keynes via south east London and a muted move to the Republic of Ireland.

However, there was no escaping the fact that many fans of Woolwich Arsenal were booing their club's performances on the pitch rather more than any plans to leave the area.

Rumours of the club moving persisted throughout that season, including suggestions that the club had bought a piece of land in Harringay, which was eventually used to develop Harringay Stadium. (The stadium opened in 1927 and was used as a greyhound and speedway venue for the next 60 years.)

The press speculation was not too far out. Norris knew that cheap, regular and reliable public transport would be key to any move. If based in a residential area, then many fans would also be able to walk to home matches.

During his research, Norris had noted far better transport links in parts of Islington in North London.

The Great Northern, Piccadilly and Brompton Railway (GNP&BR) had built a deep-level underground railway - known as the 'tube' - which connected Hammersmith in West London with Finsbury

Park in the North.

It served 22 stations when it opened in 1906 and, crucially, for Norris, connected an area adjacent to Gillespie Road station with Strand station such that it would only take some 12 minutes to travel there from Central London. This was a far cry from the long, meandering journey by train out to Plumstead and had the further advantage of joining up with overland lines serving all of the major North London suburbs.

This underground line still forms a core stretch of London Underground's Piccadilly Line today, though some of the station names have since changed or trains no longer stop there.

It also won't have escaped Norris's attention that no other club was based as close to one of the new underground stations and, just as importantly, direct transport links here were much better than at the other end of the Seven Sisters Road where Tottenham Hotspur were based.

The area of land that Norris had discovered was adjacent to Avenell Road in Highbury: specifically, a patch of land used as playing fields in the grounds of St John's College of Divinity, based at St John's Hall, a grand old building, built in 1825 and originally hosting Highbury College (of Divinity).

He paid £20,000 initially for a 20-year lease of the six-acre site; the club subsequently bought out the freehold on the land in 1925 for £64,000. The Church of England officials in charge at St John's Hall viewed football as 'ungodly' but took Norris's money anyway.

£20,000

Amount paid to secure a 20-year lease on land at Highbury

The Church demanded that no matches could take place at Highbury on Holy Days nor could 'intoxicating liquor' be sold on the premises (neither of these restrictions was adhered to for long with the ban on Good Friday and Christmas Day games at Highbury finally lifted in 1925 with the purchase of the land's freehold).

Norris's old friend the Archbishop of Canterbury personally signed the deed and so the disastrous 1912-13 season proved to be the club's last in South London.

Ironically, the football club that had been founded in a foundry devoted to the production of the weapons of war had found a new location devoted to the teaching of love and peace.

If two generations of football fans who had grown up supporting Woolwich Arsenal were aggrieved at the proposed move north of the river, there is evidence that many still viewed it as their 'local club.'

The club arranged for coaches to bring fans from Woolwich to Highbury and there is evidence that they continued to do so, building on the 'away' following they had been part of for more than 25 years. George Robertson, a regular fan summed it up:

> *"The Manor Ground was a backwater really. An odd, out of the way place. Highbury, on the other hand, was in the centre of things. It had a real buzz and a real draw."*

However, the club's imminent arrival in Islington was met with disbelief and then downright horror by residents and other London clubs alike

Highbury

It is alleged that Norris received personal death threats over the Highbury move and it was certainly opposed by other London clubs including Clapton Orient (then playing at the nearby Millfields Road ground), Tottenham Hotspur and Chelsea - all of which felt that Woolwich Arsenal's arrival would damage their own home attendances.

In an echo of Paul Donaldson's earlier letter in the Kentish Gazette the Clapton Orient Chairman - Captain Henry Wells-Holland (who was to be instrumental in helping to form 'The Footballers' Battalion' in the fast- approaching World War One) – argued that one of the first principals of the Football League was for a club to represent a certain district and is supposed to have declared that:

"...if...any millionaire can buy up a poverty-stricken club...and... form a company, where does the sport come in?"

They and Tottenham - based at the other end of the Seven Sisters Road from Highbury - provided the key opposition to the move, as they would in the Modern era too when West Ham United planned to move to the Olympic Stadium in Stratford, and for much the same financial reasons.

It is somewhat ironic that Clapton Orient sided with Tottenham Hotspur in 1913 as, eight years earlier, Spurs had opposed their joining the Southern League on the grounds that:

"We are not going to have them on our doorsteps."

There were many squabbles and problems on the pitch during that immediate pre-war period. Clapton Orient themselves were fined

£25 for fixing the kick-off time in a game against Leeds City in 1914 to be so late that the latter part of the match was played in almost complete darkness. The Leeds goalkeeper claimed to be literally unsighted as he conceded two late goals but the result was allowed to stand.

The Tottenham Herald described Henry Norris as an 'interloper' and Spurs fans still refer to Arsenal fans as 'gypsies.' Tottenham director Morton Cadman criticized Norris for being on the boards of both Woolwich Arsenal and Fulham at the same time. Norris left Fulham's management board about a month later.

Woolwich Arsenal fans who had followed their club across the river were unrepentant and a popular poem appeared in the Islington Gazette in September 1913 which confirmed their 'we shall not be moved (again)' attitude:

"'We're only Second Leaguers,
Can Chelsea really jeer?
At one time – late last April –
The Bottom they were near.
But with our faults admitted
We still remain the Reds.
Although we've quitted Woolwich,
We're not among the 'deads.'
In spite of the move from Woolwich:
You'll find us up and doing,
To keep the Highbury Height
Eye on the First Division
And no more sleepless nights.
We'll show the hateful Hotspur –
In spite of all its crows –
The Gunners can still shoot

If only with long bows."

If this was a period when rich and powerful men controlled football's destiny and events on the pitch resembled the Wild West at times, it was still the case that The FA and Football League had the final say.

The League Management Committee rejected a demand – proposed by Tottenham Hotspur - for a vote on Arsenal's move from Plumstead to Highbury and also a subsequent appeal and demand for an Extraordinary General Meeting on the issue, declaring, in March 1913, that:

"under the rules and practice of the League, we have no right to interfere."

It is suggested that Tottenham also helped residents to form a Highbury Defence Committee to oppose the move, describing it as a potential 'football invasion,' and persuaded a majority of members on Islington Council to their point of view; but there were also accusations that some of the same Councillors had shares in Tottenham Hotspur Football Club and hence the real reason for their opposition.

The Football League stood firm on its original decision, representing as they did many clubs from the North and the Midlands, for whose fans journeys to Highbury would be considerably easier than they had been to Plumstead, throughout both Victorian and Edwardian eras.

The League also felt that, though unusual, North London was a densely populated area which should be able to support three football league clubs. As a member of the League's Management Committee, the assertion by William Hall that crowds had been falling at the Manor Ground for some time due to economic decline in Woolwich, may also have been a factor.

On 4th March, 1913, with George Leavey having left the club and there being no real, remaining opposition to the move from the Board, Henry Norris publicly confirmed that the move would take place and tried to convince residents, now helpless to prevent it, that it would bring jobs and prosperity to the area.

4 March 1913

Move to Highbury officially confirmed

Many remained unconvinced. The Daily Gazette and North London Tribune (later renamed the Islington Gazette) declared - in echoes of the protests from the middle classes of Kent nearly 30 years earlier - that:

"...big football matches will attract thousands of people. Some of the tradespeople in certain lines may rejoice at the prospect of increased business, but, on the other hand, the occupiers of the better class houses may object very strongly to the invasion of a quiet locality by crowds, a portion of which is always composed of the rough element."

Finally, they turned on the Church and, in the 2nd April 1913 edition of the same paper, one correspondent declared, somewhat hysterically, that:

"...clergymen of the Church of England, the Church of Rome and the Nonconformist bodies have compromised with conscience in helping clubs; letting ground to them; in pleading for them, and in attending matches in every part of the country..."

However, the land had originally passed to St John's Hall for 'recreative purposes' but without any restricting covenants and so this last line of defence had been breached.

Norris appointed Archibald Leitch – who, ironically in view of their protests, had also worked on the football grounds at Chelsea and Tottenham Hotspur – to work with the club again. Norris also employed local builders, roofers and other tradesmen in a continuing attempt to win over local residents and prove that commercial benefits of the move would outweigh any social opposition; perhaps also building a new fan base in the process.

The land was, at this time, composed of thick grass and hillocks and largely covered by trees backing on to Highbury Hill. In the summer of 1913, reminiscent of that summer ahead of the move back to the Manor Ground exactly 20 years earlier, frantic attempts were made to have some kind of stadium in place for the start of the 1913-1914 season.

One end of the bumpy 'pitch' had to be raised by 11 feet, the other lowered by 5 feet. New turnstiles were erected and terraces were constructed with mud – much of it excavated for the building of the Piccadilly Line.

Leitch usually designed football stadiums with one main stand and three banks of open terracing. 'Arsenal Stadium' - or just plain 'Highbury' as it quickly became known – was built according to the same template.

The stand constructed on the East side was different though in that it had two tiers and, with some 9,000 seats, was the largest in London at that time and topped with a heavy multi-span roof. Each gable of the roof had a letter of the name 'Arsenal' painted on it.

9,000

Seats in the new East Stand at Highbury

The banking on the West side was named the 'Spion Kop' in another echo from the Manor Ground or perhaps a welcome continuation of the club's history in hostile territory? The South Terrace was known from the outset as the 'College End' paying reference to the original use of the site.

A steam laundry stood between the new stadium and Gillespie Road and so the North Terrace – the name preferred by the club – was known by fans as the 'Laundry End' well into the 1960s.

A story was told at the time that, when the foundations of the North Terrace were being built, a coalman's horse and cart had fallen into the rubble. The horse had to be put down and was buried forever under the new terrace. When this terrace was rebuilt 80 years later, no traces of it were found and the story was largely discredited.

However, 13 years on, when the club left Highbury, much more extensive building work was required to convert the site into residential buildings and, a long way below the surface, two horseshoes were found by workers next to timber remains, thought to be the cart in question. The horseshoes were put on display in Arsenal's museum.

It was estimated that Norris had invested more than £125,000 in the club by the time they played their first match at Highbury.

6 September 1913

Arsenal play their first league match at Highbury

This came on 6th September 1913 against Leicester Fosse (later to be renamed Leicester City FC) in the Football League Second Division.

Tommy Benfield scored the first ever goal at Highbury (for Leicester) but new centre-forward George Jobey scored Arsenal's first goal there in reply.

Scottish International Archibald Devine won the match with a penalty for The Gunners just 12 minutes from the end after a Leicester defender had handled the ball.

Jobey – signed from Newcastle United that May - was injured during the game and had to be wheeled home on a milk cart borrowed from David Lewis, a dairyman based in Gillespie Road.

Building work was still in progress and half of the stand seats were missing - and would remain so until Christmas. The players had to wash in bowls of cold water but the club had made a winning start at their new home and Norris would have felt vindicated with an opening crowd of 20,000 fans.

Those crowds continued to flock to Highbury. On 1st November 1913, a 3.2 win against Nottingham Forest was watched by 25,000:

"a sea of flat caps"

as the London Evening Standard described it.

Did you know?

The first crossword puzzle, compiled by a journalist - Arthur Wynne – from Liverpool, was published in the New York World newspaper in December 1913

In fact, attendances at Highbury in the club's first season there never went below the 20,000 mark. From being one of the worst supported club's in the league, Arsenal went to being one of the best.

Success continued on the field as well. The club won 20 of their 38 games and finished third, only failing to win immediate promotion back to the First Division on 'goal average.'

They scored 54 goals compared to Bradford Park Avenue who won the same number of points (49) but scored 71 goals and so finished in second place.

54

Goals scored by Arsenal in their first season at Highbury

Goal average (the number of goals scored, divided by the number of goals conceded) was used before 'goal difference' was introduced in England in 1976, after a successful trial at the 1970 World Cup.

Goal average had always been a controversial system of deciding promotion and relegation when two teams had finished level on points as, even if they also had the same goal difference, it would favour teams scoring and conceding fewer goals rather than those who scored and conceded more. Goal difference was introduced to favour a more attacking approach to football.

Ever since their move to North London the club had become unofficially known as 'The Arsenal' and records suggest that this was shortened to just 'Arsenal' when referring to the team during the following season.

The name was not officially changed though until 6th May 1915 when the Board of Trade confirmed that the club would now be known as 'The Arsenal Football Club Limited.'

Still referred to as The Arsenal by many, it was during the time of Herbert Chapman's management in 1927 that the simple form of 'Arsenal' really became the norm although, officially, the name has never changed from The Arsenal Football Club. Fans retained 'The Gunners' nickname but their original collective nicknames of 'The Reds' and, of course, 'The Woolwich Reds' were now left firmly behind in South London.

Programme Notes:

Arsenal club names:

1886: Dial Square

1887-93: Royal Arsenal

1893-1913: Woolwich Arsenal

1913 - Arsenal

Arsenal finished fifth in the 1914-15 season, winning only one game less (19) than in 1913-14 but losing five games more (14). At the time their official position was recorded as sixth due to a mistake in calculating goal average – a mistake that was only officially rectified by the Football League in 1975. They shared 43 points with Birmingham City and Hull City but had a better goal average than either of those clubs.

The last match of the season saw a 7.0 home win against Nottingham Forest with Henry King scoring four of the goals that day, almost thirty years since Forest had supplied the Dial Square team with its first redcurrant kit.

That game would be the last that Arsenal played in the Second Division. Played in front of just 10,000 spectators it reflected the fact – in a terrible echo of the Woolwich Arsenal experience towards the end of the Nineteenth Century - that the country was at war again. Indeed, it had been at war with Germany before the season had even begun.

Germany under Wilhelm II - the last German Emperor and King of Prussia (and eldest grandchild of Queen Victoria) - had overtaken Britain in becoming the leading military and economic power in Europe and it and others had looked to build overseas empires of their own since around 1880, expanding into Africa and China in particular.

Europe had effectively become divided into two great power systems, or 'alliances': The 'Triple Alliance' comprised of Germany (allied with a declining Ottoman Empire), Austria-Hungary (also known as 'The Habsburg Empire') and Italy.

The 'Triple Entente' was made up of Britain, France and Russia. New regional and old historical tensions, including resentment that had lingered from the end of the Franco-Prussian war in 1871, saw a number of 'Crises' between the two alliances throughout the early years of the twentieth century, especially in the Balkan region, until an event in June 1914 provided the spark that ignited the First World War.

28 June 1914

Archduke Franz Ferdinand and his wife Sophie were assassinated in Sarajevo – the spark that caused the outbreak of World War One

On 28th June 1914 Gavrilo Princip – a Serbian terrorist – assassinated the heir to the Austria-Hungary Empire, Archduke Franz Ferdinand, and his wife Sophie in the Bosnian capital, Sarajevo.

Ferdinand was the nephew of the Emperor, Franz Josef. The Austrians had been worried about the threat to their empire from Serbia for some time and, knowing that the Germans would support them due to their alliance, saw the opportunity of a pre-emptive strike and, on 28th July 1914, declared war on Serbia.

Russia mobilised its armies in support of Serbia and so German declared war, first on Russia on 1st August 1914 and then France two days later. German troops promptly entered Belgium on their way to invading France.

As far back as 1839, Britain had promised Belgium that it would defend their neutrality and so, when German forces failed to withdraw, declared war on Germany on 4th August 1914.

Austria-Hungary declared war on Russia two days later at the same time as the first British Expeditionary Forces landed in France. And so the fronts of the war – later to be called The Great War' - were formed and football was officially suspended for the duration of the hostilities.

INTER-WAR YEARS (1919 – 1939)

Post-war carnage

It is estimated that some seventeen million people died in World War One – including eleven million military personnel – and a further twenty million people were wounded before Germany signed The Armistice on 11th November, 1918 – an event which ended fighting on the Western Front and effectively confirmed a complete defeat for Germany and victory for the allied countries of the Triple Entente.

The German, Austria-Hungary and Russian empires had all been destroyed during the conflict.

28 June 1919

Germany was forced to sign the Versailles Treaty

On 28th June 1919, exactly five years after Archduke Ferdinand's assassination, Germany was forced to agree to the terms of and sign the Versailles peace treaty. The terms were harsh and meant to be a further punishment of the German nation.

The French leader, Georges Clemenceau, wanted Germany's economy and military forces to be completely ruined so that it could never again threaten French borders.

Seeing a future role as trade partner for Britain, the Prime Minister, David Lloyd George (newly-elected in November, 1918) was more sympathetic to Germany's recovery, as was US President Woodrow Wilson initially; but many Germans maintained that they were not solely to blame for the war and nor had they actually surrendered. This tended to harden attitudes among the allied nations.

Russia had been transformed by the workers' revolutions of February and October 1917 and many new countries had emerged from the decline of empires, especially in Eastern Europe, but the building or rebuilding of nations from the rubble of war was an enormous challenge, especially with so many young men having been killed during the war.

Did you know?

A flu outbreak between January 1918 and December 1920 is estimated to have killed between 50 to 100 million people worldwide

A flu epidemic of such huge and widespread proportions that it is now referred to as a 'pandemic' had also emerged in January 1918 while the war was still in progress.

To preserve wartime morale, reports of its spread across Britain, France, Germany and, further afield, in the USA were censored.

However, because Spain had been neutral in World War One newspapers tended to focus on reports of outbreaks there and so the impression was that this was somehow local to that country and it thus became known as 'Spanish Flu.'

Until it began to die out again in December 1920 the virus infected around 500 million people across the world and was estimated to have killed between 50 to 100 million people, or between three to five percent of the entire world population at that time. If World War One had been one of the deadliest military conflicts in history, then this flu virus was certainly one of the worst natural disasters.

It is estimated that around one million British people died in World War One, 9,000 of whom were linked in some way to Islington.

On 13th June 1917 German planes took part in London's first daylight bombing raid. 150 women and children are thought to have fled from a factory in Central Street, Finsbury before a PC Smith ushered them back inside to relative safety, almost certainly saving their lives. Unfortunately, Smith was killed in the raid.

The first German Zeppelin attack on London, on 31st May 1915, also included targets in Islington - on Mildmay Road and Balls Pond Road in Newington Green.

Edith Cavell worked locally, as a nurse at Highgate Infirmary (now the Highgate Wing of the Whittington Hospital). At the start of the war, she travelled to Brussels to serve as a matron at the Red Cross hospital in the city. When Belgium was invaded and Brussels occupied, she helped allied soldiers escape into the neighbouring Netherlands but was eventually found out, tried and found guilty by the Germans of assisting the enemy. She was shot by firing squad on 12th October 1915.

The Honourable Artillery Company in City Road, Finsbury, is estimated to have provided 13,000 men for 'Islington's Own' battalion and five of these were awarded the Victoria Cross.

Players from Arsenal who signed up for service included Percy Sands who enlisted in the Royal Army Medical Corps and served as a sergeant on the western front.

Reserve team player Jack Butler served in France with the Royal Artillery.

Former player James Maxwell served with the Royal Scots until he was killed in France in September 1915, while Spencer Bassett was killed on the Western Front in April 1917.

Programme Notes:

The following Arsenal players were among those who enlisted for wartime service:

- **Percy Sands**
- **Jack Butler**
- **James Maxwell**

Leigh Roose – an erratic goalkeeper for the club who perfected the wobbly knees technique of putting strikers off and who was described by Athletic News as 'mad' - was awarded the Military Medal for bravery during the Battle of the Somme before being killed at Gueudecourt during an attack on German trenches.

Many promising youth team players from the club were also killed in battle.

Henry Norris was knighted in 1917 for his services as a relentless recruitment officer during the war. He helped to assemble three artillery brigades from the Fulham area who were then also deployed on the Somme.

He rose to the rank of Colonel and in 1918 had been elected as a

Conservative Member of Parliament for the Fulham East Constituency based on a popular campaign focusing on 'common decency,' 'family values' and 'moral strength.' He also worked after the war to help solve the London housing problems of Belgian refugees.

However, for Norris and the club in which he had invested so heavily, things were looking pretty grim. Gate revenues from home matches were critical to financial stability for the club and promotion to the top tier of English football – much as it is today – seen as essential.

Given Arsenal's narrow failure to achieve promotion before the war and the fact that there had been no football at all for four years, Norris had been able to recoup barely any of his huge outlay on the club. Not only that, but the club were now £60,000 in debt and paying interest at the crippling rate of 10% on their overdraft.

1919

The history of post-war football began on 13th January 1919 with a meeting at the Grand Hotel in Manchester where the Management Committee of the Football League decided to expand its First Division by two clubs.

There was a precedent here in that when the Division had been expanded previously – in 1898 and 1905 – the two bottom clubs from the previous season had survived.

At the end of the 1914-15 season, those two clubs were Chelsea and Tottenham Hotspur (who had finished in last place). If both of these teams had actually been relegated there would have been no London club in the First Division for the first time since the 1903-04 season (Woolwich Arsenal's promotion that same season had meant they were the only London club in the First Division in 1904-05).

On 22nd February 1919 Chelsea were officially re-elected and allowed to remain in the First Division, with Derby County and Preston North End joining them, having finished first and second in the Second Division respectively. However, there was some debate about which would be the fourth club to complete the new Division's total of 22 clubs.

Although Arsenal had finished a full seven points behind Preston North End in the 1914-15 season and so nowhere near promotion, Henry Norris argued that it hadn't been a normal season, not just because of the murky pre-war suggestions that the likes of Clapton Orient fixed match times to suit themselves, but with allegations of real corruption and the fixing of match results.

One of the most notorious of these concerned a game that had taken place between Manchester United and Liverpool on Good Friday, 1915. Players on both sides - facing financial hardship or the trenches of the Western Front - agreed to rig the result at 2.0 to United which eventually saw them avoid relegation, finishing one place higher than Chelsea.

Leeds City had made illegal payments to players – an extra two months' wages to persuade them to stay with the club after the war. The club was expelled in 1919 and its players put up for sale but an FA enquiry found that manager Herbert Chapman had not been directly involved in the key decisions and so was absolved of any responsibility. He had resigned the previous year anyway and moved to Huddersfield Town.

Norris used these examples to paint a picture of the unsuitability of pre-war football results to be used as a basis for promotion decisions in 1919. He also argued that Arsenal were heavily in debt but that First Division football and the club's proximity to the bright lights of Central London would help to bring post-war fans back to Highbury.

He argued further that the club had been in the Football League 15 years longer than Tottenham Hotspur and should be rewarded for its long service to the League (though Wolverhampton Wanderers who had finished one place above Arsenal could have made a more compelling argument, having been one of the 12 founder members of the Football League in 1888).

What probably swung it for Norris and Arsenal was his close friendship with fellow freemason and businessman, the Irishman John McKenna.

'Gentleman' John McKenna had been Liverpool's first joint-manager (though his title remained as 'Secretary') and Chairman. Though somewhat compromised by the corruption case against Liverpool he had also been elected President of the Football League in 1917 and stood up for Arsenal's case.

In the end, it came down to a vote at a Special Meeting of the League, again at the Grand Hotel, on 10th March 1919, which Arsenal won with 18 votes to 8 for Spurs.

10 March 1919

Arsenal were voted back into the First Division, at the expense of Tottenham Hotspur who were relegated

Arsenal were duly promoted to the First Division – the first and last club to win promotion other than on merit.

Like Arsenal's founding fathers who had persevered against so much opposition in Kent, turned professional and joined the Football League, Norris did not care at all about fitting in or doing what was expected.

He wanted only success for Arsenal – his club – and breaking rules set by others in order to achieve that success was something he, Danskin and Humble had very much in common, in spite of their different backgrounds and social standings.

For one of the League's most respected clubs at the time - Tottenham Hotspur – the decision was perceived as a great injustice; the ruling was perceived as corrupt then as it still is by many people today.

Not only had Arsenal suddenly arrived in their homeland of North London; not only had White Hart Lane been requisitioned by the Army during the First World War meaning Tottenham had to play wartime matches at Highbury, now Arsenal had been promoted at the expense of Tottenham who were relegated.

Tottenham's immediate reaction was played out on the football field, the club winning immediate promotion back to the First Division in the 1919-20 season, coming top of Division Two by seven points from Chapman's Huddersfield Town (who were also promoted); winning the FA Cup in 1921 and finishing above Arsenal in the league in both 1921 and 1922.

Only in the 1922-23 season did Arsenal (11th) finish ahead of Tottenham (12th) and by just the one point.

Before the war Tottenham had finished ahead of Woolwich Arsenal in the league on only two occasions and in seasons when they and Arsenal both did pretty badly:

In 1909-10 – Tottenham's first season in Division One – the Gunners escaped relegation by just two points and Tottenham finished just one point ahead of them.

In 1912-13 Woolwich Arsenal were relegated and Tottenham were themselves fourth from bottom.

The early 1920s

Arsenal's first match in the 1919-20 season took place on 30th August 1919 against Newcastle United – the same opponents they had faced almost 26 years earlier.

40,000 fans attended this first post-war game at Highbury which Newcastle won 1.0 with a goal from winger James Henderson.

40,000

Attendance for Arsenal's first post-war match

As Arsenal struggled to make head way back in the First Division, so the country struggled to deal with a postwar economy that had been so badly damaged during the war.

Social welfare for the masses and poor and overcrowded housing conditions were little better than those being experienced at the time of the formation of Dial Square.

As then, working-class people who protested loudly were considered to be 'Communists' or, ironically in this case, 'Reds.' The country at large was well aware of the Russian Bolshevik and other revolutions and the threat of the same thing happening in Britain was never far from peoples' minds – a threat sometimes amplified by politicians in order to preserve a system where the few continued to control most of the country's wealth.

A new 'triple alliance' was the phrase coined to describe the three key sets of industrial workers who now sought to change things more radically: the railwaymen, miners and transport workers.

However, its natural political representatives the Labour Party -

coming to power for the first time in a minority government in 1924 under Ramsay MacDonald - saw little appetite for revolutionary change.

Even the General Strike of 1926, when workers went out on strike up and down the country in support of the miners, did not bring the country to its knees as predicted - largely due to willing volunteers operating essential services until the workers went back to work.

Unemployment continued to rise during the decade though, as did extreme poverty for many families, for whom the only other form of real protest outside of the ballot box and the vote to strike was to take part in hunger marches up and down the land.

In June 1919 Norris appointed a new secretary-manager: Leslie Knighton. Knighton, from Swadlincote in Derbyshire, had been assistant manager at Manchester City and Huddersfield Town where he had also had a spell as caretaker manager before the war.

June 1919

Leslie Knighton was appointed as new secretary-manager

Despite their return to the First Division Norris was still a long way from recovering his huge financial investment in Arsenal and the early years of the 1920s were still a financial struggle for the club - as they had been for long periods of its existence.

Norris was keen to keep a lid on transfer fees, supposedly fixing a ceiling of £1,000 for the transfer of any individual to the club (though evidence suggests this was sometimes exceeded).

Norris also made it clear to Knighton that he wanted big, strong players and so wouldn't be interested in players less than five feet eight inches tall or less than eleven stone in weight.

Clearly, these financial and physical limitations gave Knighton little room for manoeuvre and he described his situation thus:

"I had to make bricks without straw."

However, he was adept at spotting new, young talent and also, much like Danskin and Humble some 35 years earlier, had a pretty good, informal network of friends and people he had previously worked with to call upon – many in the football heartland of the North of England.

Anecdotal evidence suggests that Norris bullied Knighton endlessly – given his own legendary networking skills and especially after becoming a top Freemason (Grand Deacon of the Grand Lodge) – with their relationship being punctuated by arguments and fallings out.

For Knighton, it was additionally an often dangerous job. When travelling to different parts of Great Britain in pursuit of other clubs' players, English managers were very often attacked and beaten up by opposition fans.

1922

The Irish Free State was established, ending the Irish War of Independence

Toby Mercer who ran Belfast United in the early 1920s spotted a young right-back – Alex Mackie - and Knighton travelled to a rough part of Belfast (in the midst of a civil war over nationalist demands for 'Home Rule' at the time) to watch and eventually invite him to Highbury for a trial.

One story suggests that when Mackie was signed by the club he asked for a pet monkey rather than a signing-on fee; Norris was able to supply a monkey from his international trade contacts and the deal was done – though there is no hard evidence to support the monkey story.

Knighton signed defender Alf Baker, a miner, also from Derbyshire, after allegedly meeting him at the pit where he worked, whilst representatives of rival clubs trying to sign him were waiting at his home.

He also went 'undercover' wearing a false moustache and glasses supplied by Norris when seeking to sign another defender in Cardiff – Bob John – also in early 1922. John played for Caerphilly Town at the time and, after his move to Arsenal, played 470 times (still in the Top 20 of all-time appearance-makers for Arsenal) over the next 15 years and was capped 15 times by Wales.

Knighton signed a striker in 1923 - Jimmy Brain - who was also playing in Wales at the Ton Pentre club. He played for Arsenal over the next eight years becoming their top scorer in four consecutive seasons from 1924–25 to 1928–29 including 39 goals in 1925–26 (and four hat-tricks).

Brain was to become one of the club's most successful goal-scorers of all time, with 139 goals in 232 matches. He was also the first Arsenal player to score 100 goals in the league.

Programme Notes:

Jimmy Brain was the first Arsenal player to score 100 league goals

Knighton also signed another striker, James 'Tom' Whittaker, who played as a centre-forward before Knighton converted him into a left-half.

An even more bizarre story than the pet monkey incident surrounds the 'signing' by Knighton of another 'Jimmy.' James Paterson was a trained doctor who had won a Scottish League Championship medal with Rangers before the First World War.

Having also won a Military Cross in that war for bravery in action in France he moved south to join his brother-in-law – who served as the Arsenal club doctor at the time - in a medical practice in Clapton and found his way into the side playing on the left wing.

In one match he allegedly ran with a bunch of daffodils, handed to him by a girl in the crowd, as he couldn't bear to put them down!

Knighton's ways and means did not always work. He had also apparently signed a player in 1923 who stood at just five feet tall – Hugh 'Midget' Moffatt from Workington AFC - but Norris found out about it and sold him on to Luton Town before he had played a single game for Arsenal.

It wasn't uncommon for players to be signed, fail to impress, and then released again before playing for their 'new' clubs though Knighton's memoirs suggesting that size was everything may have an element of truth about it.

1923

The first Nazi Party rally was held in Munich, at which Hitler addressed huge crowds

Highbury had grown in stature in the capital through this period and was considered to be a key London football venue. It became the first club ground to act as a venue for an England international against opposition from outside Britain – Belgium – who visited on March 19th, 1923. England won 6.2.

Highbury had hosted its first ever international match three years earlier, on 15th March 1920, when England played Wales. Wales won 2-1 with England's solitary goal scored by Charlie Buchan.

This was the same Charlie Buchan whose travel costs Woolwich Arsenal had refused to pay before the war. Now playing for Sunderland, Norris instructed Knighton to re-sign him but he failed to do so and it is thought that this marked the beginning of the end of Knighton's reign as manager.

Apart from a few notable exceptions, it was not a successful period for Arsenal.

They did win 2.1 against Tottenham Hotspur at White Hart Lane on 23rd September 1922 in front of 40,582 fans with Reg Boreham – another Knighton signing – scoring both goals, but the match almost ended in a riot. A player was sent off on each side; players were pelted with missiles and the referee was threatened.

The Times reported that:

"It was not a satisfactory game from any point of view."

The Herald went further, confirming the same view of the two clubs as first formed some forty years earlier:

"Here was another example of Spurs' artistes being bullied out of it by 'grim Arsenal.'"

An FA Committee of Enquiry was set up to investigate events and threatened to close the ground if this behaviour on and off the pitch happened in the future. Unlike at the Manor Ground in 1895, this did not happen at White Hart Lane.

Norris may have cared little for how the press or opposition teams viewed his club: hadn't this always been the case? However, he would have been gravely concerned – if only due to his financial stake – that the club's ninth position in the league in the 1920-21 season was the best they had achieved under Knighton and the situation was getting worse, not better:

In the 1923-24 season the club finished fourth from bottom, just a point clear of relegation. In 1924-25 they finished just one place above the relegation places (though seven points clear) including five defeats in a row.

One of those defeats came against local rivals West Ham United on 26th January 1925.

Apart from a brief FA Cup run to the Quarter-finals in 1921-22 when they lost out 2.1 to Preston North End after a replay, Knighton had been unable to find any form of sustained success in that competition either.

This latest defeat came in the second replay of a First Round tie; the third game against the Hammers in twelve days.

3

Number of times Arsenal played West Ham United in 12 days in the FA Cup

Worse was to happen on 14th February 1925 when Arsenal suffered their biggest ever home defeat in the top tier: 5.0 to the mighty Huddersfield Town

Norris sacked Knighton at the end of that season (allegedly just before he was due to receive a £4,000 'golden handshake' for his service to the club). The job was advertised in Athletic News with the following, somewhat eccentric, job description:

"Arsenal Football Club is open to receive applications for the position of Team Manager. He must be

experienced and possess the highest qualifications for the post, both as to the ability and personal character. Gentlemen whose sole ability to build up a good side depends on the payment of heavy and exorbitant transfer fees need not apply."

Herbert Chapman

Later that summer, Norris made Herbert Chapman the new Arsenal manager – supposedly on a salary of £2,000 per year (footballers were paid around £300 per year at the time so Chapman's reputation to date had clearly been recognised and rewarded by the same Chairman who had tried so hard to control Knighton's purse strings).

4: Image of Herbert Chapman

Herbert Chapman was born in Kiveton Park, near Rotherham in South Yorkshire on 19th January 1878. His father was a coal miner but Herbert won a place at Sheffield Technical College to study mining engineering and so avoided having to go down the pit himself.

Two of his brothers played professional football, including Harry who won two League Championships and an FA Cup while playing for The Wednesday in the 1900s.

Chapman had an undistinguished career as a footballer - much of it as an amateur so that he could continue with his engineering career including managing a munitions factory during the war in a strange, early connection with Arsenal, given their origins in the armaments factories in Woolwich.

He played for local teams in the North and South Midlands, including Northampton Town. Wearing trademark yellow boots, he also played inside-left for Arsenal's major rivals, Tottenham Hotspur, in the Southern League.

It was while sitting in the bath after Tottenham's final match of the 1906-07 season that he first considered becoming a football manager. He had recommended a fellow player - Walter Bull - to take up the player-manager job at his old club, Northampton Town, but Bull had a change of heart and recommended Chapman. So Chapman duly took up the role instead.

At Northampton Chapman began to appreciate the lack of organisation or tactical coaching that took place in matches. He was especially concerned that all-out attack often did not bring the rewards for the team that dominated games.

He began to work out a tactical scheme where midfielders would drop back to give his forwards more space and defenders would try to pass their way out of trouble rather than just hoofing the ball upfield. Effectively he was developing an organised, counter-attacking style of football that had rarely been seen before.

Having taken 'The Cobblers' to the Southern League title he moved onto Leeds City and then to Huddersfield Town – Knighton's old club. Huddersfield had been in dire financial trouble in the post-war years and, at one point, plans had been formulated to merge Huddersfield with the team that had risen from the ashes of Chapman's Leeds City: Leeds United. However, such was the opposition to this locally that it never became a reality.

Chapman and Huddersfield won the FA Cup in 1921-22 (his first season there) beating Preston North End 1–0 in the Final at Stamford Bridge – the last Final to be played there before it moved to the new Empire Stadium in Wembley, London - and the club's first major trophy.

Chapman imposed the same style on the Huddersfield Town team as at Northampton and Leeds based on strong defending, inside passing and fast counter-attacking play which did not rely on wingers that were so popular elsewhere at that time.

All of the club's teams played in the same fashion so that players could easily fit into the first-team if called upon. Like Leslie Knighton, Chapman also believed in a strong scouting network from where he could spot the best young players, sign them before other clubs could, and mould them into his style of play.

His Huddersfield team won its first (and Chapman's first) League title in 1923-24 but only by having a goal average 0.024 better than runners-up, Cardiff City.

Huddersfield retained their title under Chapman the following season, being the first side to win the title having gone through the whole season without conceding more than two goals in any game.

Programme Notes:

Huddersfield Town were the first English club to win the league title without conceding more than two goals in any game

On Chapman's foundations, Huddersfield would go on to win a third successive championship in the 1925-26 season, after he had left for Arsenal, becoming the first English club to win three successive league titles.

In one final, non-Chapman Arsenal connection, on 27 February 1932 Huddersfield Town achieved its record home attendance at their then home ground at Leeds Road: 67,037 during their FA Cup Sixth Round tie against Arsenal.

Soon after signing for Arsenal, Chapman – now dubbed 'Yorkshire's Napoleon' by The Examiner newspaper - declared:

"I am going to make this the greatest club in the world."

He is also quoted as saying at the time:

"What a chance there is in London! I would like to build a Newcastle United there."

He also told the Arsenal board that it would take five years for Arsenal to become a force in the First Division and that he would need simultaneously money for players and – in a particular swipe at Norris - for them to leave him to get on with the job without interfering

One of his first acts was to go one better than Knighton and sign Charlie Buchan from Sunderland who had scored 209 goals in 379 league games for the Wearside club and remains their top league goalscorer of all time.

Sunderland manager Bob Kyle wanted Arsenal to pay £4,000 for Buchan but Chapman negotiated a fee of £2,000 initially – Arsenal's first four-figure transfer fee – to be followed by £100 to be paid to Sunderland for each of Buchan's goals in his first season at Highbury.

In the event, Buchan scored 21 goals for Arsenal that season and so it turned out that Chapman was worse off for his gamble to the tune of £100.

Chapman also set about persuading the press and Arsenal fans to refer to the team as simply Arsenal – even though, as we have seen, the company name remains, officially, The Arsenal.

Chapman's first league game in charge of the team – and Buchan's second coming - was at Highbury on 29th August 1925 against old rivals Tottenham Hotspur in front of 53,183 passionate North London fans.

Tottenham won 1.0 with a goal from Jimmy Dimmock, a winger who had also scored their winning goal against Wolverhampton Wanderers in the 1921 FA Cup Final.

Arsenal did not lose again in their next seven games but on 3rd October 1925 they were thrashed 7.0 by Newcastle United at St James's Park with inside-right Bob Clark grabbing a hat-trick.

A tactical discussion took place following this defeat, led by Buchan and Chapman.

Programme Notes:

After a 7.0 defeat at Newcastle, a tactical re-think was required and the new 3-4-3 formation was born

The offside law had just been changed – and actually trialled by the FA at Highbury – in that the three opponents needed to put an attacking player onside had now been reduced to two (including the goalkeeper).

The FA had wanted to encourage a more attacking game and had not been impressed with Chapman's defensive tactics, successful though they had been with Huddersfield Town.

Forwards now had more space in front of them to move into and the game became more stretched with long balls often replacing the short passing game favoured by Chapman and others.

At Sunderland, Buchan had witnessed former centre-forward Charlie Thomson not only playing as a centre-half just behind the forwards but also dropping into the back line and having a far more defensive role - effectively a defensive 'stopper' or third back.

Chapman built on this by bringing the inside forwards back to help out in midfield and so the formation changed from 2-3-5 to 3-4-3. The shape formed by the players now looked like a 'W' on top of a 'M' and so became known as the 'W-M' or 'Third Back' formation.

The offside trap was really now the responsibility of the centre-half in his new, deeper position and with instructions to rarely if ever cross the halfway line as the full-backs were encouraged to play wider on the wings.

If the authorities had wanted to see more open play then, with typical Arsenal belligerence, Chapman and Buchan had found a way to close it down again.

Did you know?

To keep food cool in the 1920s it was usually kept in a separate room; one with a north-facing wall.

Chapman was though a great innovator in the game and this formation evolved to include a fast attacking front line with wingers cutting inside and a creative midfielder role through which many of the attacks would begin.

Chapman also introduced rubber studs for boots, to be used on hard pitches; the monitoring of every player's diet and the use of club physiotherapists to help players recover more quickly from injuries; the use of a white football on gloomy, wintry afternoons and team 'bonding' holidays.

He also suggested a 10-yard penalty arc be introduced to pitch markings, as had been used overseas, but the FA refused to implement it until 1937.

Did you know?

A.A. Milne published the first 'Winnie-the-Pooh' story on 14th October 1926

Despite criticism levelled at his use of whatever tactics which were required to win matches, Chapman was also one of the great football entertainers and, in the words of The Times, wanted to:

"make football attractive to the shilling paying public."

At Huddersfield he had introduced the playing of gramophone records over the tannoy system during half-time and, in a reflection of that first Woolwich Arsenal game against Thames Ironworks some thirty years previously, Chapman had floodlights installed at the club's training ground.

He loved the idea of evening football matches played under floodlights, but he would not live to see the night that Arsenal would first play under the lights at Highbury – in 1951 after the FA had lifted its ban on their use a year earlier.

Chapman would also have loved the theatricality of these occasions. Moments before the players came onto the pitch, the lights would dim momentarily – just as in theatre performances in Islington or down the road in London's West End – to alert fans to the drama about to unfold.

28 August 1928

The 'Clock' arrives at Highbury; installed initially on the North Terrace

Many football fans did not possess wristwatches at the time and so, on 28th August 1928, Chapman had a clock measuring almost eight and a half feet in diameter placed on the North Terrace.

Its hands originally counted down the 45 minutes of each half but the Football League felt this caused far too much barracking of the referee by the crowd towards the end of matches and it had to be changed to an ordinary clock.

The clock was moved to the opposite end – The College End - in 1935 and that terrace was known by many fans forever after as 'The Clock End.'

Three days earlier, Arsenal had played Sheffield Wednesday wearing numbers on the back of their shirts for the first time, to aid commentators and fans alike.

At Highbury against the other Football League club from Sheffield – Sheffield United – the club had played in the first ever match to be broadcast live on the BBC.

Recognition of where on the pitches players were actually located was also key for fans. To help with this the Radio Times had published a diagram of the pitch – actually eight rectangles and known as 'snakes and ladders' or 'hopscotch' until it was abandoned in the mid-1930s – which commentators would refer to during the game so that listeners would know where players and ball actually were.

The goal area was known as 'square one' and so, when players kicked the ball back to their goalkeepers it was referred to as going 'back to square one.'

That match ended in a 1.1 draw with Charlie Buchan scoring the first goal ever to be heard on radio.

Programme Notes:

Charlie Buchan scored the first goal ever to be heard on radio

Such was the success of the experiment that The Spectator declared:

"that type of broadcasting has come to stay"

For all these early innovations on the pitch and off of it, Chapman was not – as he himself had predicted - immediately successful at Arsenal.

True the team did get to its first FA Cup Final that same year – 1927 – with eight of the players recruited by Leslie Knighton, but now captained by Buchan.

Having beaten Southampton 2.1 in the Semi-final at Stamford Bridge with goals from Buchan again and one from new winger, Joe Hulme, they faced Cardiff City in the fifth Final to be played at Wembley Stadium (originally known as the British Empire Exhibition Stadium or simply the 'Empire Stadium') on 23rd April 1927.

Cardiff City had beaten the holders Bolton Wanderers – who had already won two FA Cups – on route to the Final.

23 April 1927

Arsenal reach the FA Cup Final for the first time

91,206 fans saw Cardiff win the match 1.0 and take the trophy out of England for the first and only time in the competition's history. While additional trains had been laid on to get Cardiff's fans to Wembley, many Arsenal fans had been caught up in traffic on London's North Circular Road, as had the Arsenal players who were on edge as a result.

The game that followed was poor with a draw being seemingly inevitable until a late mistake by, ironically, Arsenal's Welsh international goalkeeper Dan Lewis cost them the match.

The ball had slipped underneath his right arm and Cardiff's (Scottish) striker Hughie Ferguson knocked the ball into the net, seemingly with his elbow. Lewis blamed both the shine of the ball and the gloss or sheen of his new jersey.

As a result, Arsenal have washed the goalkeeper jersey before every subsequent Wembley cup appearance so as to at least remove the offending sheen.

The 1927 Final was the first where football fans joined together before the match to sing 'Abide with me' which has become an FA Cup Final tradition and known to some as the 'Cup Final Hymn.'

It was also the first FA Cup Final to be broadcast live on BBC Radio with George Allison - the same sports journalist who had reported on Woolwich Arsenal's matches during their days in Kent and who had produced propaganda for the War Office during the First World War – the first BBC FA Cup Final commentator.

Also in 1927, Henry Norris was forced to leave the club and, in 1929, received a lifetime ban from football over an expenses scandal which included alleged illegal payments to Buchan over his transfer from Sunderland and proceeds from the sale of the club's team bus apparently reaching his wife's personal bank account.

Founder Jack Humble also left the club as a result of this. Though innocent of any wrongdoing, he was judged to be negligent along with other Directors of the club for not spotting such irregularities earlier.

Norris would die from a heart attack in 1934 - a week after his 69th birthday – but, in spite of his years of bullying Leslie Knighton, left money to him in his will and also to groundsman Alec Rae who Norris had mercilessly criticized when the Highbury pitch had failed to come up to his exacting standards.

If Chapman felt liberated with Norris (who he also argued with frequently) now gone, his total control over all playing matters still wasn't reflected in glory on the pitch during the 1920s.

The Club passed into the control of Eton-educated Samuel Hill-Wood, also a businessman and Conservative politician and significant investor in the local mill town club of Glossop North End before the war.

Glossop subsequently failed to gain re-election to the Football League and disappeared without a trace while the Hill-Wood dynasty at Arsenal saw both Samuel's son Denis and grandson Peter eventually serve as Chairmen of the club, but it wasn't until the 1930s that Hill-Wood was able to preside over sustained Arsenal success.

After the club's best ever league performance, finishing second in Chapman's first season at Highbury – five points behind Huddersfield Town – his Arsenal teams finished no higher than ninth in the following three seasons. This wasn't for any lack of competitive spirit from the team, being true to its origins, or its new manager.

2nd

Arsenal's best-ever league performance to date - in what was Chapman's first season at Highbury

On 2nd February 1927, during a Fourth Round replay in the FA Cup against Port Vale, Chapman sent his trainer George Hardy (who had been one of Norris's and Hall's first 'signings' in 1910) to the training room for shouting out team tactics from the touchline during the match.

Hardy left the club and went to work for Tottenham Hotspur. He was replaced by Tom Whittaker while Charlie Buchan put the Gunners through on their way to that Wembley meeting with Cardiff City.

Did you know?

Alexander Fleming announced his discovery of penicillin on 30th September 1928

Tough and innovative in his approach to coaching and management, Chapman was also ruthless and uncompromising with his players – determined to keep their feet very firmly on the ground.

A regular team meeting took place on Friday afternoons at midday during which Chapman used toy players that could be moved around a magnetic table's football field layout (another innovation).

On one occasion, after previously winning 7.1 at Wolverhampton Wanderers, Chapman substituted criticism for praise, reminding the players that:

"If our forwards hadn't scored, we'd have lost that match."

It could be said that Chapman was recruiting key players and perfecting the W-M formation during this time. Unlike so many previous seasons in the club's Football League history, the club finished comfortably in mid-table and, if there was no sign of league success, there was similarly no serious threat of relegation either.

To be fair to Norris (and persistence from the bullish Chapman) funds had now become available for players and this continued under Hill-Wood's chairmanship.

Adding to the likes of Alf 'Doughy' Baker who played in all eleven positions during his time at the club, Jack Lambert - a robust centre-forward - arrived from Doncaster Rovers.

Born in Rotherham, South Yorkshire, and also having played for Leeds United, Chapman had spotted him when at Huddersfield Town.

Lambert would go on to score 18 times in just 20 league appearances in the 1929-30 season and then 38 goals in 34 league games in 1930-31, including no less than seven hat-tricks.

Lambert was joined by defenders Tom Parker – who would be an ever-present right-back for over three years - Herbie Roberts and a young George Male from West Ham via Clapton Orient. Male had been rejected by West Ham and signed for Arsenal over a cup of coffee in the Lyons Teashop on Wood Green High Road.

Another especially robust defender to join Arsenal's 'defence-in-depth' project was 'Eddie' Hapgood. Hapgood – who supplemented his wages in a nod to the Modern Era by modelling for fashion magazines and advertising chocolate - would go on to captain both Arsenal and England.

Lambert was also joined up front by three of the greatest attacking players to ever play for the club: David Jack, Cliff 'Boy' Bastin and Alex James.

Programme Notes:

Chapman signed some of Arsenal's best ever players during the late 1920s:

- Jack Lambert
- Tom Parker
- George Male
- Eddie Hapgood
- David Jack
- Cliff Bastin
- Alex James

Jack arrived on 13th October 1928 for a transfer fee of £10,890 – the first player ever to be sold for a five-figure fee. He was also the first player to score in an FA Cup Final at Wembley – in the first of those Bolton Wanderers Cup wins – after two minutes against West Ham United, and after knocking a spectator unconscious as the huge crowd (controlled by mounted police including the legendary 'White Horse') pressed against the goal net.

Cliff Bastin signed for Arsenal from Exeter City in 1929 at the age of just 17, thus earning the nickname of 'Boy.' Though initially reluctant to leave Devon he became a prolific striker for the club and probably the first 'golden boy' of English football.

He scored 178 goals in 396 games, making him Arsenal's all-time record goalscorer at the time; the record stood from 1939 until 1997, when his total was surpassed by Ian Wright and subsequently Thierry Henry. A left-winger, he scored 33 league and cup goals in the 1932-33 season – more than any other out-and-out winger.

178

Goals scored by Cliff Bastin for Arsenal – a record that stood for almost 60 years

'Alex' James from Lanarkshire in Scotland was the creative midfielder Chapman's evolving W-M formation needed to make it complete.

Signed from Preston North End as a goal-scoring inside-forward, like Hapgood he was advised to supplement his wages – the maximum wage set by The Football League was £8 per week at the time – with a 'sports demonstrator' job at leading department store Selfridges as well as ghost-writing a weekly article for a London evening newspaper.

James was one of Arsenal's first great showmen; in his 'baggy pants,' heavily gelled hair parted down the middle and long-sleeved shirt he often clashed with Chapman's disciplinarian approach.

However, he became one of the most outstanding players of his generation and was the midfield link that would make the whole team tick.

Matt Busby, playing for Manchester City at the time and later famous manager of Manchester United, said of James:

"Alex James was the great creator from the middle. From an Arsenal rear-guard action, the ball would, seemingly inevitably, reach Alex. He would feint and leave two or three opponents sprawling or plodding in his wake before he released the ball..."

If Chapman's arrival at Arsenal, having left the reigning league champions to do so, was sensational then news of his signings was greeted with excitement, expectation and not a little jealousy from other clubs. Chapman was supposed to have boasted that he could pay £2,000 more than other clubs for any player he wanted.

Arsenal's spending earned them the nickname of 'The Bank of England Club' but, as in so many previous periods in the club's history, expenditure, excitement and expectation had rarely formed their own holy trinity of success. This would all change in the 1930s

The 1930s

Although hunger and poverty remained for many during the decade, the 1920s have been named the 'Roaring Twenties' or the 'Golden Age.' These years of glamorous excess were depicted in Hollywood films and high society dances in the new 'Jazz Age.'

New innovations such as motor cars, telephones and electricity illuminated peoples' lives as the darkness of the war years receded. The new Republican President of the United States of America, Herbert Hoover, boldly announced in 1928 that: ***"We in America today are nearer to the final triumph over poverty than ever before in the history of any land."***

Encouraged by this, many ordinary people gambled on the stocks and shares of new businesses which seemed to be growing rapidly, though often manufacturing more goods than there were people to buy them.

Unfortunately, prices were artificially high and, in October 1929, they began to fall rapidly as speculators tried to sell and at least get their money back or take their savings out of banks to pay essential bills such as housing and food.

This was known as the 'Wall Street Crash' and caused a run on America's banks – of which 5,000 went out of business in the three years of the 'Great Depression' that followed. Many ordinary people lost their homes, their jobs and their life savings.

Since the end of the First World War, the USA had been lending heavily to European countries – including Britain. As a direct result of the banking crisis at home, they recalled these loans which, in turn, caused a banking crisis across Europe and plunged much of the continent into the worst economic depression it has seen – before or since - with unemployment in Britain racing to over two million people by August 1930.

Did you know?

An average semi-detached house cost £450 in the 1930s – equivalent to two years' salary for a professional man such as a doctor or lawyer

If football attendances are a barometer for the state of a country's economy or peoples' general well-being, then the 1930s represented a boom time not dissimilar to that experienced in the early years of the century.

Crowds flocked to Highbury in their tens of thousands as fans, looking to rebuild their lives outside of the stadium, tried to escape worry and hardship for at least ninety minutes on Saturday afternoons.

Crowds regularly topped 70,000 during the 1930s. In Islington's long tradition of entertainment, the must-see players were performing for Arsenal and Highbury was the most glamorous theatre in the Borough.

Arsenal had become a winning team and, if Huddersfield Town had dominated much of the 1920s, then Chapman's newly constructed team with its new playing style were so successful in the 1930s that it became known initially as the 'Chapman Era' and, enduringly, as the 'Arsenal Era.'

Although the club struggled again in the league in the 1929-30 season, only finishing fourteenth, they were involved in an astonishing 6.6 draw with Leicester City at their Filbert Street ground on 21st April 1930.

This was the first-ever 6.6 draw and the highest-scoring draw in Football League history; Arsenal's goals came from Bastin with two and Scot David Halliday with four.

Halliday scored eight goals in just fifteen performances for Arsenal. Later, as a football manager, he was one of only two people (Alex Ferguson was the other) ever to guide Aberdeen to the Scottish League Championship.

Arsenal fared better in the FA Cup reaching their second Cup Final, this time against Chapman's old giants of the game – Huddersfield Town – on 26th April 1930.

In Chapman's honour, having managed both teams, this was the first Final when the teams entered the Wembley Stadium side-by-side, led out by captains Tom Parker and Tom Wilson (known in the game as the 'Gentleman of football' or 'The dauntless Tommy Wilson').

Arsenal went on to win the game – and thus their first major trophy - 2.0, with goals from James and Lambert (in a move also created by James).

It was also the first trophy of any kind to be won by the club since that London Senior Cup triumph back in 1891.

That evening saw Upper Street swamped by Arsenal fans; traffic all the way back to the West End itself had to be diverted because of the celebrations.

The 1930 FA Cup Final was also remembered for an appearance by the German airship – the Graf Zeppelin – which hovered over Wembley Stadium. At the time it was the largest airship in the world, measuring around 776 feet in length.

A few years later it and another airship – Hindenburg – would be used by the new German government (the Third Reich) to distribute propaganda leaflets in the lead up to the Second World War. In retrospect, the huge airship's eerily quiet movement would be used as a metaphor for German stealth and massive military rebuilding after its surrender during World War One.

For Arsenal though, it was a case of moving from football strength to strength.

Programme Notes:

Gerard Keizer was the first foreigner to play for Arsenal; and the first in English football

During the summer of 1930, they signed a Dutch goalkeeper called

Gerard 'Gerrit' Keizer who was the first foreign player to appear for the club and, indeed, the first player outside of Great Britain or Ireland to play in English football.

Keizer had first played in England in Kent – not so far along the river from Woolwich - in Margate. In those days Margate played the role of what we would now call a 'nursery' club, developing players for Arsenal.

It was here that Chapman spotted him and he made his debut for the club in their opening game of the 1930-31 season on 30th August 1930, in a 4.1 away win at Blackpool.

Keizer never kept a clean sheet for the first team and his approach was flamboyant in the vein of later 'crazy' goalkeepers who would grace the English game, but it wasn't this that made his part of the Arsenal story unique.

Keizer would play for Arsenal on Saturday afternoons then fly back to Amsterdam in his native Netherlands in the evenings in order to play for the Ajax second team the next day. He soon earned the nickname of 'The Flying Dutchman.'

After the German occupation of their country during World War Two and possibly not helped by their location and identity with Jews in the borough of Amsterdam-Oost during the 1930s at the same time as Hitler's Holocaust, the club found itself in severe financial trouble.

As Nottingham Forest had done for them sixty years earlier, so Arsenal supplied kit and footballs to Ajax, which is why the Dutch team's first games after the war were played in the same red and white shirts as Arsenal.

Chapman added white collars and sleeves around 1933, supposedly having spotted a fan at the ground wearing a red, sleeveless sweater over a white shirt.

After securing their first FA Cup trophy they won the First Division title in the following season becoming champions of England for the first time.

In an echo of 1893, they were also the first southern club to win the Football League Championship; Herbert Chapman made his own history as the first manager to guide two different teams to the title.

1930-31

Arsenal were league champions for the first time, and the first team from the south to win the title

That 1930-31 football team was considered by many to be the best club side of all time - let alone in Arsenal's own football history – and all in a season when Tottenham Hotspur would finish third in Division Two and just miss out on promotion back to the First Division.

Arsenal won 28 of their 42 games that season and lost only four. In the process, they amassed 66 points, six more than any other team had previously scored when winning the title.

They also scored huge victories: 7.1 against Blackpool in the return match at Highbury and 9.1 against Grimsby Town on 28th January 1931 in which David Jack scored four goals; this remains Arsenal's record home win of all time in the top tier of English football.

Such was their dominance that Aston Villa, who finished second, were seven points behind Arsenal who secured their title on 18th April 1931 with a 3.1 home win over Liverpool. Their scorers on that momentous day were three of Chapman's key imports: Lambert, Jack and Bastin.

Arsenal scored an incredible 127 league goals that season, yet Villa scored 128 – a record in the top tier of English football.

60

Arsenal's record number of away goals

Arsenal also scored a record number of 60 away goals, such was their dominance outside of London as well as within the capital.

Buoyed by this success and the ongoing gate receipts from huge crowds at Highbury, Arsenal were, for the first time in their history and despite the large transfer fees Chapman had paid to sign the best players available, in good financial health.

Their players now travelled by train to away matches in a private carriage and mixed with stars of other sports in the 'soft south.'

They were dismissed – especially in the North – as arrogant and rich; pitch invasions were a regular occurrence as opponents on the terraces as well as on the pitch tried to, quite literally, boot them off of it.

Did you know?

The Empire State Building opened in New York on the 1st May 1931 - at the time it was the tallest building in the world

Chapman's tactics on the field also weren't to everybody's taste and one of the origins of the 'boring Arsenal' and 'lucky Arsenal' chants from opposing supporters may have come from Chapman's teams' tactic of defending for long periods and then hitting their opponents on the break with deadly efficiency.

'Lucky Arsenal' is more likely to be a relic of how Norris contrived to have them promoted back to the First Division in the first place.

In the 1931-32 season, the jealousy of opposition fans was raised to even greater heights. Arsenal came closer than any other club in the twentieth century to completing the 'Double' of League Championship and FA Cup wins in the same season.

Only Preston North End with that first League title-winning season in 1888-89 and Aston Villa in 1896-97 had ever achieved it. Indeed, when this great Arsenal side failed to follow suit in 1932, many football commentators believed that no club would ever achieve it again.

They only just missed out on the title, critically losing 2.1 to Liverpool at Anfield on 9th April 1932, with Liverpool's Merseyside rivals, Everton, taking advantage to win the league by just two points from Arsenal.

In the FA Cup itself, Arsenal almost repeated that record scoreline against Ashford United some forty years earlier when they beat Darwen 11.1 on 9th January 1932, though it was still their record win at Highbury. Jack scored a hat-trick and Bastin went one better with four goals.

Their 'lucky Arsenal' label held firm in the FA Cup Semi-final of that year. At Villa Park on 12th March 1932, they beat Manchester City 1.0 with Bastin scoring the winner in the dying seconds of the match after City had been denied two earlier penalty appeals.

Bastin would eventually score more FA Cup goals (26) than any other Arsenal player. The Daily Mail labelled the occasion as:

"Cup-tie Murder" and "Bastin's Dagger Thrust."

And, somewhat joylessly:

"Naturally, as the scorer, Bastin was the hero of the game. At Snow Hill station a woman kissed him impulsively and called him one of those soft names that women use..."

Arsenal met old foes Newcastle United in the Final at Wembley on 23rd April 1932 and Bob John scored an early goal for The Gunners but the game hinged on an incident just before half-time.

Winger Jimmy Richardson of United chased a long ball towards the bye-line and crossed it for Jack Allen to score the equaliser. Arsenal players – and Hapgood in particular, being closest to it – protested that the ball had already gone over the line before it could be crossed but the referee disagreed and so the goal stood.

Newcastle's manager, Andy Cunningham said, simply:

"From my position, I could not see whether it had gone out of play or not."

This would often be the media stance taken by another famous Arsenal manager more than sixty years later when asked to comment on controversial incidents in matches and sometimes unwilling or unprepared to do so.

Allen got his and Newcastle's second with twenty minutes to go and sealed Newcastle's victory and their third FA Cup triumph in total.

In their third visit to Wembley Arsenal became the first side to score first and go on to lose the match. However, the match would forever be caught up in the controversy of Richardson's cross and known in football history as the 'over-the-line' Final.

Queen Mary, attending with King George V, seemed far more taken with Cliff Bastin, exclaiming that:

"it is extraordinary that a boy so young should be such a good player."

This was reported in a London Star article on the Monday after the Final alongside a piece on the opening of a new football stadium in Paris – the Parc des Princes – and an article on German election results which had ***"staggered political experts"*** amid a warning from France that the Reich is: ***"pushing Germany's youth on to avenge her country's defeat (in World War One)."***

Adolf Hitler's re-armament plans and preparations for another war were gathering pace as the world stood by and watched.

Later that year, Chapman approached the London Electric Company and lobbied for the name of the local London Underground station at Highbury – Gillespie Road – to be changed.

This was a huge undertaking given that the tickets, signs and maps across the whole network would all have to be changed, not just at Gillespie Road.

Chapman had first had the idea when visiting with his Leeds City team in 1913 and, like Norris, had been impressed by the location of such a key transport link - but one that few people outside of Islington had ever heard of.

October 31, 1932

Gillespie Road Underground Station was renamed Arsenal (Highbury Hill)

As with Woolwich Arsenal he wanted Arsenal's fame to spread throughout the land and beyond and thanks to his tireless campaign the station was renamed 'Arsenal (Highbury Hill)' – the first and only tube station to be named after a football club (the 'Highbury Hill' suffix disappeared in the early 1960s when the station's name became, simply, Arsenal.

The football ground was also officially renamed as 'Arsenal Stadium' though, not unlike their old London rivals, West Ham United's Boleyn Ground being forever known as Upton Park, so Arsenal's stadium in North London would be referred to by home and away fans as Highbury – even those travelling there by tube.

Later in 1932 a new double-decker West Stand was built, at a cost of £45,000 – easily the most expensive grandstand ever seen - with seats for 4,000 spectators and standing for a further 17,000.

£45,000

Cost of the new West Stand at Highbury

The stand was opened by the Prince of Wales (later King Edward VIII who would rule the country for less than a year before abdicating in favour of his brother in 1936) on 10th December 1932 before a match with old London derby rivals, Chelsea. Arsenal won the match 4.1 in front of a crowd of 53,206.

This was one of many convincing home league wins that season: 6.1 against Sunderland in September 1932; 8.2 against Leicester City in the October; 9.2 against Sheffield United in December, and 8.0 against Blackburn Rovers the following February.

Did you know?

Fred Perry, one of Britain's greatest tennis players, who won Wimbledon three times, often joined in fitness training with the Arsenal team

There were also some convincing away wins including a 7.1 victory at Wolverhampton Wanderers (who, incredibly got their revenge at Highbury, 2.1) but defeat to their West Midlands neighbours, Aston Villa, 5.3, in November 1932.

Villa would go on to be runners-up to Arsenal, just as in 1930-31 but this time by just four points to Arsenal who duly won their second league title, scoring another century of goals (118) in the process.

118

Goals scored by Arsenal in winning their second league title in 1932-33

The elusive Double seemed to be on again but, in the third round of the FA Cup (the first round in which Arsenal and other leading clubs now entered the competition), it all went badly wrong in one of the biggest shocks in Arsenal, FA Cup and football history.

Walsall

On 14th January 1933, Arsenal travelled to Walsall of the Third Division North, just down the road from Villa Park.

If Arsenal had pipped Villa in the league twice in the past three seasons, their near neighbours took advantage of a one-off cup tie at their narrow ground and won 2.0 in front of a crowd of just over 11,000.

Arsenal were missing key players such as Hapgood, Hulme, John and Lambert through either injury or illness and perhaps Chapman had underestimated the strength of the opposition, playing at the top of their game to further the romance of the underdog in the FA Cup competition.

Walsall scored their first goal after an hour of play through Gilbert Allsop and then Tommy Black – drafted in to replace Hapgood and who had already made several bad tackles on Walsall's Bill Sheppard - gave away a clear penalty from which they scored their second goal.

As with trainer George Hardy almost six years earlier, Chapman never forgave Black who made no further appearances for Arsenal and was soon transferred to Plymouth Argyle.

It is hard to really do justice to the shockwaves caused by the result of this match. Not only did nobody – even the most die-hard Walsall fan – see it coming but Arsenal were generally considered to be streets ahead of their First Division rivals, let alone those from two leagues below

The Arsenal team had been assembled for what was then a huge sum of £30,000, whereas Walsall's had cost just £69.

£30,000 v £69

Cost of Arsenal's playing squad compared to Walsall's

Winning the league with Arsenal for a second time was some

compensation for Chapman. His wingers Bastin and Hulme contributed 53 goals – far more than other clubs who tended to use them primarily as a supply line for their centre-forwards.

Alex James was the key provider in these early 1930s teams and with the wingers starting or cutting inside at speed, Chapman's counter-attacking strategy was deployed to perfection.

However, in spite of all their recent success, he also saw in that raw, physical game at Walsall the need to rebuild a side that could then survive his retirement and not just

"collapse like a pack of cards."

He signed inside-right Ray Bowden from Plymouth Argyle for £4,500 in March 1933, but only after several meetings as Bowden was initially reluctant to leave the West Country (he had been born in Looe in Cornwall) as had the young Cliff Bastin four years earlier.

Chapman viewed him as a natural replacement for the ageing David Jack. In the event, he was to be Chapman's last major signing for the club.

Bowden made his debut in a home game against Wolverhampton Wanderers on 18th March 1933 which Arsenal lost 2.1. They lost 2.1 in their following league match at Newcastle as well and were struggling in the league, having won only three matches since being knocked out of their stride in that shock defeat at Walsall.

Things fitted back into place on 1st April 1933 though when they made up for the away defeat at Aston Villa with a 5.0 win at Highbury and a subsequent run of four successive league wins to carry them to the title.

1933

Hitler came to power as Chancellor of Germany

The 1933-34 season began well with the team winning 14 of the 23 league games before the turn of the year and heading towards a second, consecutive league title (and ultimately a third the season after that) but, as at Huddersfield, Chapman failed to see through either hat-trick of titles.

After watching matches featuring Sheffield Wednesday – Arsenal's next league opponents – and an Arsenal third team game against Guildford City while nursing a head cold, it quickly developed into pneumonia.

Chapman died on January 6th, 1934, aged just 55.

The Times described his career as being so successful and innovative that:

"a novelist would reject it as being too far-fetched."

The six pallbearers at Chapman's funeral on 10th January 1934 were Cliff Bastin, Alex James, Eddie Hapgood, David Jack, Joe Hume and Cliff Bastin. His assistant, Joe Shaw, wrote a poem – 'The Lost Captain' in his memory:

"The last whistle has sounded, the great game is over,
O was ever a field left so silent as this;
The scene a bright hour since, how empty it is;
What desolate splendour the shadows now cover.
The captain has gone. The splendour was his."

Finishing the job

After the shocking and totally unexpected death of Chapman Shaw took over as caretaker manager in a bid to continue the success of the team that Chapman had first put together and had started to rebuild.

He was assisted by Tom Whittaker and George Allison – the media journalist who had already played his part in the Arsenal story – who would formally take over as manager of the club at the end of the season.

One of the first post-Chapman signings came in March 1934 and was a player Chapman had been tracking for some time but without success as, again, 'Ted' Drake preferred to play in his native South of England.

Drake did eventually sign for £6,500 from Southampton where he had scored 47 goals in 71 appearances.

Also an occasional cricketer for Hampshire, he was a powerful and ruthless centre-forward and went on to become Arsenal's top scorer for each of the five seasons from 1934–35 to 1938–39. After retiring as a player he led London rivals Chelsea to their first ever League Championship in 1955.

Drake scored on his Arsenal debut – a 3.2 home win against Wolverhampton Wanderers – and went on to score in four of the final nine league games, including both goals in the last game of the season – a 2.0 win against Sheffield United at Highbury which was also David Jack's last game for the club before moving to Southend United as their new manager.

Programme Notes:

Ted Drake would become Arsenal's top scorer for five consecutive seasons from 1934-35 to 1938-39

In the year of Chapman's death, it was perhaps appropriate that Huddersfield Town would be runners-up, just three points behind Arsenal who promptly clinched their third league title, though scoring markedly fewer goals than in previous winning campaigns: just 75.

If the dream of the Double had again looked likely, especially after a 7.0 home thrashing of Crystal Palace in the Fourth Round, it was snuffed out at the Quarter-final stage. Arsenal lost 2.1 at Highbury to an Aston Villa team finally gaining some revenge for those near misses in the league championship campaigns of recent years. The attendance was a colossal 67, 566.

During the summer of 1934, Allison sought to strengthen the team further and once more followed up on signings that Chapman had been pursuing before his death.

'Jack' Crayston signed for £5,250 from Bradford Park Avenue and would become the team's first choice right-half, effectively replacing Charlie Jones.

Accompanying him at right-half was Wilfred 'Wilf' Copping, also signed from a Yorkshire club - Leeds United, where he had made 162 appearances - for £8,000 as a replacement for Bob John. This new centre-back partnership became known as 'Beauty and the Beast' and Copping was most definitely the Beast.

Programme Notes:

In the summer of 1934 Arsenal signed Jack Crayston and Wilf Copping: they became one of the most formidable defensive partnerships Arsenal had yet seen

Well-built, Copping had been born into the tough mining community of Barnsley in South Yorkshire and was absolutely fearless on the football field. Quickly labelled 'Iron Man Wilf' he would not have been out of place in the Royal Arsenal team of Morris Bates, the original 'iron-headed' man and his tackling and shoulder barges were ferocious in the Arsenal cause.

The Examiner understated his contribution somewhat:

"...he became rather over-zealous in the tackle."

With this new partnership at the back and Drake up front, Allison's team began another assault on the First Division Championship and a Double that had by then taken on almost mythological proportions.

The league programme started well enough with Arsenal losing only four of their first 20 league matches. One of these was at home to key, 1930s league rivals, Aston Villa, at Highbury in November 1934. Another was at Sunderland's Roker Park just three weeks earlier. Sunderland would prove to be Arsenal's main challengers that season.

The Battle of Highbury

Also in November came an international match at Highbury that would become known as the 'Battle of Highbury.'

Innovator and visionary as he was, Herbert Chapman had been a huge fan of international football and, thirty years before the first regular European club competition as we know it today, had dreamed of a competition that would pitch him against old friend, Austrian Hugo Meisl, similar to the Metropa Cup that was contested by Central European club teams.

Chapman had been furious with the FA after they had pulled out of FIFA – football's world governing body – in 1928 over compensation payments for loss of earnings during major tournaments, championed by the British Olympic Association.

As a result of this England failed to appear in the first three World Cup competitions – in 1930, 1934 and 1938. Italy had won the 1934 competition in their own country (beating Czechoslovakia 2.1 in the Final) but it had been as much a propaganda campaign as a football competition.

Following the infamous 'March on Rome' in October 1922, Benito Mussolini had become at that point the youngest Italian Prime Minister in history. His National Fascist Party strengthened its grip on power through purges of all political opponents, often with the help of feared secret police, until the country became effectively a one-party state.

In the mid-1930s he would form an alliance with Hitler's Germany that would eventually threaten all of Europe's stability and ultimately lead to a Second World War.

On 14th November 1934 in the midst of a typical London fog the opportunity to spread his country's influence – especially as newly-crowned World Champions – was too good to miss, though the English press responded by calling it 'the real World Cup Final.'

Mussolini is alleged to have offered his players a package of inducements to win the game including money, a new Alfa Romeo car each and being excused from military service. In the event, it turned into a political if not a football own goal.

Chapman would have been delighted to see seven Arsenal players selected for an England team (the most players from one club to play for England in a single match) that also included a young Stanley Matthews, winning his second England cap.

In fact, in 58 international matches played by England between April 1933 and November 1948 at least one Arsenal player was represented in the England team.

With radio commentary once again provided by George Allison and watched by 54,000 expectant spectators, the Italian players seemed determined to kick anything that moved, especially centre-half Louis Monti who sustained a broken toe and eventually had to leave the pitch.

Amid similarly robust challenges from Wilf Copping, England raced into a 3.0 lead with goals from Eric Brook of Manchester City and one from Ted Drake. Italy fought back in the second half but the match finished 3.2 to England.

The match will be remembered far more for its violence than the scoreline, with three players suffering broken bones and the Italians generally thought to have lost their heads – certainly in the first half. It was not a beautiful game and neither did it reflect Italian nationalism in anything but a sinister and ugly light.

Eddie Hapgood, who was captaining England and who had to have his nose reset after a clash with right-half Attilio Ferraris, later described it as:

"the dirtiest football match I had ever played in."

The Guardian was more circumspect describing it as:

"a match of unusually robust character."

Back in domestic football, violence often spilled over in Arsenal matches too. Contempt for their counter-attacking style - continued by Allison after Chapman's death - resulted in much jeering and baiting of players at away grounds across the land.

In a match at Everton on 16th March 1935, the Arsenal players were continually barracked as 'southern poofs' whereupon Wilf Copping (apparently single-handedly) took out two opposition players, hurting his knee in the process. Arsenal also won the game 2.0.

Did you know?

The first Monopoly Board Game was produced by Parker Brothers in 1935

The league battle with Sunderland continued and the sides met in the return match at Highbury on March 9th, 1935 to contest a 0.0 draw in front of a crowd of 73,295: the record attendance ever recorded at Highbury.

Three days earlier on 6th March 1935 Arsenal had scored their biggest-ever away victory over Tottenham Hotspur with a 6.0 win at White Hart Lane and this momentum continued with another huge win over Middlesbrough – 8.0, to match the 8.0 home win over Leicester City earlier in the season – and the team going on to score 115 goals in total in winning the title by four points from Sunderland.

Ted Drake had been the star of the campaign with 42 goals in 41 league matches and a record 44 goals for the season including three hat-tricks and four four-goal hauls.

Arsenal's joy at winning a third consecutive league title was completed with Tottenham simultaneously finishing bottom of the First Division that same season.

Arsenal had been knocked out of that season's FA Cup by Sheffield Wednesday – 2.1 in the Quarter-final at Hillsborough. Wednesday would go on to win the Cup that year – their third Cup Final triumph.

1935

Dust storms in the prairies – the agricultural heart of the USA - led to drought and extreme hardship over some ten years. It is known as the 'Dust Bowl' or 'Dirty Thirties'

In 1936 Arsenal got to the Cup Final again against the city's other professional club – Sheffield United – who were determined to match the success of their fiercest rivals the previous season. Arsenal's progress to the Final had been relatively smooth, though in the Fifth Round they had to go to a replay against the team that had beaten them in the Final four years earlier – Newcastle United.

In the previous round, they met Liverpool at Anfield just five days after the death of King George V. The crowd of around 60,000 stood up before the match to sing 'Abide with Me' and 'God Save the King' before the players appeared wearing black armbands.

The Cup Final itself on April 25th, 1936 was a physical affair with United setting up plenty of attacks which the Arsenal defence absorbed in its usual business-like way.

Ted Drake scored the only goal of the game about a quarter of an hour from the end to give Arsenal their second FA Cup triumph.

The Times highlighted a superb defensive display by Arsenal, describing George Male as having:

"the game of his life."

Ted Drake had also scored a record seven goals in a top-tier match at Aston Villa on 14th December 1935 but had been unable to equal his goal-scoring total of the previous season.

7

Goals scored by Ted Drake in a single First Division match

Arsenal lost him to a knee injury for 10 weeks and also lost 12 matches in the league. They eventually slipped to sixth place, a full 11 points behind the champions - and the previous season's closest rivals - Sunderland.

So, Arsenal failed to make it four League Championships in a row. No English team has ever achieved this record and Arsenal had still failed to win the Double in what was, until that point, the most sustained period of success in their football history.

Some of the profits from that success were now ploughed into ground improvements. Apart from the new West Stand, Highbury had remained pretty much the same as when the club first arrived in 1913 and both accommodating the vast crowds of the 1930s and the club's desire to emulate the grandeur of such historic grounds as Aston Villa's Villa Park meant that a huge rebuilding programme off of the pitch was needed.

The North Terrace, known popularly as the 'North Bank,' was covered with a new roof as was the 'Clock End.'

In April 1936 work began on a new East Stand with the tip-up seats being sold to Ipswich Town. This almost certainly followed a visit by Captain Ivan Cobbold to fellow Old Etonian Samuel Hill-Wood. As a result of that meeting, the Cobbold family became key

Board Members of Ipswich Town and pushed them towards the professional ranks. A stand at Portman Road is still named after them.

1936

The Spanish Civil War began

Archibald Leitch designed a new East Stand for Tottenham Hotspur that year but Arsenal had moved from his structural engineering approach to a far grander, architectural vision from Claude Waterlow Ferrier for the building of the West Stand four years earlier.

Embracing an Art Deco design, the late Ferrier's partner, William Binnie, sought to build an almost identical stand on the eastern side of the ground, with the previous stand and its expensive-to-maintain, multi-span roof now demolished.

Art Deco is shorthand for *Arts Décoratifs* and, as its name suggests, emanated from France just before World War One. Aiming to add modern elements to traditional themes it was hugely popular in the inter-war years and marked Highbury as a distinctive product of its time for the rest of its life as a football ground.

The East Stand cost some £130,000 to complete – more than twice the cost of Leitch's latest creation; a crowd of more than 51,000 witnessed its official opening before a 0.0 draw against Grimsby Town on 24th October 1936.

A bronze bust of Herbert Chapman stood in what was to become known as the 'Marble Halls' and a huge red cannon was set into its floor, both reflecting the club's origins and its most recent successes.

The Boardroom, just above the players' new dressing rooms, would be decorated on match days with flowers in the colours of the visiting teams.

Holding 4,000 fans on its top tier, a further 4,000 below that and then a paddock in front, the new East Stand completed Highbury's re-development as the most fashionable football stadium in the country.

For only the second time since 1930 Arsenal failed to win either League or FA Cup in the 1936-37 season and it was clear that key players such as Bastin and Hulme were past their best; Drake's injuries became more regular and took longer to heal, while Bob John and Alex James retired at the end of that season.

Allison found James in particular and the creativity and dynamism he had brought to the side especially difficult to replace.

However, the team still finished in third place behind Charlton Athletic and champions Manchester City.

Younger players were given their opportunities in the first team and goalkeeper George Swindin, Alf Kirchen and the Compton brothers made their debuts alongside inside-forward Leslie Jones who had joined from Coventry City along with another striker, George Hunt, who had crossed the divide from Tottenham.

16 September 1937

Arsenal appeared in the first football match to be televised live

On 16th September 1937 these players had the opportunity to make further history by taking part in the first match ever to be televised live by the BBC when the first-team played the reserves in a game specially arranged for the occasion.

Herbert Chapman may have been one of football's first showmen but George Allison, with his journalism background, was one of its first experts in manipulating the media and it is impossible to believe that Allison hadn't somehow instigated this 'first' for Arsenal.

Although old foes Preston North End beat them in a Fifth Round FA Cup tie at Highbury, 1.0, on 12th February 1938 in front of another massive crowd in excess of 72,000, Arsenal did go on to win the league that season by one point from Wolverhampton Wanderers.

Wolves had to win away at Sunderland on the last day of the season to clinch the title but could only draw 1.1 while Arsenal were thrashing Bolton Wanderers at Highbury 5.0 to make sure of a fifth league championship in eight years.

Such was the strength in-depth of the 1938 Arsenal team that they had no less than five players who had scored 100 league goals by then: Cliff Bastin, Ray Bowden, Ted Drake, Joe Hulme and George Hunt.

Along with their two FA Cup wins, Arsenal had simply dominated the 1930s.

As in the 192os before it, the 1930s ended in crisis. The re-armament of Germany through Hitler's Nazi Party, fuelled by the German's treatment at Versailles and his expressed need for more 'Lebensraum' (literally, living space) for the German people - and thus annexing of Austria and occupation of Czechoslovakia - had been accompanied by Mussolini's fierce nationalism at home and expansion into Africa.

Ironically, Britain and other western nations had dealt with such empire-building ambitions by doing very little. Their policy of appeasement meant trying to avoid war at all costs and seeking peaceful, diplomatic solutions in the face of the aggressors.

However, similar to the situation before the First World War when Britain had assured Belgium of its support, so it now guaranteed Poland the same and, therefore, when the Germans invaded Poland on 1st September 1939 and refused to withdraw, Britain declared war on Germany two days later and the Second World War began.

Programme Notes:

Arsenal in the 1930s:

1930: Won FA Cup

1931: Won First Division

1932: Runners-up in First Division

Runners-up in FA Cup

1933: Won First Division

1934: Won First Division

1935: Won First Division

1936: Won FA Cup

1938: Won First Division

POST-WAR PERIOD (1946 – 1992)

Post-war austerity

Ending in 1945 this was the third major war to play its part in the Arsenal story and, as in the aftermath of the previous two, the club was left in a terrible financial state with no gate receipts and overall debts this time estimated at around £150,000, while devastation was all around in the country – and Europe – at large.

The country had turned up to 55% of its economy over to armaments production during the war – including in the remaining workshops at Woolwich, which were damaged during 'The Blitz' when London was bombed for 57 consecutive nights by the German Air Force or 'Luftwaffe.'

Long years of austerity lay ahead. Wartime rationing of food and other essential goods did not end completely until nine years later, in 1954.

The balance of the worlds' economies had changed once again. The USA was the world's largest creditor and set about sending aid on a huge scale to desperate European countries, including Britain, through such recovery initiatives as the Marshall Plan.

Without such funding it had no chance of its debts being paid – decimated economies were of no use to the Americans any more than they were to native governments.

The aid and re-development programmes would also continue to create export markets for new American consumer goods such as cars, television sets and washing machines which flooded into Britain from the 1950s and signalled a new purchasing power for ordinary families to aspire to - whilst simultaneously indicating the end of the post-war years.

For the USA, the rebuilding of western European nations was also political. The war had ended with the Germans surrendering to the Western Allies and the Soviet Union. The allies, consisting of Britain, France and the USA were deeply distrustful of Josef Stalin and the Soviet Union – a huge regional bloc of formerly independent countries that had allied with Russia in 1922 and professed to be a socialist state run by the Communist Party (as the original Bolshevik-led revolutions of 1917 had intended).

However, it became increasingly clear that Stalin had effectively become a dictator in a one-party state. All opposition was banned – in the style of Hitler and Mussolini who had now been vanquished – and millions of his own people either starved to death on the land through gross economic mismanagement or were deported to camps, or 'gulags,' for 'political correction.'

The Cold War

If fears of communism were rife in the 1920s they were widespread and largely unstoppable in the post-war years. Winston Churchill declared, in a speech in Fulton, Missouri, USA on March 5th, 1946 that:

"From Stettin in the Baltic to Trieste in the Adriatic, an iron curtain has descended across the continent."

This mistrust became known as the 'Cold War' and countries in Europe until the late 1980s were either behind the 'iron curtain' - and therefore 'communist' - or not.

On the global stage, conflicts such as the Korean War in the 1950s and the Vietnam War in the 1960s were as much about the tension between the world's superpowers – the USA and the Soviet Union – as they were about the local needs of ordinary people.

What made matters especially frightening was the possession and development of nuclear weapons by the world's superpowers: the USA and the Soviet Union. The dropping of atomic bombs by the USA on Hiroshima and Nagasaki in Japan had effectively ended the war in the east in 1945 and effectively brought an end to the Second World War.

By 1952 the USA was testing its hydrogen bomb – or H-bomb - capability, obliterating an island in the Pacific Ocean. This new weapon was deemed to be some 1,400 times more powerful than the bombs in 1945 and, by the early 1960s the Soviet Union was testing its own hydrogen capability with their Premier, Nikita Khrushchev remarking that,

"the explosion of one hydrogen bomb releases more energy than all the explosions effected by all countries in all the wars in the history of mankind."

The Cold War was essentially an exercise in propaganda, playing on the very real fears of nuclear and conventional military strength. One of the first components in the propaganda stand-off actually involved Arsenal but happened at White Hart Lane on 21st November 1945.

Highbury had been used as an ARP (Air Raid Precautions) centre during the war, offering storage for a barrage balloon unit, first-aid facilities and a safe house for refugees. Because of this, it became a target for the German Luftwaffe which bombed both the North Bank, which was pretty much totally destroyed and the Clock End in an attack during which two RAF personnel died.

The damage was so great that Highbury was declared unsafe and forced to close. Tottenham Hotspur, with football hostilities being suspended during wartime, offered White Hart Lane for the remainder of Arsenal's friendly and other wartime matches.

Just after the war, the Soviet Sports Ministry contacted the FA with a view to one of their leading clubs – Dynamo (or Dinamo) FC of Moscow - playing representative club sides on a short British tour.

They also issued a list of 14 demands, one of which was that one of the clubs involved had to be Arsenal FC: the most famous British club in the world and even more so after its achievements in the 1930s.

Although suspicious of this - it was later revealed that Dynamo were the adopted team of Stalin's secret police – and at a time when the USA was being pressed to share atomic weapons secrets with the Russians, the FA decided that this would be an early strike in the Cold War in demonstrating British superiority on the football field.

The British press weren't convinced by this argument. The Sunday Express haughtily dismissed it:

"They are not nearly good enough to play our class of professional teams. Their players are simply a set of very earnest amateurs..."

However, in the days before proper European club competition, which had so frustrated Herbert Chapman in the 1930s, and eager for more colourful entertainment in the largely black and white post-war period, the British public flocked in their tens of thousands to see the first Russian team ever to play in Britain.

After a 3.3 draw with Chelsea at Stamford Bridge in which the Russians had presented their opponents with bouquets of flowers in gestures of goodwill, Dynamo beat Cardiff City 10.1 at Ninian Park and, after the Arsenal match, would go on to draw 2.2 with Rangers at Ibrox Stadium in Glasgow.

21 November 1945

Arsenal played Dynamo Moscow at Highbury – the first Russian football team to visit Britain

So, the most eagerly-awaited match of the tour came at White Hart Lane on 21st November 1945 with the media suitably mobilised by George Allison.

Some 40 of Arsenal's 42 professional players had joined the armed forces in one capacity or another, as did most of the administrative staff. Eight of the players and a member of the club's ground staff were known to have died in the conflict.

At the end of the war, those who had survived were dispersed literally all over the world and so six 'guest players' were drafted in, two of whom happened to be future England greats Stan Mortenson and Stanley Matthews (who had played in that 'Battle of Highbury' in 1934).

The Russians were particularly aggrieved by Matthews' inclusion but were appeased when it was suggested they would want to play against the very best players England had to offer.

It was also suggested that his inclusion was at the request of a 'higher authority,' thought to be King George VI himself. (Tom Whittaker would later try to sign Matthews for Arsenal on more than one occasion amid suggestions of bribes being offered but, if this was a similar scenario to when Leslie Knighton had tried to sign Charlie Buchan, then the result was the same: failure).

In the event, and officiated by a referee the Russians had brought on tour with them, the match was shrouded in an even worse fog than in the Italy game at Highbury eleven years earlier, such that very little of the match could be seen by the 54,000 spectators.

As the fog got worse, it was expected that the match would have to be abandoned but was allowed to continue as the Russians won 4.3.

The Mail later described it as:

"the most farcical match which has ever been played."

Cliff Bastin added that:

"so long as the Dynamos got the ball in the net, even if they carried it there, the referee was going to award them a goal."

Amid accusations of betting scandals and foul play and even that Dynamo had 12 players on the pitch at one point, it should perhaps be remembered that Dynamo were actually an extremely good football team with gifted and technically very capable players.

They too had been a dominant domestic football team in the 1930s, winning two Soviet Championships and a Soviet Cup. Ironically they had also modified Herbert Chapman's original W-M formation under the coaching of Russian guru, Boris Arkadiev.

He advocated an attack based game based on quick, incisive,

passing football, known as 'passovotchka' and supplemented by clever movement off of the ball in a revolutionary 4-2-4 formation where the front players were constantly interchanging.

This fluid way of playing was labelled 'organised chaos' by the Russian press but Arkadiev himself suggested that:

> *"Our players worked to move from a schematic W-M, to breathe the Russian soul into the English invention, to add our neglect of dogma."*

Some claim this technically advanced way of playing would be the foundation for Dutch 'total football' in the late 1960s and early 1970s.

The Russian coaches offered to discuss innovative football tactics with their British counterparts but the British were having none of it, considering themselves superior to the 'ideas of 'foreigners.' If this old Empire attitude put back the tactical development of the game in Britain for many years, it would also come back to haunt them in the 1950s.

Arsenal under Chapman had always been open to international innovations – the training ground floodlights were installed after a trip to Belgium – and foreign players.

Following on from the success of Gerard Keizer they signed striker Albert Gudmundsson in 1946. Though then playing for the club as an amateur – as Keizer had done – Gudmundsson would become Iceland's first professional footballer. Retiring from football in 1954 he enjoyed a successful business career before entering politics, becoming Mayor of Reykjavik and subsequently the country's Finance Minister.

Service is resumed at Highbury

Also in 1946, a fire destroyed much of the old College of Divinity's remaining buildings including its library. Arsenal were determined to continue to write their own chapters of Islington's history and Highbury duly re-opened the same year - and in time for the first post-war FA Cup competition.

Given that the Football League programme would not recommence for another year, it was decided that each FA Cup tie in that season's competition would be played over two legs – home and away.

The main reason for this was to try to raise attendance money for all cash-strapped clubs – including Arsenal – until regular league football returned. It was the only season in FA Cup history when home and away legs featured, with a return to the traditional one-off matches the following season.

For Arsenal, the postwar era could not have started much more badly. They lost to West Ham United 6.0 in the first leg at Upton Park and, though Horace Cumner scored the only goal in a 1.0 win for Arsenal at Highbury in the second leg, they were knocked out 6.1 on aggregate.

Leslie Jones played his last match for Arsenal that day while Jimmy Logie and Henry Waller made their debuts for the club. Logie had been brought in to try and bring midfield creativity to the team in the huge gap left by Alex James.

Did you know?

French designer Louis Réard unveiled a new two-piece swimsuit in Paris in July 1946. He called it a 'bikini' after hearing reports of a U.S. atomic test which had taken place off the Bikini Atoll in the Pacific Ocean earlier in the week

Derby County won the FA Cup that season but, in the receding shadow of six years of armed conflict, that year's competition's is remembered far more for the 'Burnden Park Disaster' which occurred just two months after Arsenal had played their first post-war match.

On 9th March 1946, in a Quarter-final tie against Stoke City at Burnden Park - then home of Bolton Wanderers - a crowd estimated at some 85,000 were in attendance, eager to watch a game of football in the sunshine after the dark days of war.

Massive overcrowding on the terraces eventually caused a stampede in which 33 people were crushed to death and hundreds of other fans injured. Up until that time, it was the worst disaster ever to occur in a football stadium.

9 March 1946

The 'Burnden Park Disaster' occurred at Bolton in which 33 football fans died

The 1946-47 league season began for Arsenal with a First Division match at Wolverhampton Wanderers on 31st August 1946. In a disastrous echo of their Cup defeat to West Ham earlier in the year, Reg Lewis scored their only goal in a 6.1 defeat.

They didn't fare much better at Highbury four days later when – seven years and one day since the war had been declared – Reg Lewis scored again but the team still lost 3.1 to Blackburn Rovers.

In fact, the first half of the season went badly with Arsenal losing 11 of their 20 league matches before Christmas and relegation looking a distinct possibility.

True to form, manager George Allison was more focused on the club's relations with the media and also its transfer dealings, including how to replace the recently retired Ted Drake, than day-to-day training and match day tactics. He certainly wasn't a hands-on manager in the style of Herbert Chapman.

Mercer and Whittaker

Nevertheless, the arrival of Joe Mercer from Everton and 35-year old centre-forward Ronnie Rooke from Fulham helped to steer the team away from danger and a 13th place finish.

Mercer had fallen out with Everton manager Theo Kelly who had accused him of not trying, and he had even been forced to pay for his own surgery following a cartilage injury.

During transfer negotiations with Arsenal in London it is alleged that Kelly brought Mercer's boots with him so that he had no reason to return to Everton but, after signing, Mercer continued to commute from Liverpool on match days.

Initially signed as a wing-half he played a more defensive role for Arsenal, soon becoming club captain and a hugely influential post-war player despite his Everton teammate, the great Dixie Dean, once telling him in the 1930s that:

> *"your spindly legs wouldn't last the postman on a morning round."*

Now in his mid-sixties, George Allison retired and was replaced by Tom Whittaker as Secretary-Manager. Whittaker, awarded the MBE for waterproofing RAF vehicles involved in the Normandy invasion during the war, had also acted as trainer for the England national team.

Under his coaching Arsenal made a far better start to the 1947-48 season, going 17 matches unbeaten from the start of the campaign and winning twelve of them.

Joe Mercer had helped to bring more discipline to Arsenal's defence and Ronnie Rooke's goals were a revelation at the other end. He had been Fulham's leading goal-scorer in three consecutive seasons at Craven Cottage in the 1930s and his 21 goals in 24 matches had helped Arsenal to reach safety the previous season.

33

Goals from Ronnie Rooke – a post-war scoring record

In 1947-48 he scored 33 goals on his way to becoming the league's highest goalscorer that season and a post-war scoring record for Arsenal in a single season that has never been beaten.

Reg Lewis would capitalise on his uncanny ability to find space in the box and deadly accuracy to continue to score many goals for the club too and at a remarkable strike rate – eventually scoring 118 league and cup goals in a total of 176 appearances.

George Swindin only conceded 32 goals that season and they flew in at the other end at Highbury and away grounds around the country as they had done in the 1930s as Arsenal swaggered to the First Division title – their sixth - topping the table with 59 points – seven clear of nearest rivals Manchester United.

The away game against Manchester United that year, on 17th January 1948, had set an all-time Football League attendance record of 83,260.

The match was played at Maine Road (home of Manchester City) because United's ground at Old Trafford had been damaged in the war and would not see football action again until 1949.

Incredibly, for all their domination once more – winning 23 of their 42 league matches and losing just six – Arsenal failed at the first hurdle of the FA Cup for the second successive season; in a 1.0 home defeat to Bradford Park Avenue.

8 January 1949

Arsenal met Tottenham Hotspur in the FA Cup for the first time

They met Tottenham Hotspur in the FA Cup for the first time on 8th January 1949 in the Third Round and won comfortably 3.0 at Highbury but would lose 1.0 again in the next round at Derby County.

For Arsenal, there were individual success stories such as striker Doug Lishman who had scored one of the goals in that Cup victory over Spurs and who had signed for the club in 1948 from Arsenal's famous cup conquerors, Walsall.

Lishman had served as a Royal Marines Commando during the war and had no fear of opposition defences. He was the club's top scorer during the 1950-51 season and, in the next, included in his

30 goals were hat-tricks in three consecutive home games against Fulham, West Bromwich Albion and Bolton Wanderers. He went on to score 137 goals in 244 matches for Arsenal.

Whittaker also brought in goalkeeper 'Jack' Kelsey in August 1949 from non-league side Winch Wen in South Wales. Given the superb form of George Swindin, Kelsey's opportunities were initially limited but, after three years or so, he did become the number one keeper at the club and went on to make 352 appearances in total.

He also played 41 times for Wales – a record for a British goalkeeper at the time - making his debut in 1954 and appearing in their first World Cup Finals tournament in Sweden in 1958.

In fact, it was in an international match four years later that his career effectively ended when saving at the great Brazilian Vava's feet. In doing so he displaced two vertebrae at the base of his spine and was never able to fully recover. Many consider him to have been one of the greatest Welsh goalkeepers of all time and, in another period, might have won many trophies with Arsenal.

The Compton brothers also made their mark for both club and country. Like Andy Ducat and Ted Drake before them, they were also accomplished cricketers.

An outside-left, Denis struggled with a knee injury which would persistently hamper his football career but he played 78 Test Matches for England and scored over one hundred centuries in first-class cricket.

In 1947 they helped Middlesex to win the County Championship and then Arsenal to the league title a year later. They thus became the only brothers to have won national titles at the highest level in both cricket and football.

Denis was very much the charismatic star. Like Hapgood and

James before him – and his contemporary, Stanley Matthews - he was encouraged to use his status and personality in selling.

U.S. marketing and advertising agencies were pushing consumer goods ever harder and advertising on television would open many new opportunities for companies and the individuals they paid to sell their goods directly into Britain's front rooms.

Denis – supposedly a secret favourite of Queen Elizabeth, the Queen Mother - fronted a series of sports annuals but really made his name as the original 'Brylcreem Boy' endorsing a range of hair products.

30 January 1948

Indian nationalist Mahatma Gandhi was assassinated in New Delhi, one year after the British had granted independence to India and its partition to eventually form the republics of India and Pakistan

The brothers, though now well into their thirties, were instrumental in Arsenal reaching the FA Cup Final for the fifth time in the 1949-50 season. Finishing back in sixth place in the league they nevertheless enjoyed their best Cup run since the war.

In the Semi-final they faced Chelsea at White Hart Lane on 18th March 1950. In front of a crowd of 67,752 Leslie, who had great ability in the air and now played at centre-half, headed in a last-minute equaliser from a corner delivered by Denis.

The match finished 2.2 and Arsenal won the replay (also at White Hart Lane) and headed for Wembley on 29th April 1950 where they beat Liverpool 2.0 with two more goals from Reg Lewis.

Arsenal had played all seven of their FA Cup games in London that season.

Later that year Leslie Compton, known affectionately as 'Big Head' became, and remains at 38 years and 64 days, the oldest player to make his England debut since the war when selected to play against Wales on 15th November 1950.

The following year, on 19th September 1951 Arsenal played that first match under the floodlights at Highbury, which Herbert Chapman could only dream about, when beating Hapoel Tel-Aviv of Israel in a friendly match 6.1.

Unfortunately for Arsenal, after a series of injuries to key players, they lost by the same margin against Manchester United at Old Trafford in their final league match of the 1951-52 season in what was effectively a championship decider.

It was also Reg Lewis's last game for the club. They would finish third in the First Division, four points behind United and level on points with Tottenham Hotspur but with a worse goal average of just 0.179.

In the FA Cup, they beat Chelsea in the Semi-final again but faced old Cup rivals Newcastle United on 3rd May 1952 in what was their 11th Final and Arsenal's sixth.

Injuries continued to play a major part in Arsenal's season. Arsenal right-back Walley Barnes twisted his knee in the thick Wembley turf and had to be carried off after just 35 minutes.

This was followed by further injuries to Holton, Roper and Daniel and Logie suffering internal bleeding from a leg wound.

In the end, in this era of no substitutions being permitted (they weren't allowed in Football League matches until 1965-66 and not in the FA Cup until 1967), Arsenal had just eight fit players on the pitch. Despite this numerical advantage Newcastle only managed to win the match by a single goal, scored by George Robledo.

As when losing the Cup Final to the same opponents twenty years earlier, Arsenal had come so close to winning the elusive Double but failed once more.

Programme Notes:

Charlie Buchan set up his own publishing company in 1951 and produced a *Football Monthly* magazine, priced at one shilling and sixpence. The first issue sold 60,000 copies which rose to 250,000 when England won the World Cup in 1966

The following season they won the league title for the seventh time but only just. At the end of the season, Arsenal were tied on 54 points with nineteenth-century rivals Preston North End who had beaten them in the last but one game of the season – 2.0 at Deepdale.

Arsenal held their nerve though and beat Burnley at Highbury 3.2 (despite going behind inside the first ten minutes) to equal Preston's points tally. This time the goal average metric worked in Arsenal's favour: they won the league with a goal average just 0.099 better than Preston's.

0.099

Arsenal's superior goal average over Preston North End to win the 1953 league title

In direct contrast to those newspaper reports condemning the Arsenal team's tactics, their supporters and their location in Kent, and also conveniently forgetting about the opposition that their move to Islington in 1913 had raised, The London Star reported on Thursday, August 6th, 1953 that:

> *"A flair for showmanship has always been part of Arsenal's appeal to the soccer public. The smartness of their kit, the fine organisation at Highbury, the sense of the spectacular and the publicity accorded to their moves have all whetted the interest of the man in the street."*

Sixty years after turning professional and joining the Football League, perhaps Arsenal had finally been accepted? Either way, although nobody could possibly have known it at the time, this tiny margin of victory in the league as well as the world at large was to mark the end of Arsenal's long line of success since 1930 and they would fail to win another trophy for 17 long seasons.

Decline and fall

A key part of the historical and geographical backdrop to this story has been the building and then decline and fall of empires such as the British Empire which now morphed into the far less imperial British Commonwealth; the Habsburg dynasty and the end of expansionist plans by Germany and Italy – mostly due to the major military conflicts that had so halted the progress of Arsenal Football Club.

Programme Notes:

Arsenal won seven league titles and three FA Cups in the 17 seasons from 1930 - 1953

In football, the ageing of players and managerial decisions in terms of selection and coaching add to the competitive nature of clubs and countries alike.

Arsenal had to face a major rebuilding programme of their own and their fans had to understand that the glory days of seven league titles and three FA Cups in the previous 17 seasons were over for now and until something equally special on and off the football field could kick off a new cycle of success.

It would have been difficult for any set of players or manager to have matched or even continued the success of such a golden age for the club.

The England national team was also struggling on the pitch. Having previously only ever lost at home to the Republic of Ireland – 2.0 at Everton's Goodison Park ground in a 1949 friendly – they had competed in their first World Cup in 1950.

The Mighty Magyars

In that tournament in Brazil, they had suffered the humiliation of a shock 1.0 defeat to the USA in Belo Horizonte. Despite this and displaying an arrogant complacency as 'originators of the game' they invited Hungary to a play a friendly match at Wembley on 25th November 1953 in what the British press built-up as the 'Match of the Century.'

The Hungary team were known as the 'Mighty Magyars' having become Olympic football champions in Helsinki the previous year. With England sticking to the Chapman W-M formation and Hungary playing 2-3-3-2 the visitors, under captain Ferenc Puskás (known as the 'Galloping Major and one of the greatest Hungarian if not world players of all time) scored in the very first minute and went on to win 6.3.

England had similarly not heeded the same warning as when Hungary's communist neighbours, Russia, had sent their technically superior Dynamo Moscow team to play Arsenal almost exactly eight years earlier.

2 June 1953

Queen Elizabeth II was crowned at a coronation ceremony in Westminster Abbey, London

Worse was to follow. England played a return match at the Nepstadion in Hungary's capital – Budapest – on 23rd May 1954 and lost 7.1. They were simply out-thought and outplayed in both matches and this finally led to respect for how far the football of 'lesser nations' had come, as well as a major tactical re-think of how the game could and perhaps should now be played.

Perhaps symptomatic of this period was Arsenal's failure to beat a non-league team at home for the very first time. It came in a third-round FA Cup tie against Bedford Town of the Southern League.

Watched by over 55,000 fans Arsenal could only draw 2.2 but did go on to win the replay five days later 2.1.

Did you know?

Roger Bannister broke the four-minute mile at the Iffley Road track in Oxford on 6th May 1954

That replayed match on 12th January 1956 was the first football match to be covered live by ITV - the new independent television rival to the BBC which had launched just under four months earlier.

7 January 1956

Arsenal failed to beat a non-league team – Bedford Town – at Highbury for the first time

Later that year Tom Whittaker died of a heart-attack and Arsenal turned to their former player 'Gentleman' Jack Crayston who had formed such a formidable defensive partnership with the combustible Wilf Copping in the inter-war years.

The team finished fifth in his first season winning 21 of their 42 games including a 7.3 drubbing of Manchester City and 6.3 beating of Sheffield Wednesday. However, they were also well beaten by Manchester United 6.2 at Old Trafford and had lost six of their first 11 league games which meant they were never serious title contenders.

The team went backwards the following season. On 4th January 1958 they travelled to Northampton Town in the third round of the FA Cup and were knocked out 3.1.

The Cobblers were 19th in the old Third Division South at the time and, though a considerable shock, only Arsenal's own status – they were thirteenth in the First Division at the time – prevented the news from being as dramatic as the upset against Walsall 25 years earlier.

1956

The Hungarian Revolution or Uprising was a nationwide revolt against the Soviet-backed Hungarian government – the first major protest within one of the so-called 'Warsaw Pact' countries behind the Iron Curtain

Crayston resigned in May 1958 complaining that the club had refused to buy several new players that he had identified. He was replaced by another former player – George Swindin. His management again started off fairly well with a third place finish in the 1958-59 season behind Wolverhampton Wanderers and second-placed Manchester United but mid-table mediocrity would follow.

The Busby Babes

It is hard to mention the year 1958 in football circles without also thinking about Manchester United. Matt Busby, who, as a player, had been so impressed with the creativity of Alex James before the war, had now built a youthful side in his image, known generally as the 'Busby Babes.'

One of its stars was Duncan Edwards who had scored in their thrashing of Arsenal in 1957 and who was now part of the United team that arrived at Highbury on 1st February 1958.

Black armbands were worn out of respect for Manchester United director George Whittaker who had died in his sleep at the team's hotel that day. Perhaps this was a grim portent of further tragedy.

Edwards scored one goal and Tommy Taylor scored two others in a 5.4 win, with Jimmy Bloomfield scoring two in reply for Arsenal. Not only was this a thrilling match – United were 3.0 up at half-time - played in front of 63,578 football fans, but it was the last league game that the Busby Babes would play.

Less than a week later, on 6th February 1958 Edwards and Taylor – as well as Roger Byrne, Eddie Colman and Mark Jones who all played in that match at Highbury - would be among the eight players and 23 in total who died in what is now known as the 'Munich Air Disaster.'

Matt Busby had managed the Great Britain soccer team to fourth place in the 1948 Olympic Games in London and, like Chapman before him, was a strong advocate of international club football. Though the Football League opposed it, he had taken Manchester United into the second European Cup competition the previous season.

On this fateful day the United team, along with some supporters and football journalists, were on their way back from a European Cup Quarter-final match against Red Star of Belgrade in Yugoslavia (now Serbia).

Their British European Airways flight had to refuel in Munich but then crashed on its third attempt to take off in worsening weather conditions and a runway covered in snow and ice.

6 February 1958

The Munich Air Disaster claimed 23 lives including eight players from Manchester United

Busby was badly injured yet survived to build a new team, but a generation of fine football talent had been wiped out and – though it pales into insignificance in the midst of such horror - Manchester United's plans to complete three successive English league title wins that season – as Huddersfield and Arsenal had done previously – effectively ended in Germany.

George Swindin

George Swindin had left Arsenal in 1954 to become player-manager at non-league Peterborough United with whom he won three Midland League championships. Born in Doncaster he was an archetypal tough-talking Yorkshireman and was duly quoted in the press:

"If I've got something to say, I'll say it."

After just three months at Peterborough 13 players were sacked and a further 13 the following season but under his management their replacements would form the nucleus of a successful league and cup-fighting team which would eventually be elected to the Football League in 1960, replacing Gateshead.

His assistant for much of his time at Arsenal was ex-Chelsea half-back and trainer of the England under-23s team, Ron Greenwood.

Did you know?

By the 1950s around 15% of British households owned fridges and 33% had washing machines

It is clear that Greenwood's radical theories on a new style of playing were not fully understood by the players or appreciated by the new manager although he did try to break away from the more defensive, counter-attacking approach that had prevailed at the club since Chapman had first joined it.

In an Observer interview on 22nd August 1959 he explained that he had:

"thrown away the defensive concept of 'one goal up and the iron curtain down' synonymous with Arsenal sides."

favouring one-touch football where:

"the player doesn't cling to the ball, he passes it on at once and then moves into the open so that it can be passed back to him"

in order to produce much more entertaining football.

Entertaining it might have been and the Islington Gazette reported on 9th December 1960, that there were still 200 people on the waiting list for season tickets and asking why so many people should be:

"anxious to pay in advance and risk the season's entertainment being worth the money."

Club Secretary, Bob Wall, had replied cheerily that

"...the seats are good and wide. They are covered with Sorbonne cushions – only three clubs in England have that. Then our refreshment and toilet facilities are about the best in the League."

When the major ground improvements were made at Highbury in the 1930s success on the field had continued. Unfortunately, this was not the case in the 1960s and after taking Arsenal to third place in the league in his first season in charge, Swindin could never repeat or better it and resigned in May 1962.

At the start of the decade though another personnel change would have far-reaching repercussions. In April 1960, 65-year old trainer, Billie Milne, left after 39 years of service, including over 100 league games for the club as a wing-half. He once said:

"you should only limp if you have broken a leg."

The London Standard announced his replacement on 23rd April 1960 as Bertie Mee – another 'Gentleman' figure who was:

"a qualified physiotherapist who runs a hospital clinic under the National Health (Service)... He brings a more scientific, up-to-date and – frankly – colder approach to the job of getting players fit."

The 1960s

If many people consider the key events of the early 1960s to include the failed 'Bay of Pigs' invasion of Fidel Castro's communist Cuba by USA-backed paramilitaries in 1961 or the Cuban Missile Crisis of 1962 when Soviet missiles were placed there and the Cold War seemed almost certain to explode into action, or even the assassination of U.S. President Kennedy the following year, for Arsenal fans, the outbreak of a new decade will be remembered for the 1960-61 season when their nearest rivals, Tottenham Hotspur, won the Double.

1960-61

Tottenham Hotspur did the Double – the first team in the twentieth century to do so

Never before in the twentieth century and not since Aston Villa had won both First Division and FA Cup in 1896-97 had one team won both trophies in the same season.

Arsenal had come so close in 1932 and then again in 1952 without achieving it that it was unthinkable that Bill Nicholson's team should be the one to finally break the football mould – beating Arsenal home and away to boot.

If George Swindin had been under pressure beforehand with yet more injuries and the lack of an effective youth programme providing new talent for the first team, then it was held up all the more in contrast to the jubilation at White Hart Lane.

He had signed Tommy Docherty from Preston North End in 1958 but he was at the end of his career and moved to Chelsea who he also went on to manage as well as a host of clubs including Manchester United and the Scottish National Team.

Swindin also signed George Eastham from Newcastle United in 1960. Although money had poured into football in the 1940s and 1950s players were still paid low wages and a maximum wage of £20 per week was in force. They were also discouraged from taking out pensions to provide regular income for then they retired and so many former players were almost destitute as a result.

Alex James had become a pig farmer in order to make ends meet.

1961

The maximum wage cap for players was abolished

Under Jimmy Hill's chairmanship of the Professional Footballers' Association (PFA) the maximum wage cap was abolished in 1961 with Fulham's inside-forward and England captain Johnny Haynes becoming the first player to earn £100 a week.

There was, however, another equally pressing issue for footballers at this time. A system called the 'retain and transfer' system effectively bound players to their clubs.

Club chairmen could decide whether to keep players or transfer them to other clubs and, if they did decide to keep them, place them in the reserves and sometimes not even pay them.

George Eastham was an inside forward for Newcastle United and, because he felt the house provided to him was uninhabitable and the club continually tried to block him from playing for the England Under-23s team, refused to sign a new contract in 1959. The club refused to transfer him and so Eastham went on strike before Swindin persuaded Newcastle to sell him to Arsenal for £47,500 the following year.

21 March 1960

The Sharpeville massacre took place in South Africa when state police opened fire on black people protesting against racial segregation ('apartheid'). 69 people were killed and 180 injured in what came to be seen as a symbolic moment in the fight for freedom

Eastham took Newcastle to the High Court in 1963, claiming that he had been the victim of a 'slavery contract' where his rights as a footballer were practically zero and that it, therefore, represented a restraint of trade.

Although he was not granted wages he felt had been due to him the judge agreed and, as a result of the case, club chairmen found it far harder to retain footballers unfairly.

George Eastham made his Arsenal debut against Bolton Wanderers at Highbury on 10th December 1960 when a crowd of more than 30,000 saw him score two goals in a 5.1 victory.

He also scored in a 3.3 draw on his return to Newcastle two months later when he was simultaneously pelted with apples and called 'Judas' by Newcastle fans who had been less than impressed by one of their best players refusing to play for the club before moving south to an Arsenal team which was still as hated in northern outposts as much as it had been thirty years earlier.

The 1960s would become a decade similarly defined by protests against social restrictions at home and 'unjust' military disputes abroad. A widespread questioning of the rights of women and racial minorities in a 'new society' began to take place as the straightjacket of the 1950s years was ripped off and thrown away.

Billy Wright

Though beloved by players and fans, George Swindin had represented 'old school' Arsenal and the club decided to change tack in 1962 by looking beyond former players and coaching staff – for the first time since Herbert Chapman had been appointed – and appointing boyhood Arsenal fan Billy Wright as their new manager.

Wright had made 490 appearances for his only club – Wolverhampton Wanderers – and had been a mainstay of the great Wolves teams of the 1950s that had won the league three times in 1954, 1958 and 1959, making their mark on that decade as Arsenal had done 20 years earlier.

He had also become the first player in history to make 100 appearances for their country (eventually winning 105 caps) captaining England in three World Cup campaigns but also including the 1953 humiliation against Hungary.

If Arsenal wanted to free themselves from the pressures of past success and make a statement in this fast-changing period then Wright brought glamour and excitement as well as the promise of new success,

Wright's period in charge started well enough on 18th August 1962 with a 2.1 win in the First Division at Leyton Orient. Centre-forward Joe Baker scored one of Arsenal's goals that day in what was his debut match having been signed from Torino in Italy for a club record transfer fee of £70,000.

With Scottish parents he had nevertheless been born in Liverpool and so was eligible to play for England which he duly did while playing for Hibernian in Edinburgh. He, therefore, became the first player to play for England without, at that time, ever having played for an English club.

Baker was a tremendous purchase, scoring 100 goals in just 156 appearances for the club and was leading scorer in three of the four seasons in which he played in North London. He benefitted hugely from crosses from Alan Skirton.

22 November 1963

John F. Kennedy, President of the United States, was assassinated in Dallas, Texas

Another player from the West Country, Skirton had actually been signed by George Swindin in 1959 but had been laid low through pleurisy and pneumonia and had missed some 18 months of playing time.

Switched to the left wing by Wright he thrived when given the opportunity and was known by fans as the 'Highbury Express.' However, Wright would usually only commit to playing one winger in matches and Skirton had to share the role with Johnny Macleod from Hibernian – another Swindin signing.

Geoff Strong – a prolific forward who had actually been signed as a 20-year old by Jack Crayston from North-East amateur club Stanley United – had also come to the fore, often playing alongside Baker and Eastham. He and Baker both scored 28 league and cup goals in the 1963-64 season before Strong left for Liverpool where he won League and Cup medals.

Wright signed centre-half Ian Ure from Dundee for £62,500 in 1963. In a dispute with manager Bob Shankly, similar to Eastham's, Ure had threatened to 'strike' if the club didn't release him. Fellow defender Frank McLintock also arrived from Leicester City for a new club record of £80,000 the following year.

£80,000

New club record fee paid for Frank McLintock

Ure was not a great success at Arsenal and left for Manchester United in 1969.

McLintock also struggled under Wright citing communication problems but, like Danskin before him, he was a tough Scot whose fight and determination to win had been shaped by childhood poverty in Glasgow's Gorbals district. McLintock would go on to be one of Arsenal's finest-ever captains.

Though losing in the fifth round of the FA Cup at Highbury to Liverpool, the 1962-63 season turned out to be Wright's best in terms of league position. The team finished seventh in the First Division and the following season were London's representative in the Inter-Cities Fairs Cup – a second European club competition which, like the European Cup, had begun in 1955.

The competition was originally set up as a series of friendly matches to promote international trade fairs but only one team from each city was eligible to take part. After 1968 this rule was relaxed and teams qualified on finishing positions in their national leagues.

Some see this competition as a natural forerunner of the UEFA Cup - but UEFA (the Union of European Football Associations - effectively football's governing body in Europe) themselves do not.

25 September 1963

Arsenal played their first match in a European competition

Arsenal's first match in European competition took place in Denmark on 25th September 1963. They faced Staevnet in Copenhagen who were actually a Danish representative team with players selected from 11 clubs. Johnny Macleod scored the club's first European goal and Joe Baker its first European hat-trick as, with Geoff Strong also scoring a hat-trick they won the First Round, first leg match 7.1

Alan Skirton scored Arsenal's first European goal at Highbury a month later in the second leg match on 22nd October 1963. Arsenal lost 3.2 but went through 9.4 on aggregate.

They met Liège of Belgium in the next round which is where their first European adventure ended - going out of the competition 4.2 on aggregate.

Under-soil heating was installed at Highbury in 1964 having been first introduced at a football ground six years earlier, in 1958 at Everton's Goodison Park. This led to far less disappointment – especially for away fans – over matches being cancelled due to bad weather.

It also meant the financial impact to the club was lessened with fewer late postponements and the more lucrative Saturday matches having to be rescheduled in midweek.

Peterborough United

As with Jack Crayston, the end of Wright's reign as manager was hastened by a cup defeat. On 30th January 1965 the team travelled to Peterborough United – near neighbours of Northampton Town – for a Fourth Round FA Cup tie.

Despite leading at half-time they went out by two goals to one. Derek Dougan equalised for George Swindin's old club and winger Peter McNamee scored the winner just five minutes from the end.

Goalkeeper Bob Wilson had signed for the club on 16th July 1963. He went on to play 308 games for Arsenal and was the first English-born player to play for Scotland having played previously for the England schoolboys team).

1965

The U.S. sent ground troops into Vietnam for the first time, to support the South Vietnamese regime against the communist North

However, without a solid enough defence, not yet seeing the best days from Wilson and despite such fine attacking riches, Arsenal never really looked like achieving their goals under Billy Wright's management.

Some said he was 'too nice' to be a manager while others claimed that he did not have the authority to manage such a huge and diverse club as Arsenal, having been a one-club man for the whole of his career.

Certainly selling leading scorer Joe Baker to Nottingham Forest (where he continued his goal-scoring success as Forest finished runners-up in the league the following season) did little to endear him to the other players in the dressing room and was probably the final straw as far as they were concerned. Wright also struggled with alcoholism in later life.

One thing is certain: whereas Herbert Chapman had been a far better manager than a player, the opposite was the case with Billy Wright. As he himself had been, he relied far too much on his 'star players' and perhaps the biggest indictment of his time as Arsenal's manager was that only one Arsenal player – George Eastham – made the England squad for their successful 1966 World Cup win.

Like another fine individual 'flair' player, the prolific Jimmy Grieves of Tottenham Hotspur, Eastham failed to make the team for the Final: a far cry from 1934 when Arsenal had supplied so many England players in that match against Italy.

Bertie Mee

England's World Cup win against Germany – winning 4.2 in the Final - lifted the national team to new heights and gave a huge economic lift to the entire nation. It also marked the beginning of the end of the chasm between working-class players and middle-class managers/owners.

After the 1966 Final England's players celebrated at The Royal Garden Hotel in Kensington, London, where the FA insisted on their wives dining in a separate room and being each presented with a celebratory pair of scissors in their roles as 'Housewives.'

England's and clubs' players would join in the common protests against such stuffy, outdated social practices though, by the same process, often became superstar celebrities in the Modern Era and so were similarly separated from ordinary football fans.

The mood around Highbury was also given a lift with the departure of Billy Wright. His team had struggled to fourteenth place in the league in the 1965-66 season – their worst finish since 1930 – and just four points above the relegation zone.

In their penultimate game of the season, on 5th May 1966, they had recorded their lowest ever attendance at Highbury, losing 3.0 to Leeds United in a First Division match watched by just 4,554 people.

4,554

Arsenal's worst-ever attendance at Highbury

To be fair it was a cold night accompanied by torrential rain and Liverpool's European Cup-Winners' Cup Final match was being screened live on television that same evening.

Such television events were still quite rare at that time, though Arsenal had featured in the first episode of BBC's 'Match of the Day' highlights programme nearly two years earlier when they themselves had been playing Liverpool (they lost the game at Anfield 3.2).

National boxing hero Henry Cooper failed to win the World Heavyweight crown from Muhammad Ali, 16 days after that Leeds defeat in a bout at Highbury in front of 46,000 fans who were treated to far more fight and determination from two individuals than the entire Arsenal football team had displayed.

Billy Wright had failed on points and left the ring. If relieved to see him leave the club, Arsenal fans were probably underwhelmed at trainer/physiotherapist Bertie Mee being appointed their new manager – their fourth in the almost ten years since the death of Tom Whittaker - in that glorious summer of 1966.

20 June 1966

Bertie Mee appointed as Arsenal manager

It could be argued that even if the Wright experiment had failed, the previous policy of recruiting from within had been similarly unsuccessful in recent years with Swindin's time as a manager still fresh in supporters' minds; but at least he had been a successful player and, much more importantly, part of a winning Arsenal team.

Any victories achieved by Bertie Mee to date would have been achieved on the training ground or the medical couch in the back room and so were largely unknown about. Certainly, they didn't seem to have led to any obvious first-team success.

5: Image of Bertie Mee

From Bulwell in Nottinghamshire, Bertie Mee's own football career at local club Mansfield Town and just down the road at Derby County had been cut short by injury and he had moved on to train as a physiotherapist in the Royal Army Medical Corps.

Obviously inexperienced in football management he made the clever move of appointing two men as his assistants, both of whom would become great coaches in their own right.

Dave Sexton, born in Islington, had started off as a coach at Chelsea before moving to Leyton Orient as manager in 1965. Favouring exciting, attacking football, Mee made him his first-team coach. Though he left in 1967 to replace Tommy Docherty as manager of Chelsea, his hands-on impact on team strategy helped Mee to fill the vacuum left by Wright.

Don Howe was a right-back who had played for most of his career for West Bromwich Albion in his native West Midlands. A contemporary of Jimmy Armfield he might have played many more times for England than just the 23 matches, including in the 1958 World Cup, had he not been playing during the same era.

Howe had been signed by fellow Midlander Billy Wright and made club captain but broke his leg in a match against Blackpool in March 1966 and struggled to play first team football after that. Mee made him reserve team coach and he stepped up when Sexton left, going on to become Mee's number two.

With both ends of the pitch being addressed by these new tactical experts and Mee, a specialist in training and physiotherapy, the only ingredients missing were the players to carry out their instructions and it was here that Mee was fortunate in inheriting a successful youth team.

That team had just won the 1966 FA Youth Cup for the first time in the club's history - beating Sunderland's youths over two legs - and a wave of young talent had become available which Mee would introduce to the first-team over the next few years.

Winger George 'Geordie' Armstrong had been understudy to Johnny Macleod and Alan Skirton during the Wright years but Mee was quick to give him first-team opportunities as he did Jon

Sammels. A forward, Sammels had scored on his first-team debut at Blackpool but was well back in the pecking order behind Geoff Strong and George Eastham.

Another young fringe player was Peter Storey who had been a boyhood apprentice with the club. Originally a defender, he became a midfielder with an excellent record as a dispassionate, consistent penalty taker.

It was as a defensive midfielder that Storey would become known as one of the hard or 'hatchet' men of football in the 1960s, alongside 'Nobby' Styles at Manchester United, Ron 'Chopper' Harris at Chelsea, Tommy 'Anfield Iron' Smith at Liverpool and Norman 'Bites Yer Legs' Hunter at Leeds United.

Storey, nicknamed 'Cold Eyes,' would rank closely with Wilf Copping as one of the toughest players ever to wear an Arsenal shirt.

Like Storey, Pat Rice had been an apprentice at the club, originally working in a greengrocer's shop on Gillespie Road and, as Storey moved into midfield, so Rice, who turned professional in 1966, took on the right-back role, eventually making over 500 appearances for the club.

Another apprentice, John Radford from Hemsworth in Yorkshire, had made his debut two years earlier and become Arsenal's youngest ever hat-trick scorer, against Wolverhampton Wanderers on 2nd January 1965.

He was aged just 17 years and 315 days. Later that month he would score Arsenal's goal in the cup defeat at Peterborough.

2 January 1965

John Radford became Arsenal's youngest hat-trick scorer

Another member of that Youth Team success was Sammy Nelson from Belfast in Northern Ireland. He was originally a winger until Don Howe converted him into a left-back. He also had to wait for opportunities though as Mee signed Bob McNab from Huddersfield Town in October 1966 who would hold down the position, playing almost 70 times in the following three seasons.

Terry Neill - another defender from Northern Ireland – had also been signed by Billy Wright and would eventually become part of the preferred centre-back pairing with McClintock.

So, things looked bright for the new regime and it was at Roker Park, Sunderland that the Bertie Mee revolution began with a 3.1 win – the Arsenal goals coming from Armstrong and two from Skirton.

13 September 1966

Arsenal played their first League Cup match

On 13th September 1966 Arsenal played Gillingham at Highbury in a Second Round League Cup tie – their first match in that competition.

The idea of a second cup competition had first been muted by Stanley Rous, Secretary of the FA and later President of FIFA (Fédération Internationale de Football Association – football's world governing body).

Against a background of falling attendances at football matches, he thought it would provide much-needed revenue for those clubs who had already been knocked out of the FA Cup. Moreover, with floodlights installed at many clubs during the 1950s - as at Highbury - it would provide an opportunity for regular midweek matches.

Alan Hardaker, Secretary of the Football League at the time, also felt that the League should try to rekindle the nation's interest in its football clubs but saw it very much from the point of view of those clubs being firstly and foremost Football League members.

There were various arguments with the FA about how revenues from the new competition would be split; football journalists and commentators generally felt that the Football League had missed the point, adding to potential fixture congestion at home rather than recognising that the future lay in the new European competitions - which the same Football League had opposed and originally discouraged more visionary men such as Matt Busby from entering.

The Times protested that:

> *"Where a drastic reduction is required in an attempt to raise quality, no doubt quantity and a further spread of mediocrity will be the dose. Where (other) men... think in terms of a European-league for the future in which a lead could surely now be given jointly by our leaders, the Football League propose next season to implement their useless Football League Cup to be played in midweek. It gets the players, the clubs and the public nowhere."*

Despite this opposition, the tournament began in 1960-61 with

Aston Villa being the cup's first winners. Leading clubs such as Arsenal continued to oppose it though and it was only once qualification for European competition was offered to the winners and a Final at Wembley Stadium that they all participated. By the 1971-72 season entry to the competition was made compulsory.

Did you know?

In the 1960s:

- **A loaf of bread cost 5p**
- **A pint of milk cost 7p**
- **A dozen eggs cost 30p**

Arsenal's first League Cup match ended in a 1.1 draw and was the last match in which Don Howe turned out as a player for Arsenal.

Tommy Baldwin scored for Arsenal as he did in the two subsequent replays of the tie with Arsenal eventually progressing 5.0. They were his last goals for the club as on 30th September he moved to Chelsea with centre-forward George Graham heading to Highbury as a result of the deal, which also included a transfer fee to Chelsea.

This transaction was especially galling for Bob Shankly's brother – Bill – now manager of Liverpool, as he too was interested in Graham and had also just missed out to Bertie Mee on the Bob McNab signing.

Having clashed with Chelsea manager Tommy Docherty, the lure of new coach Dave Sexton was clearly an important factor for Graham and he was quoted in the Daily Mirror to that effect:

"I wanted to leave Chelsea, but I didn't want to leave London. Arsenal are a fine club. They have Dave Sexton as their coach, and he did more than anyone for me when he was at Chelsea."

George Graham was another Scot who had grown up in poverty - in Bargeddie, near Coatbridge, North Lanarkshire - and seen both his father and sister die from tuberculosis. Later moving from centre-forward to inside-right to allow John Radford to play through the middle, George Graham's style was laid-back, to say the least and he quickly earned the nickname of 'Stroller.'

However, his apparent lack of effort was clearly deceptive as he became Arsenal's top scorer in his first two seasons with the club and would play a key part in the Arsenal story.

As with all team re-building programmes it took time for these exciting new individuals to gel and for them to be moulded into a competitive team.

Arsenal finished seventh in Bertie Mee's first season then ninth and fourth, but a full 11 points behind the 1968-69 champions Leeds United.

Did you know?

The first heart transplant was carried out on 3rd December 1967 by South African surgeon, Dr Christiaan Barnard

For two seasons in a row, they lost to Birmingham City in the fifth round of the FA Cup including a 2.1 replay defeat on 12th March 1968 at St Andrews with Arsenal's goal coming from Bobby Gould. Ten days earlier they had contested their first League Cup Final.

After beating old adversaries, Huddersfield Town, 6.3 on aggregate over the two legs of the Semi-final Arsenal lined up in front of almost 98,000 fans at Wembley on 2nd March 1968. This was their first appearance at Wembley since losing the FA Cup Final in 1952.

2 March 1968

Arsenal reach their first League Cup Final at Wembley

Fully 16 years later they lost again – to their other West Yorkshire rivals, Leeds United, 1.0, with Terry Cooper scoring the winning goal.

It was Leeds United's first major trophy win and they would be one of Arsenal's closest and keenest rivals over the next six years.

The match was a very physical affair with Peter Storey involved a running battle with Leeds's Johnny Giles and a major brawl breaking out between the players in the second half.

4 April 1968

American civil rights leader Dr Martin Luther King Jr. was shot dead by a sniper in Memphis, Tennessee

Adding attacking midfielder Ray Kennedy - who had been rejected by Stanley Matthews' Port Vale as being 'too slow' - to his squad, the same year, Mee's team reached their second, consecutive League Cup Final the following season.

In the Semi-final they faced Tottenham Hotspur over two legs; this was the first time the North London rivals had clashed at such a late stage in a major competition.

With so much at stake, both matches were aggressive affairs with particular flashpoints occurring between John Radford and Cyril Knowles, and Tottenham's Mike England clashing with Ian Ure on the pitch. Violence was also prevalent in the stands and outside both grounds.

20 November 1968

Arsenal faced Tottenham Hotspur in the Semi-final of a major competition for the first time

Arsenal took a 1.0 lead from the first match at Highbury with a John Radford goal, in front of 55,000 fans.

Radford scored in the second leg too as Arsenal held out for a 1.1 draw, again in front of over 55,000; Jimmy Greaves scored Spurs' only goal of the tie but it wasn't enough to stop Arsenal going back to Wembley with a 2.1 aggregate win (they also beat Tottenham home and away in the league that season).

Swindon Town

The euphoria gained from local bragging rights did not last. The Final on 15th March 1969 represents one of the most humiliating defeats in a major Final that Arsenal have ever succumbed to.

The Wembley pitch had been badly cut up by the recent 'Horse of the Year' show and wasn't helped by heavy rain since then. Arsenal also had several players suffering from the flu. However, they were up against Swindon Town of the Third Division and still widely expected to win.

In the event, Swindon took the lead through Roger Smart who capitalised on a moment of Arsenal confusion between defender Ian Ure and goalkeeper Bob Wilson. They held the lead until four minutes from time when Gould scored an equaliser and forced the match into extra time. However, two Don Rogers goals against a tiring Arsenal team secured a 3.1 win for Swindon.

Two years earlier Queens Park Rangers had become the first team from the Third Division to win a major trophy when they beat West Bromwich Albion to win that year's League Cup but, despite winning the League Cup, hadn't been able to enter the European Inter-Cities Fairs Cup because only sides in the First Division were allowed to do so at the time.

The same rule applied to Swindon Town in 1969 and so Arsenal took their place in the following season's competition. As a direct result of this, the Anglo-Italian League Cup and Anglo-Italian Cup competitions were introduced for those who had won a domestic cup but were still ineligible for major European qualification: Swindon Town promptly went on to win both trophies in the following two seasons.

For Arsenal, Bob Wilson saw light through the gloom of defeat:

> *"It's never going to remain the happiest day of my life but I will go to the grave telling people that what we achieved in the years following that League Cup defeat we owe to Swindon. There were certain players who dropped by the wayside, but those who were part of the abuse we got from the London press – who thought there was no way we could lose to a Third Division side – used it as a spur."*

Peter Marinello and Charlie George

The 'British Invasion' of the USA through music from groups such as The Beatles and The Rolling Stones was accompanied in the late 1960s by psychedelic drug and music experimentation from the likes of Cream and Pink Floyd back in Britain.

The 'Swinging Sixties' featured new designs in fashion from designers like Mary Quant and all of it was recorded by celebrity photographers such as Terence Donovan and David Bailey.

Into this whole culture of drugs, drinking and celebrity fame strode two more players who would be part of the Arsenal story in the early 1970s.

20 July 1969

Astronaut Neil Armstrong became the first man to walk on the moon

At the turn of the decade, Arsenal paid out their first six-figure sum - £100,000 – to bring the 19-year-old Peter Marinello to Highbury from Hibernian.

Hailed by many as 'the Scottish George Best,' unlike previous Scottish players who have entered our story since its outset, Marinello wasn't noted for his toughness or determination; rather it was his flamboyance in the mould of Alex James and his heavy drinking that hit the front pages of newspapers far more often than the back.

He had a promising debut at Old Trafford on 10th January 1970, scoring a solo goal in Arsenal's 2.1 defeat to Manchester United. Sadly, though, he was out of his depth and was soon swallowed up in the bright lights of London never truly making the grade and settling for seedy modelling and fashion shoots instead.

To make matters worse he often clashed with Don Howe and then a knee injury ruled him out for much of that season, after which he found it hard to break back into the first-team.

This was to prove especially hard, given the maturity and altogether greater work-rate of those players who were now repaying Bertie Mee and the club for its initial faith in their abilities and patience in them fulfilling their potential.

Another individual who was far more concerned with style and flair than working hard was Charlie George who had always been an Arsenal fan and, born in Holloway, had played for Islington Schoolboys before joining the club and making his first-team debut four months before Marinello: on 9th August, 1969 in a 1.0 home loss to Everton.

George had the looks and the attitude to act out his attacking role with flair – a skinhead with swagger who liked a drink and, in a violent era, could be violent on the football field.

He was the latest in a long list of Islington entertainers and the Highbury crowd loved him as 'one of their own.' Some of the older fans may have seen elements of another Charlie – the young Buchan – in Charlie George. If he was closer in cultural terms to the pop group 'Slade,' what was beyond doubt were his quick feet, first touch and natural ability with a football.

Celebrity culture was magnified not only by photography in a world where image rights still came second to playing football, but by the introduction of colour television and the first 'experts panel' for live matches introduced by the same Jimmy Hill – now Head of Sport at ITV - who had led the crusade against the maximum wage cap for players.

Did you know?

Colour television arrived in Britain on 1st July 1967

Colour television had first arrived in Britain on 1st July 1967 when, BBC2 launched Europe's first colour service with the Wimbledon tennis championships, presented by David Vine.

On 15th November 1969, the remaining two channels - BBC 1 and ITV - also started broadcasting in colour and coverage of those able to receive colour signals (and then have to pay double the License Fee) quickly increased across the country.

George and Marinello could now be beamed in full colour into ordinary people's homes up and down the country: both their highlights and their misdemeanours.

By now Bertie Mee was under severe pressure to deliver a trophy for Arsenal. Despite the embarrassment of youthful talent which he had inherited, or brought in, here was another 'old boy' who had enjoyed three seasons in which to stop the rot, including defeats in two major Finals - one against a Third Division team.

Largely leaving player involvement and coaching to Don Howe he was often a remote, almost socially awkward figure – not unlike England manager Alf Ramsey – for whom things had to be done his way alone and where brute force rather than maverick showmen was sometimes required to win football matches. Bob Wilson echoed this approach:

"The better sides put the opponents under pressure throughout, not by just a brilliant forward line...just one slip and the game is won."

The 1969-70 season was Mee's worst yet in the league as Arsenal finished 12th and were knocked out of the FA Cup by Blackpool in a Third Round replay. This was also the last match that Terry Neill played for Arsenal before moving to Hull City as player-manager at the end of the season.

European glory

Mee's job was almost certainly saved by success in Europe and the Arsenal Board; the players; the fans and possibly Bertie Mee himself probably believed that this could actually be possible after the events of 8th April 1970.

In front of 46,271 fans, they faced Ajax of Amsterdam in the first leg of the Semi-final of the Inter-Cities Fairs Cup.

The Dutch were the keenest advocates of the 'total football' concept – the first glimpse of which the Highbury crowd had seen when that Moscow Dynamo team had visited Highbury nearly 25 years earlier – whereby any outfield player can play in the position of any other player in the team if called upon to do so.

It would lead Ajax, inspired by the world's best player at the time, Johan Cruyff, to three consecutive European Cup wins in the following seasons and the Dutch National Team to two World Cup Finals in the 1970s.

Charlie George scored two goals that night and Jon Sammels the other as Arsenal won 3.0. They went through to the Final 3.1 on aggregate after losing the away leg 1.0.

If Bertie Mee's 'team over individual' philosophy had ever been put to the test, this was it and he and his team had passed it.

After beating such a fine team, they might have thought Anderlecht of Belgium would provide much easier opposition, but the Belgians had beaten mighty opponents of their own in the Semi-final – Internazionale of Milan. They had lost their first leg tie 1.0 but, astonishingly, won 2.0 in the return in Italy with Gerard Bergholtz (also a Dutchman) scoring both goals.

This momentum was maintained in the first leg of the Final on 22nd

April 1970 when they beat Arsenal 3.1 with yet another Dutchman – Jan Mulder – getting two of Anderlecht's goals. They were also known for having an excellent away record – as witnessed by that match at Inter's San Siro stadium.

Mercifully for Arsenal, Ray Kennedy pulled a goal back just eight minutes from the end.

More than 51,000 packed Highbury for the second leg on 28th April, 1970 to see Eddie Kelly – a midfielder from Glasgow who had only made his debut earlier that season – and John Radford score to make it 2.0 on the night and 3.3 on aggregate but with Arsenal having the vital away goal that would win them the Final (the 'away goals rule' stated that 'the team that has scored more goals 'away from home' will win if scores are otherwise equal').

In the event, just a minute after Radford's goal, Sammels scored a third and, with the match ending 3.0, Arsenal won their first European competition and ended the 17-year wait for a trophy.

This was also the third season in a row that an English team had won the Inter-Cities Fairs Cup after Leeds United had won it in 1968 and then Newcastle United in 1969.

Just to keep their feet on the ground and prevent their fans from thinking that, as in 1930, a new era had dawned for the club, Arsenal lost their final match of the season just four days later: 1.0 at White Hart Lane against Tottenham Hotspur who thus finished one league place above them.

The Double

If not the beginning of a new period of success, the 1970-71 season certainly represented a moment in Arsenal's football history story that had been so long in coming.

After the world had watched the fabulous Brazil national side win the World Cup in Mexico during the summer of 1970 the Arsenal club decided to wear gold away shirts in homage to their South American brilliance. Bertie Mee was optimistic about domestic success following their European trophy win:

"Some of our critics say we are functional, but I would point out that Charlie (George) and George (Graham) would lighten up any sides with their skills."

Arsenal started their league season at Goodison Park, home of champions Everton, with a 2.2 draw – and, sure enough, Charlie George and George Graham scored their goals.

Charlie George was injured in that game though, in a clash with Everton goalkeeper Gordon West, and would miss several months of the season before being converted into more of an attacking midfielder and playing a vital role in unlocking stubborn defences in the run-in for the league title.

Arsenal were unbeaten in their first four league games before Chelsea beat them at Stamford Bridge. They went a further four league games without being beaten before a 5.0 thrashing at Stoke City on 26th September 1970.

In the meantime, the team had begun the defence of their Inter-Cities Fairs Cup in Rome on 16th September 1970 against a Lazio team roared on by 60,000 fans.

John Radford scored both of Arsenal's goals in a 2.2 draw. Radford scored again in the return leg and Armstrong added another to take Arsenal safely through to the next round but safety had been in short supply after the first match in Rome.

The Lazio team were managed at the time by Juan Carlos Lorenzo, an Argentinian who had played in a stormy Quarter-final match against England in the 1966 World Cup. Whether encouraged by him or not, his players attacked members of the Arsenal team during the post-match banquet in a Roman restaurant and it is alleged that armed Lazio fans were heading to the same restaurant to join in.

With Eddie Kelly being held at gunpoint by Italian police at one stage, it was somewhat unsurprising that Frank McLintock and Peter Storey led the fight back and, though aloof and impersonal he might have seemed to many, it was Bertie Mee who jumped into the fray, fighting to protect his players and ensuring they got onto the team coach before serious injuries could be sustained.

Arsenal made it all the way to the fourth round of that season's European competition and were looking increasingly good to retain the trophy. It was McLintock and Storey who scored their goals in a 2.1 win against FC Köln in the first leg. However, Köln grabbed the vital away goal and then won the second leg in Cologne 1.0 to go through on the away goals rule.

Progress in the First Division had been pretty consistent since losing to Stoke at the Victoria Ground. Arsenal went 14 matches unbeaten in the league until – almost inevitably given the history between these great clubs – lost 2.1 to Huddersfield Town at Leeds Road on 16th January 1971.

15 February 1971

Known as 'Decimal Day' when the UK changed its currency from pounds, shillings and pence to decimal coinage

Their major threat that year also came from West Yorkshire in the form of Leeds United who had been knocked out of the FA Cup in a shock result of their own – 3.2 at Fourth Division Colchester

United - and would score 72 league goals that season: one more than Arsenal.

Losing at Elland Road 1.0 on 26th April 1971 with just two games left made it look more and more likely that the league title was heading north for the third consecutive season.

However, Arsenal rallied to win their final league game at Highbury to Stoke City (again) 1.0 before travelling two days later to White Hart Lane for their final match of the season against Tottenham Hotspur, just as it had been the season before.

Just under 52,000 attended that final match of the season on 3rd May 1971 and tens of thousands more were locked outside the ground at kick off.

Arsenal trailed Leeds by one point and needed either a win or a scoreless draw. It looked like the match would finish 0.0 and so make Arsenal champions but, as in the previous season in the Inter-Cities Fairs Cup Final second leg, they made certain with a goal just three minutes from time.

After Tottenham's goalkeeper, Pat Jennings had somehow prevented John Radford from scoring, George Armstrong crossed for Ray Kennedy to head the winning goal.

3 May 1971

Arsenal clinch the league title at White Hart Lane

Arsenal were on top of the league by just a single point and League Champions again for the first time since Tom Whittaker's team had achieved it in 1953. The scenes after the match were very different from 12 months earlier and winning the title at the home of their closest rivals was a scenario even Henry Norris would have struggled to conjure up in the almost sixty years since their controversial move to Highbury.

The team celebrated in the aptly-named White Hart pub in Southgate, North London. The following day's Daily Express reported, under a title of 'Fan-Tastic:

> *"Arsenal are champions...but 50,000 locked outside couldn't see a thing."*

In the FA Cup progress had been relatively straightforward as two Charlie George goals knocked Manchester City out at Maine Road in the Fifth Round.

In the Quarter-final it took another George goal to beat Leicester City after a replay and then Peter Storey scored twice, including a penalty in extra time, to hold Stoke City to a 2.2 draw in the Semi-final at Hillsborough.

In the replay at Villa Park, 62,500 fans saw Arsenal win 2.0 with goals from Graham and Kennedy and so compensate for that earlier defeat in the Potteries.

Arsenal, therefore, reached Wembley for the first time in the FA Cup since their injury-hit defeat to Newcastle United 19 years earlier. This time they would face Bill Shankly's emerging Liverpool team.

8 May 1971

Arsenal won the FA Cup and finally achieved The Double

In baking sunshine on 8th May 1971 the two teams played out a close match which ended 0.0. Steve Heighway put Liverpool ahead within two minutes of the first period of extra time. Eddie Kelly –

who had come on as a substitute for Peter Storey – then equalised (the first substitute ever to score in an FA Cup Final) before Charlie George, aged just 20, struck a superb drive from 20 yards past Liverpool goalkeeper Ray Clemence and into the net for the winner.

As in 1950 Arsenal had beaten Liverpool to win the FA Cup: their fourth.

The team had played 64 matches during the season but this was the win that finally gave them the elusive Double; the pressure of Spurs being the only other team in the twentieth century - ten years earlier - to have previously achieved it was finally relieved.

At an earlier Civic Reception, Arsenal were awarded the Freedom of the Borough – the first time a football club had received such an honour - ahead of the Honourable Artillery Group which had been turned down amid councillors being accused of seeking votes from Arsenal fans. Either way, it was ironic given Arsenal's origins in Dial Square.

Along with another 'double' - captain Frank McLintock was named 'Player of the Year' and Bertie Mee 'Manager of the Year' – a young Arsenal team had also beaten Cardiff City to win the FA Youth Cup for the second time.

200,000 people turned out in Islington the following day for Arsenal's victory parade. Surely this heralded a new period of success and domination for Mee and his team?

The 1970s

Soon after the Double celebrations had died down Don Howe left Arsenal to join his former club, West Bromwich Albion, as manager. The move wasn't a success for Howe and some say it was a key factor in why Arsenal failed to achieve further success in building on the 1970-71 momentum they had created.

Having said that, it was always going to be difficult to follow such a successful season as the previous one where they had put down such a famous marker in the club's history.

They did play their first match in the European Cup (later reformed and restyled as the UEFA Champions League) against Strømsgodset IF in Norway in the First Round on 15th September 1971.

Programme Notes:

Peter Simpson scored Arsenal's first goal in the European Cup

Peter Simpson scored Arsenal's first European Cup goal after just two minutes and two more were added by Peter Marinello (in a rare start) and Kelly.

Arsenal lost to eventual competition winners (for the second consecutive year) Ajax, losing both legs of their Third Round tie and unable to repeat their winning ways against the Dutch of two years previously.

In the league, it was service resuming as usual on 14th August 1971 when they beat Chelsea 3.0 at Highbury with goals from Kennedy, McLintock and Radford but they would go on to lose three of their first five league games.

There were some big wins, with the 5.0 away win at Sheffield United on 29th January 1972 – including two Charlie George goals – being their most emphatic. There were also some big defeats such as a 5.1 loss at old rivals Wolverhampton Wanderers.

The old champions eventually finished fifth, six points behind the new: Brian Clough's Derby County side.

It was against Derby County in the FA Cup that some of the season's key incidents occurred. The teams met on 26th February 1972 in the fifth round. Charlie George scored both of Arsenal's goals in a 2.2 draw and flicked a V-sign at Derby supporters.

If his youthful arrogance was to blame, the irresponsibility he displayed almost led to a riot and many travelling Arsenal fans – Nick Hornby among them and recalling in his book 'Fever Pitch' – literally feared for their lives.

These were unsettled times. Edward Heath's Conservative Party had come to power in 1970 and almost immediately clashed with the same industrial powerhouses as the government had faced fifty years earlier: the railwaymen, miners and transport workers (including militant dockers).

Aspirations were high after the falling barriers to freedom and sheer optimism of the previous decade. These groups not only wanted to buy food from living wages and live in decent housing, they wanted a share in the country's new prosperity.

In 1972 the country was in the midst of industrial strikes and, after oil-producing countries in the Middle East had dramatically raised the price of oil, an energy crisis occurred, accompanied by power cuts and irregular plunges into darkness.

For this reason, the replay of the cup tie against Derby had to be played on a Tuesday afternoon – 29th February 1972 - when an incredible 63,000 fans turned up to watch a 0.0 draw.

63,000

Fans turning up for an FA Cup replay on a Tuesday afternoon

Unfortunately, a surge from the crowd caused a crush barrier to break (many fans had claimed beforehand that it was loose) and 50 people were injured.

The incident took place in the shadow of Britain's worst stadium disaster that had occurred a year earlier. If Archibald Leitch – architect behind the rebuilding of Arsenal's Manor Ground – had been involved in the first Ibrox Stadium disaster in Glasgow in 1902, then he had nothing to do with the second 69 years later.

On 2nd January 1971, a similar crush at Ibrox Park took place on the notorious 'Stairway 13' towards the end of a match between Rangers and 'Old Firm' rivals Celtic, watched by 80,000. 66 people including many children and teenagers died and more than 200 were injured that day.

Arsenal did get past Derby County eventually with a Ray Kennedy goal sufficient in the second replay at Leicester City's Filbert Street ground.

1971, 1972

Arsenal faced Stoke City in FA Cup Semi-finals in consecutive seasons

They faced Stoke City again on 15th April 1972 in the Semi-final at Villa Park. Goalkeeper Bob Wilson badly injured his knee but had to continue as no substitute goalkeepers were allowed in those days. Again, the tie went to a replay where, four days later at Everton's Goodison Park, George and Radford helped Arsenal to a 2.1 win.

They played fierce contemporaries Leeds United in the Centenary FA Cup Final at Wembley on 6th May 1972 and lost to a single Allan Clarke goal in the second half.

30,000 Arsenal fans had applied for their allocation of 21,000 tickets and although the defeat was a disappointment, season ticket applications for the following season soared with 1,000 remaining on the waiting list.

In a return to the Kentish distaste of the nineteenth century and the residents of Islington protesting against Arsenal's arrival in 1913, the Islington Gazette remarked on 16th October 1973 that:

> *"A constant barrage of noise throughout the night prevents the local people from sleeping; a large quantity of rubbish...is left lying about and various acts of obscene and anti-social behaviour take place as members of the queue try to relieve their boredom."*

In 1973, Heath would take the nation into the European Economic Community, resulting in both a wider choice of imported goods and pressure on the UK economy but also the desire by many to travel further afield and visit some of the places their football teams had been playing in since 1955.

At home, the economic malaise continued with clubs forced into early kick-offs through cutting back on lighting.

Under a Daily Mail headline – 'Arsenal count every penny' General Manager Bob Wall talked about cutting back on light bulbs and confidently predicted that:

> *"This is the end of six-figure transfers..."*

It was a far cry from the Bank of England club of the late 1920s and 1930s.

In fact, Arsenal had paid Everton £220,000 for the 26-year old England midfielder Alan Ball at the end of 1971 but the Double side never did build on their success.

There was nearly a repeat of the 1972 FA Cup Final in 1973 but though Leeds United did get back to the Final, Arsenal lost to eventual winners Sunderland 2.1 in the Semi-final at Hillsborough with Charlie George inevitably getting the Arsenal goal.

They had been pretty close to another Double at one point but eventually finished as runners-up in the league to Bill Shankly's Liverpool side who, along with the rise of teams such as Derby County and decline of others such as Leeds United, became the new life force in English football.

At the end of that season Mee sold Frank McLintock to Queens Park Rangers; Bob Wilson retired in 1974 and, after playing 179 times for Arsenal and scoring 49 goals, Charlie George was sold to Derby County at the end of the 1974-75 season and returned to the Baseball Ground where he had made his infamous 1972 gesture.

Did you know?

Arthur Ashe became the first black man to win the Wimbledon tennis tournament on 5th July 1975 in the first all-American Final

The Class of 1966 had matured and aged; the Double team was being broken up and their league positions reflected it: having finished tenth and then sixteenth they briefly flirted with relegation in the 1975-76 season before eventually finishing seventeenth.

The pressure on Bertie Mee was immense and he eventually retired in the May of that year citing 'pressures' and 'personal strain' after ten years in the job.

The 'Double Years' were in an increasingly distant past as was a general optimism in the country that ushered in those early years of the 1970s. The England national team had failed to qualify for the

1974 World Cup which ultimately cost Alf Ramsey his job, to be replaced by Don Revie from Leeds in an unsuccessful period for him personally and the team he left behind.

Football hooliganism had been a part of the Arsenal story since the earliest days of fights on Plumstead Common and the Manor Ground closure in 1895. In the glory days of the 1930s, an ambulance shuttle service had run regularly between Highbury and the Royal Northern Hospital.

In the mid-1970s though, fan crews were often infiltrated by right-wing groups such as the National Front and it was becoming much more widespread: an unwanted backdrop to the nation's economic struggles.

In 1975 plans had been mooted for a moat to be built around the Highbury pitch instead of a wire fence. On June 28th, 1974 the Islington Gazette (in an eerie denial of Boer War atrocities 75 years earlier) had made known its protest at a wire fence being installed at Highbury to help to separate fighting fans and keep them off of the pitch:

"Not only does the fence obscure vision...(but) we have the situation where British people abhor any scheme which smacks of the 'concentration camp'"

The reporter went on to say:

"What is more important...is the possibility of a situation arising on The Terraces when innocent people might want to spin on to the pitch in order to avoid a major hazard."

This was to be a horribly prophetic warning for events in the following decade.

The return of Terry Neill

After apparently courting the then Real Madrid manager, Yugoslav, Miljan Miljanic, Arsenal looked closer to home for Mee's replacement – another old boy who had managed their fiercest rivals, Tottenham Hotspur, for the previous two seasons: Terry Neill.

Moves between the two North London rivals were rare and to move from Arsenal to Spurs (via the Hull City position) and back to Arsenal again was unheard of.

Equally unheard of was for someone so young to be considered for the role. Neill was just 34 years of age when he was appointed Arsenal manager on 9th July 1976.

34

Terry Neill's age when taking over as Arsenal manager

As with Bertie Mee, Neill benefitted hugely from the return of Don Howe the following year – this time as head coach. Howe was also part of the England coaching setup under Ron Greenwood and then Bobby Robson.

Although Alan Ball had largely underperformed for the club Neill seemed intent on making his mark as Arsenal manager by bringing in more top, highly-paid stars.

Powerful striker Malcolm Macdonald arrived from Newcastle United (he remains their fifth highest goalscorer of all-time with 121) for the equally memorable fee of £333,333.34 and Alan Hudson from Stoke City.

£333,333.34

Amount paid to Newcastle United for striker Malcolm Macdonald

Hudson had made his name as a flamboyant and highly skilled midfielder with Chelsea before moving to Stoke City – partly to help pay for the massive new East Stand at Stamford Bridge.

He enjoyed two highly successful seasons in the Potteries where Stoke's resurgent form was described by manager Tony Waddington as 'the working man's ballet' (later also the title of Hudson's autobiography).

Sadly, a major storm in January 1976 caused considerable damage to the Victoria Ground and the club had to sell its best players to pay for the huge repairs. Neill duly signed Hudson for £200,000 in December of that year.

The following year he signed physically huge but ungainly centre-back Willie Young. Born in Edinburgh, Young followed Neill from Spurs – again, one of the few players to make the move in either direction between the North London rivals. Neill once said of Young:

> *"He tried to play like Pele, George Best and Gerson rolled into one. He should have remembered that he was a 14-stone Scotsman."*

These were marquee signings for Terry Neill – statements of intent that he and the club meant business.

If Macdonald, Hudson and Alan Ball, in particular, were meant to lift and lead the mid-70s Arsenal team to star status it was a strategy that failed under Neill who many said was far too young to manage a team like Arsenal.

A drinking culture had set in at the club and Neill found it increasingly difficult to challenge such celebrity egos (Alex Ferguson would face the same issues at Manchester United a decade or so later).

More importantly, the club did not appear to improve in league or cup competitions until the latest crop of young players emerged – most a legacy of the Bertie Mee years in exactly the same way as he had inherited such promising talent when replacing Billy Wright.

Known collectively as 'The Young Ones' Mee had introduced Irishmen David O'Leary, Frank Stapleton and Liam Brady to the first team and, along with other apprentices, they quietly made their marks in the shadows of their far more glamorous team members.

Programme Notes:

Three young Irish players who made their mark at Arsenal in the 1970s:

- David O'Leary
- Frank Stapleton
- Liam Brady

After making his debut in the first match of the 1975-76 season at just 17-years old (a 0.0 draw at Burnley on 16th August, 1975), centre-back David O'Leary, born locally in Stoke Newington, would be a first-choice defender for Arsenal for most of the next 10 years and made 722 appearances in total – a club record.

Famous for his blocks and defensive interceptions he was nicknamed 'spider' as he often gave the impression of having more than one pair of legs.

Fellow apprentice Frank Stapleton also made his debut in 1975 (against Stoke City) and formed a fine striking partnership with Malcolm Macdonald with the pair scoring 46 goals between them in the 1976–77 season.

Especially good in the air, Stapleton was leading scorer in the three seasons after that and would form a similarly lethal strike partnership with Alan Sunderland, who joined from Wolverhampton Wanderers in 1977.

Stapleton scored a total of 108 goals in 300 appearances for Arsenal before leaving for Manchester United in 1981.

A midfield playmaker, blessed with skill and vision, Liam 'Chippy' Brady was sometimes described as having:

"the best left foot since Ferenc Puskás"

that could open any defence, recalling the Hungarian genius who had so terrorised England twenty years earlier.

Bill Shankly was even more fulsome in his praise:

"(he) could get into Wembley through a turnstile without touching the sides. Defenders felt him brush the palms of their hands as he goes by, but they can't hold on to him."

Brady had, like O'Leary, made his debut for the club at the age of 17 in 1973. Neill and Howe made him central to their first-team plans and he initially learned from the likes of Alan Ball before emerging as one of the great Arsenal players and one of the most gifted players of his generation.

He is remembered for a particularly fine goal at White Hart Lane on 23rd December 1978 when Arsenal beat Tottenham 5.0 – their biggest win there since the Second World War and including, largely thanks to Brady's intuitive passing, an Alan Sunderland hat-trick.

In an episode similar to those in late nineteenth century Woolwich, Brady was beaten up in January of 1979 for no reason other than that he had an Irish accent. Irish Nationalism – first witnessed by Leslie Knighton in the 1920s - had plagued Northern Ireland and mainland Britain throughout the decade with bombings and other atrocities committed by IRA terrorists.

One player from Northern Ireland who had been a regular player in North London since 1964 was goalkeeper Pat Jennings – except, as we saw in that title-clinching game in 1971, he played for Tottenham Hotspur, making 591 appearances for them in total.

Jennings himself had once said of the rivalry with Arsenal:

> *"If you were only going to win two games in the season, they had to be the two against Arsenal."*

And yet, in August 1977, believing his best days were behind him, Tottenham agreed to sell Jennings to their closest rivals, as with Willie Young before him.

1,000

Senior appearances by Pat Jennings in English football

Pat Jennings would actually play for Arsenal for a further eight years, making 327 appearances and, on 26th February 1983, became the first player to make 1,000 senior appearances in English football. He would also play 119 times for Northern Ireland.

It took time for Neill and Howe to blend youth and 'big star' experience. In Neill's first three seasons as manager Arsenal finished eighth, fifth and seventh. Signs of progress were seen instead in the cup competitions.

Going out to Middlesbrough 4.1 in the fifth round of the FA Cup on 26th February 1977 (some measure of revenge for the heavy defeats inflicted on Teesside by Arsenal teams over the years) they did better the following season, reaching the Semi-final of the League Cup.

They went out to old enemies Liverpool 2.1 on aggregate. A 2.1 away defeat did the damage. Malcolm Macdonald scored for Arsenal but Kenny Dalglish and former hero Ray Kennedy – who had moved to Anfield four years earlier - scored for Liverpool.

Arsenal did get all the way to the FA Cup Final in 1978. Having beaten Leyton Orient in the Semi-final 3.0 with two more goals from Macdonald, they faced Ipswich Town on 6th May 1978 at Wembley – their eighth Final and the first for Ipswich who were considered to be huge underdogs.

In the event, it was one of the most one-sided FA Cup Finals in football history – with Ipswich completely dominating the match and winning 1.0 with a goal from Roger Osborne just under a quarter of an hour from the end after a misplaced clearance from Willie Young.

To be fair, several key Arsenal players such as Brady, Rice, Nelson, Sunderland, Jennings and Young himself had been carrying injuries but it was their abject surrender, showing a lack of any real fighting spirit that was most disturbing; the manner of defeat would have surprised the Cobbold Family at Ipswich just as much as the result.

Macdonald, in particular, was culpable having talked up his own game prior to the Final just as he had done before his former team - Newcastle United - had faced Liverpool four years earlier. In the event, he froze on both occasions with poor performances.

The following season saw Arsenal fail to win their first three league games before opening their account against Queens Park Rangers in a 5.1 win at Highbury on 2nd September 1978 including two goals from left winger Graham Rix – another apprentice under Mee – who had effectively replaced George Armstrong.

The Inter-Cities Fairs Cup was replaced in 1971-72 by the UEFA Cup (which itself would be merged with the UEFA European Cup Winners' Cup in 1999 and then the UEFA Intertoto Cup, to be rebranded as the UEFA Europa League since 2009-10).

Qualification was now based on league placings and performance in domestic cup competitions.

13 September 1978

Arsenal played their first match in the UEFA Cup

Because they had come fifth in the First Division in 1977-78 Arsenal had qualified for the UEFA Cup and played their first match in that competition on 13th September 1978.

They beat Lokomotiv Leipzig of East Germany 3.0 with two goals from Stapleton and a third from Sunderland and would win the tie 7.1 on aggregate.

They faced Hajduk Split of Yugoslavia (now Croatia) in the next round and lost 2.1 in Split with Brady scoring their away goal. A 1.0 victory in the return match with a goal from Young saw them through on the away goals rule.

In the Third Round they faced another Yugoslav team: Crvena Zvezda, commonly known in English as Red Star Belgrade (who Manchester United had played just before the Munich Air Disaster) and lost 1.0 in Belgrade but this time it was the away team who scored in the second leg at Highbury and went through 2.1 on aggregate

Arsenal struggled in the league – eventually finishing 20 points behind champions Liverpool – but they did get to a second consecutive FA Cup Final, though they made hard work of getting to Wembley.

In the third round, they had needed five matches to get past Sheffield Wednesday 2.0 in the fourth replay. Arsenal's goals that day came from Stapleton and Steve Gatting.

5

Number of matches Arsenal needed to get past Sheffield Wednesday in the FA Cup Third Round

Gatting, who had made his debut in the Leipzig match, was another apprentice from the mid-1970s crop and brother of England cricketer, Mike Gatting.

Two Alan Sunderland goals eventually got them past Southampton – for whom old boy Charlie George was making his debut – in a Quarter-final replay, before Sunderland and Stapleton scored the goals in a 2.0 defeat of Wolverhampton Wanderers in the Semi-final.

3 May 1979

Margaret Thatcher became Britain's first female Prime Minister

Arsenal's players had the chance to make amends for 'not turning up' against Ipswich the year before. One player who would be banned for the Final though was Sammy Nelson. On 3rd April 1979 he had scored a thunderbolt of an equaliser in a First Division match against Coventry City at Highbury and celebrated by dropping his shorts in front of the North Bank.

The 1979 FA Cup Final took place on the sweltering afternoon of 12th May 1979 and it was clear from the kick-off that Arsenal were going to perform hugely better than they had done against Ipswich.

Facing a Manchester United side now managed by former coach Dave Sexton, they cruised to a 2.0 lead at half-time with goals from Brian Talbot (who had played in midfield for Ipswich in the previous year's Final) and Stapleton.

However, there was to be one of the most dramatic finishes in FA Cup history – indeed it is known as the 'Five-minute Final' because Gordon McQueen pulled one back for United just five minutes from the end before Sammy McIlroy equalised just two minutes later.

3 in 5

Number of goals in the last five minutes of the 1979 FA Cup Final

Incredibly, from the kick-off, Brady, holding his and the collective Arsenal nerve, passed to Rix on the wing whose cross was turned in by Sunderland. Arsenal did not concede again and hung on for a 3.2 victory.

This was Arsenal's fifth FA Cup success and the only trophy that Terry Neill would win in his seven years as manager.

Arsenal had appeared in four Finals in the 1970s, winning two and losing two and they made it all the way to the FA Cup Final again in 1980, making it three consecutive Finals – the first team to do this since West Bromwich Albion in 1886, 1887 and 1888, more than 90 years earlier.

Arsenal's route to the 1980 Final took almost as long as in 1979. Two Alan Sunderland goals saw off Cardiff City in the Third Round 2.1, after a Highbury replay and he scored two more, along with Stapleton, in a 3.0 win against Bolton Wanderers in the Fifth Round – again after a replay at Highbury.

Sunderland was busily forging his new partnership with Frank Stapleton as Malcolm Macdonald – along with Alan Hudson – had been effectively grounded after late-night drinking during a pre-season tour of Australia.

At the semi-final stage, they faced old Cup rivals, Liverpool. In the longest Semi-final in FA Cup history the match went to a third replay at Coventry City's Highfield Road ground where on 1st May 1980 Arsenal finally won 1.0 with another vital cup goal from Brian Talbot.

The Final took place nine days later on 10th May 1980 when a tired and weary Arsenal faced West Ham United, then in the Second Division and, like Ipswich two years previously, massive underdogs.

5

Pat Rice became the first player to play in five FA Cup Finals for the same club

Arsenal defender Pat Rice made history by becoming the first player to appear in five FA Cup Finals for the same club (1971, 1972, 1978, 1979, 1980)

In the event, Trevor Brooking headed The Hammers ahead after just 13 minutes and despite having much of the possession, Arsenal were unable to make any kind of breakthrough, losing 1.0.

Not only was this another Cup Final shock, it remains to date the last time a team from outside the top tier of English football has won the FA Cup.

Neill's team made some progress in the league, again finishing behind champions Liverpool in a creditable fourth place, though still eight points adrift of the title winners. It was in the cups that they had found the most success.

On 34th September 1979 they had got some revenge against Leeds United for the 1968 and 1972 League Cup and FA Cup Final defeats by beating them 7.0 in a Second Round, second leg League Cup tie.

Alan Sunderland scored a hat-trick in this their biggest ever home win in the League Cup competition in which all went well until the Quarter-final.

This brought them face-to-face with their old League Cup nemesis from ten years earlier: Swindon Town. Alan Sunderland again scored Arsenal's goal from a penalty in a 1.1 draw. However, history repeated itself in the replay on 11th December 1979 as, despite two goals from Brady and one from Talbot, Swindon – still in the Third Division – won 4.3.

As FA Cup Winners in 1979 Arsenal had qualified for the 1979-80 UEFA European Cup Winners' Cup competition for the first time (in 1971-72 following the Double the previous season, they had played in the European Cup).

Their first ever game in this competition came on 19th September 1979 against Fenerbahçe from Istanbul – formed when Turkey had still been part of the Ottoman Empire.

Alan Sunderland scored Arsenal's first Cup Winners' Cup goal and

Willie Young added a second five minutes from the end. Drawing 0.0 in the second leg it was enough to put Arsenal through to the next round.

They then beat German side Magdeburg, before thrashing IFK Göteborg of Sweden to arrive at a first leg Semi-final match against Italian giants Juventus at Highbury.

The match finished 1.1 in another bad-tempered game against a team from Italy before Arsenal headed for the Stadio Communale (now Stadio Olimpico, home of Torino FC) in Turin on 23rd April 1980.

A crowd of over 66,000 were expecting Juventus to go through because of the away goal they had scored in the first leg and also because no British side had won there in the 25 years of European football that had taken place so far.

23 April 1980

Arsenal became the first English team to beat Juventus at their Stadio Communale ground

In the event, the game was heading for a 0.0 draw which would have been enough to put Juventus through to the Final and so Neill introduced another young Arsenal player - Paul Vaessen - who, at just eighteen years old, scored for Arsenal from a Graham Rix pass just two minutes from the end.

It proved to be the only goal of the game and enough to put Arsenal through to their second European Final. Unfortunately for Vaessen, he would never hit this peak on the football field again and, after a series of injuries and drug-related crime, died tragically young at just 39 years old.

That Final came on 14th May 1980, just four days after the FA Cup Final loss to West Ham United and with still two First Division matches to play at the end of a long season and fixture pile-up.

As so often happens when success breeds further matches in cup competitions, this second major Final in four days was a match too far. At the fifty-year old Heysel Stadium (rebuilt and renamed in 1995 as the King Baudouin Stadium) in the north west of Brussels, Belgium, Arsenal faced Valencia of Spain – managed by former Argentine and Real Madrid great, Alfredo Di Stéfano.

The match ended 0.0 after extra-time and went to penalties. Left-footers Graham Rix and Liam Brady both missed as Valencia took the Cup 5.4.

Brady subsequently left Arsenal after their last league match of the season on 19th May 1980 – a 5.0 defeat at Middlesbrough's Ayresome Park; his destination was the team they had beaten in that heroic European Semi-final: Juventus.

After playing 70 matches that season Arsenal had lost two major Cup Finals and failed to qualify for Europe.

The long goodbye

There was little for Arsenal to shout about over the next three seasons: a nine-match unbeaten run at the end of the 1980-81 season saw them finish third, seven points behind Aston Villa, but they got nowhere in the cups (including a League Cup defeat to Tottenham in November 1980).

The following season they finished behind champions Liverpool again but 16 points back in fifth place. They were denied a major cup run by Tottenham again – this time in the Third Round of the FA Cup - and another run in the UEFA Cup ended with an away goals defeat, on aggregate, to the tiny Winterslag from Belgium (who in 1988 would merge with Waterschei Thor to form the K.R.C Genk club).

The spring of 1982 was overshadowed by a 74-day military conflict between the United Kingdom and Argentina. On 2nd April 1982 Argentina invaded and occupied one of Britain's overseas territories – the Falkland Islands – in the South Atlantic Ocean, more than 3,500 miles away from London.

The following day they did the same in South Georgia and the South Sandwich Islands. Prime Minister Margaret Thatcher approved the sending of a naval task force to retake the islands. After a bloody engagement with the Argentine Navy and Air Force in which over 3,000 were either killed or injured, Argentina surrendered on 14th June 1982 and control of the islands reverted to Britain.

1983 was to provide a bigger shock and ultimately result in the departure of Terry Neill. Neill bought Tony Woodcock from FC Cologne to effectively replace Frank Stapleton and as a partner to Alan Sunderland but Arsenal went backwards in the league, finishing tenth – 24 points behind champions Liverpool (again).

Seeking salvation in the cup competitions they suffered one of their worst nights in Europe. On 14th September 1982 they faced another team from Moscow - this time Spartak Moskva (or FC Spartak) – in the UEFA Cup and lost narrowly in Russia 3.2 in front of 68,500.

If they had expected to have a good chance of progressing in the return leg, having two away goals in the bag, things turned out very differently. On 29th September 1982 Arsenal lost 5.2 at home and so went out on aggregate 8.4.

Good progress in both domestic cup competitions led eventually to Semi-final defeats - both at the hands of Manchester United.

Left-back Kenny Sansom had joined the team from Crystal Palace three years earlier and would go on to make 394 appearances for the club as well as 86 for England.

In the summer of 1983 Neill also bought Charlie Nicholas from Celtic for £750,000 after the 21-year old had scored 50 goals the previous season. If Charlie was the new darling of Glasgow he was also stepping into the flamboyant, fashionable footsteps of Peter Marinello.

£750,000

Amount Arsenal paid to Celtic for Charlie Nicholas

Nicholas was one of the first players to have an agent (Bev Walker) who encouraged him to endorse branded products in media, music and fashion.

Like Marinello before him, he would make headlines in London far away from the football pitch and his drinking exploits quickly earned him the nickname of 'Champagne Charlie.'

Many Arsenal fans, still missing their hero, Liam Brady, loved Nicholas the model and soundbite personality and in his defence, he would score 54 goals in 184 appearances. However, he was far from being a model professional and never reached his full footballing potential, according to others.

Margaret Thatcher had become Britain's first woman Prime Minister in 1979 and sought to deregulate markets and free capitalist entrepreneurs from bureaucracy, state involvement and anti-competitive practices such as those held tightly by trades unions.

Anxious to avoid the industrial strife of her Conservative

predecessor, Heath, in the 1970s, Thatcher attacked what she saw as outdated working methods in decaying industries. The Miners' Strike of the mid-1980s represented the most serious and prolonged period of industrial action since the General Strike of 1926, involving some 142,000 mineworkers at one point.

The flip side to the old staple industries such as coal mining and shipbuilding being allowed to decline and their dependent communities die overnight was money-making for individuals on a huge scale, epitomised by bankers and financiers in the City of London.

Individual enterprise ahead of community welfare was trumpeted and, for many, quickly morphed into flagrant greed.

The drinking, gambling, womanising and full-blown egos of Arsenal's highly-paid stars fitted easily into this 'loadsamoney' landscape (especially in London) and continued to undermine Terry Neill as it had done really ever since he was first appointed.

Neill, somewhat stoically and definitely unfashionably, favoured professionalism above all else:

"These days we judge success by the size of someone's car, or which parties they go to. That's fame, not success. Success is about self-worth, being professional and, in football terms, winning things."

But Neill had only won that one trophy – the 1979 FA Cup – and was unfavourably (and perhaps unfairly) compared with Bob Paisley who had taken over from Bill Shankly at Liverpool and won twelve prizes over a similar period.

It all ended in a cup competition defeat to one of Arsenal's most famous tormentors from the past who, like Swindon Town, were out to prove that football history could repeat itself.

Third Division Walsall came to Highbury on 29th November 1983, 50 years after their shock FA Cup victory. Playing this time in a Fourth Round League Cup (Now the Milk Cup) tie the men from the West Midlands won 2.1 to knock Arsenal out and Terry Neill with them who could only remark:

"...the players don't seem to know what it is to hunger for goals and glory."

After 416 games in charge, Terry Neill was sacked in December 1983. One of Neill's detractors was the up-and-coming Arsenal director David Dein.

Dein was born into a working-class, Jewish family whose ancestors had moved to East London at the beginning of the twentieth century. His father was a tobacconist and, from starting out by helping out in the family shop, the younger Dein had progressed to the running of a huge import-export business in Shepherds Bush Market in West London.

He had played Sunday League football with another Jewish entrepreneur – Irving Scholar – who was becoming similarly influential at Tottenham Hotspur.

Head Coach Don Howe replaced Neill as caretaker and officially became Arsenal manager just over four months later on 28th April 1984.

Don Howe's new foundations

If David Dein encouraged hard work, then so did Howe. Under him, Arsenal gradually became a competitive team again rather than a group of either talented or lazy individuals (or both).

He appointed coach John Cartwright to work with him. Cartwright was himself a product of West Ham United's famous Youth

Academy and had played alongside other young players such as England greats from 1966: Bobby Moore and Geoff Hurst.

Regarded as one of the finest youth coaches of his generation with an emphasis on skill and technique, he gradually weeded out some of the drinkers at Arsenal whilst nurturing yet another round of young talent to go with new signings such as striker Paul Mariner and defender Viv Anderson.

Apprentice Paul Davis – who had made his debut against Tottenham Hotspur as far back as 1980 - had already begun to make his mark as a talented, creative midfielder.

He also made a mark on Southampton's Glenn Cockerill in 1988 when he punched him during a match and broke his jaw, earning him a nine-match ban.

1984

An IRA bomb killed four people at the Conservative Party Conference in Brighton

Another talented Arsenal youngster David 'Rocky' Rocastle turned professional in December 1984 and became one of the most popular midfielders of the era, appearing 277 times for the club, scoring 34 goals.

Blessed with natural pace he also played 14 times for England before suffering a persistent knee injury and leaving for Leeds United in 1992. Like Paul Vaessen before him, David Rocastle died much too young – of non-Hodgkin's lymphoma - an aggressive form of cancer which attacks the immune system – on 31st March 2001, aged just 33.

In another quirk of fate, later that day Arsenal played Tottenham in a First Division match at Highbury before which fans from both sides in the crowd of just over 38,000 stood in silent respect at his passing.

Another youth player to progress under Howe was Irish centre-forward Niall Quinn who had been rejected after a trial with Fulham. A hugely popular player at Highbury, Quinn would go on to score 20 goals in 94 appearances for the club and amass 92 caps for the Republic of Ireland.

At the back, two young central defenders were also beginning to make their mark. Like Quinn, Martin Keown had played Gaelic football as a boy in Oxford. Joining Arsenal as a schoolboy he made his senior debut against West Bromwich Albion in November 1985.

Tony Adams from Romford, East London, joined Arsenal on a schoolboy contract at the same time as Keown but made his debut two years earlier, against Sunderland, at just 17 years-old. He would go on to be considered one of the greatest Arsenal players ever.

Programme Notes:

Tony Adams made his debut for Arsenal at the age of 17

Blessed as he was with such promising talent, and, though the blend of the team with senior players was improving, as under Bertie Mee it took time to gel.

Arsenal never got into serious trouble in the league, finishing sixth, seventh and seventh again in the seasons when Howe was manager. They went out cheaply in the FA Cup – at Middlesbrough in the Third Round in 1984 and at Third Division York City in the Fourth Round in 1985 - as well as a Third Round League Cup defeat at Second Division Oxford United (albeit they were Second Division Champions that season).

In May 1985 plans to build a new stand over the South Terrace ('Clock End') were rejected by Islington's Planning Committee as it would be an

"unreasonable intrusion to the skyline"

Councillor Carol O'Brien added that the proposed new stand would provide:

"executive-type boxes (which) will not benefit local families"

Twenty years later, as the modern era took hold, these arguments would hold little sway as the club moved into its new Emirates Stadium.

Did you know?

The Live Aid concerts took place at Wembley Stadium in London and John F. Kennedy Stadium in Philadelphia on 13th July 1985 to raise money for famine victims in Ethiopia

In 1985, though, the season ticket optimism even in the wake of losing the 1972 Cup Final had run its course. Arsenal hadn't even contested a major Final for five years and the attendance at Highbury for their opening First Division match of the 1985-86 season was just 21,895 – the lowest recorded attendance for an opening home fixture since the Second World War.

Moreover, the skilful approach of John Cartwright looked like descending into a long-ball, results-first mentality such was the increasing desperation for success on the field

Arsenal's seventh place in the First Division in 1984-85 had seen them finish 24 points behind the champions who were from Merseyside again but, for a change, not Liverpool but Everton.

Everton under manager Howard Kendall were flourishing and the 1980s saw one of the most successful (and competitive) periods for both clubs in recent memory, both in England and Europe.

Shockingly, the first of two terrible disasters involving Liverpool fans was about to unfold.

Mid-1980s football tragedies

Liverpool had won the European Cup in 1984 for the fourth time and got all the way to the Final again in 1985 where they would face the side that Arsenal had so famously conquered in the European Cup Winners' Cup Semi-final five years earlier: Juventus.

The match was to be played at the same Heysel Stadium where Arsenal had lost on penalties to Valencia. Decrepit, unsafe and clearly not fit for purpose for a match of such magnitude, it is incredible in retrospect that UEFA had chosen it for one of their major Finals.

It seems that the local police too were insufficiently experienced or deployed properly to deal with football fans on such a scale in their city. Running battles between rival fans had taken place during the day before the match and, an hour before kick-off on 29th May 1985, rioting Liverpool fans attacked Juventus fans who tried to escape, running instead into a concrete retaining wall which eventually collapsed with the loss of 39 lives – mainly Italians – and 600 people being injured.

As a result, some top officials, the captain of police, Johan Mahieu, and 14 football fans were convicted of manslaughter. English clubs were banned from European competition for five years and

Liverpool specifically for six years.

The Heysel disaster was described subsequently as:

"the darkest hour in the history of the UEFA competitions"

Eighteen days earlier a riot occurred at Birmingham City's St Andrew's ground in their Second Division match with Leeds United. Urged on by hooligan 'firms' the 'Zulu Warriors' from Birmingham and 'Service Crew' from Leeds, more than 500 people were injured in ferocious violence and one person died: 15-year old Ian Hambridge from Northampton was attending his first-ever football match when a 12-foot high wall collapsed on top of him.

On the same day, another tragedy in an old stadium had occurred. Bradford City had won the Third Division title and had received the trophy just before their match with Lincoln City. Their Valley Parade ground was consequently packed with celebrating fans including in their main stand which had a wooden roof and, having been previously condemned as unsafe, was due for demolition.

Just before half-time, a small fire was spotted underneath that stand where piles of rubbish had been allowed to accumulate. Only four minutes later, due largely to the fanning effect of strong winds, the whole stand was on fire and panic took hold of spectators who tried to escape by breaking down locked exit gates.

56 people died – many burnt to death at the turnstiles that had also been locked – and 265 suffered injuries. It was the worst fire disaster in British football history and the worst tragedy to occur in any British football stadium since the second Ibrox disaster, fourteen years earlier.

96

Number of fans killed in three separate football tragedies

If football's product was stale in the mid-1980s it plumbed new depths off the pitch with tragic consequences.

Don Howe struggled on but Arsenal's Quarter-final replay defeat to Aston Villa in the League Cup, and Fifth Round FA Cup loss to Luton Town, hastened his departure.

It is alleged that Arsenal approached Alex Ferguson - then the highly successful manager of Aberdeen - about the manager's job at Arsenal. Liverpool are supposed to have made a similar approach when their own manager, Joe Fagan, retired the previous year.

Whether either rumour was true or not, Ferguson wanted to wait until after the World Cup of 1986 where he was in charge temporarily of the Scotland national team after the sudden death of the legendary former Celtic manager, Jock Stein, before making any decisions about his own future. He subsequently remained in Scotland until joining Manchester United as manager in November of that year.

Rumours next circulated of an Arsenal approach for former Chelsea, Tottenham and QPR player, Terry Venables, then manager of Spanish giants Barcelona. Venables did not like the dubious way in which Arsenal's directors appeared to be doing business and remained in Spain before moving to North London the following year – as the new manager of Tottenham Hotspur.

Ironically Don Howe did not like the idea of his employees going behind his back either and, after 117 games as Arsenal manager, resigned in March 1986.

Return of George Graham

After a brief caretaker role from coach (and later Chief Scout) Steve Burtenshaw between March and May 1986 the club turned again to an old boy as their next manager.

14 May 1986

George Graham returned to Highbury as manager

George Graham returned to Highbury as manager on 14th May 1986, having himself coached at Crystal Palace and QPR and managed old nineteenth century rivals Millwall to promotion from the Third Division.

It was perhaps entirely appropriate that a tough, working-class Scotsman should be appointed in Arsenal's centenary year (the legend 'Centenary Year 1985' had been added just below the club crest on Arsenal's shirts for the 1985-86 season).

If Arsenal's players were expecting Graham the manager to stroll around Highbury as he had done as Graham the player, they were in for a mighty shock.

Their new boss had already built a reputation as a strict disciplinarian where hard work and professionalism were key. Though he was not initially dismissive of flair players, the hangers-on and the has-beens were quickly moved on to other clubs or banished to the reserves. Graham was quoted as saying:

> *"...from now on, players will have to earn the right to play for Arsenal."*

He also added, rather ominously:

which was more an echo of Henry Norris and Herbert Chapman than Don Howe or even Bertie Mee.

Graham was determined to build a team around the promising youth players already at the club with Tony Adams being made club captain within a year of Graham's arrival (he would remain as captain for the next 14 years).

Apprentice Paul Merson made his debut as a right-winger in December 1986 and schoolboy Michael Thomas made his debut in defence the following year before being moved to a midfield role.

In his first season as Arsenal manager, Graham's team finished in fourth place in the First Division, one point behind Tottenham and 15 points behind Everton who were champions again.

Their centenary league match came on 27th December 1986 in a 1.0 win against Southampton at Highbury in front of more than 38,000 fans who included old boys George Male, Ted Drake and Joe Mercer; Arsenal were top of the league at that point.

Since losing 1.0 at Nottingham Forest in a First Division match on 27th September 1986 Arsenal went 22 matches unbeaten in league and cup competitions before losing 2.0 at Manchester United on 24th January 1987 with goals from Gordon Strachan and Terry Gibson

They went down to a shock 3.1 home defeat to Watford in the Quarter-final of the FA Cup but went further in the League Cup (then sponsored by and known as the Littlewoods Cup).

Beating old rivals Huddersfield Town in the Second Round they cruised past Manchester City, Charlton Athletic and Nottingham Forest to arrive at the Semi-final stage where they faced Tottenham Hotspur, just as they had done nearly twenty years earlier.

It was in the first leg on 8th February 1987 that Michael Thomas made that first-team debut in front of 41,306 at Highbury. If a promising future beckoned for him, the team's immediate prospects did not look bright as Tottenham took a 1.0 lead with a goal from Clive Allen (son of Les Allen who had also played for Tottenham in their Double success of 1961).

Clive had once been on Arsenal's books though he did not play a competitive first-team game for them before moving to Crystal Palace as part of the deal that brought Kenny Samson to Highbury.

In the second leg at White Hart Lane Clive Allen scored again but Arsenal replied with goals from Niall Quinn and Viv Anderson to level the tie. With no away goals counting in separating the sides, a replay took place three days later on 4th March 1987, again at Tottenham's ground.

The score was the same as in the second leg – 2.1 to Arsenal with a late goal from Rocastle following one from striker Ian Allison who had made his debut for the club in that shock 1983 League Cup defeat to Walsall.

Clive Allen scored in his third consecutive League Cup game for Tottenham but to no avail: Arsenal were back at Wembley for the first time since losing to West Ham United in the FA Cup seven long years before while their fiercest London rivals, Tottenham, sent congratulatory champagne to the Arsenal dressing room after the battle on the pitch had ended.

Arsenal faced Liverpool in the League Cup Final on 5th April 1987 and won 2.1. Ian Rush scored first for Liverpool (until this match Liverpool had never lost a match when Rush had scored the opening goal) but a quick reply from Charlie Nicholas levelled the match before Nicholas scored his and Arsenal's second just seven minutes from the end.

It was third time lucky for Arsenal who took their first League Cup trophy and their first win in a major Final since 1979.

Graham – who had become the first player to appear in four League Cup Finals, including the two late 60's defeats for Arsenal - did not allow his young team's winning of a major honour in his first season detract him from his desire to continue to build a competitive team that could challenge for league and cup winning medals in each and every season.

Though Charlie Nicholas had shown a brief renaissance and despite the presence of Niall Quinn in the team, Graham was rumoured to have been chasing Kerry Dixon of Chelsea before signing Leicester City's striker Alan Smith for £800,000 after he had scored 84 goals in 217 appearances for 'The Foxes.'

It was to a strong defensive platform where most of Graham's attention was drawn though. Martin Keown had asked for a pay rise but players would grow to learn that Graham would almost always tell them that there was no money in the budget. If they argued about it, they would be left out of the team or even sold. Keown was promptly transferred to Aston Villa for £100,00 before being re-signed from Everton six years later for £2.2 million.

Right-back Nigel Winterburn signed from Wimbledon in the summer of 1987 and would go on to replace Kenny Samson.

Programme Notes:

By 1988 one of the most famous back lines in football history was created: Dixon, Adams, Bould and Winterburn

Two Stoke City players arrived the following year: Lee Dixon at left-back and Steve Bould at the centre of defence. One of the most famous back lines in football history was thus created: Dixon,

Adams, Bould and Winterburn.

1987-88 opened with a 2.1 home league defeat for Arsenal on 15th August 1987 against the team they had just beaten in the League Cup Final: Liverpool. They won their first game of the season on 29th August 1987 at Highbury with a 6.0 win over Portsmouth; new striker Alan Smith getting a hat-trick.

After a poor start, this was to be the first in a 16-match unbeaten league and cup run, only ending after 14 consecutive wins in a 1.0 First Division defeat at Southampton on 21st November 1987.

Arsenal came sixth in the league that season, a huge 24 points behind champions Liverpool. As in the previous season, they went out of the FA Cup at the Quarter-final stage – this time to Brian Clough's Nottingham Forest.

As in 1968 and 1969 though, Arsenal made it to a second, consecutive League Cup Final where, having beaten Everton home and away in the Semi-final they faced Luton Town at Wembley on 24th April 1988.

Brian Stein put Luton ahead in the first half before two goals in three minutes from Martin Hayes – another striker who had started as an apprentice with Arsenal – and Alan Smith put Arsenal in control.

Danny Wilson then equalised for Luton, eight minutes from the end, before Brian Stein got his second of the match in the final minute of normal time to win the Cup for Luton Town – the only major trophy they have won in their history. Arsenal were League Cup runners-up for the third time.

Arsenal had signed winger Brian Marwood from Sheffield Wednesday for £800,000 in March 1988, initially as cover for Hayes who tended to be injury-prone. Marwood scored in the first match of the 1988-89 season, along with one from Paul Merson and another Alan Smith hat-trick as they trounced Wimbledon 5.1 at Plough Lane on 27th August 1988.

Arsenal were knocked out of the League Cup by Liverpool in a Third Round second replay at Highbury; and also went out in the Third Round of the FA Cup after a replay against West Ham United.

Hillsborough

Liverpool cruised through to the FA Cup Semi-final where they faced Nottingham Forest at Hillsborough, Sheffield on 15th April 1989. The FA Cup was the one domestic trophy that had always eluded Forest manager Brian Clough but on this fateful day, individual and collective football glory were rendered irrelevant as the second major tragedy involving Liverpool supporters in four years occurred.

At previous FA Cup Semi-finals during the 1980s concerns had been raised about safety in the stadium – especially at the Leppings Lane end where many more fans had been allowed to enter than could be safely accommodated leading to overcrowding and crushing.

38 fans had been hurt in the 1981 match between Tottenham Hotspur and Wolverhampton Wanderers and more crushing occurred in the 1987 game between Leeds United and Coventry City.

Almost exactly one year earlier, on 9th April 1988 on their way to the Final against Wimbledon, Liverpool had also met Nottingham Forest at the same Semi-final stage and were again allocated the smaller Leppings Lane end despite protests that they had the larger number of supporters.

After crushing occurred Liverpool had lodged a formal complaint about the state of the ground which had no safety certificate in place following changes made after the 1981 Semi-final injuries.

The similarities with Heysel did not end there. As with the Brussels police, the South Yorkshire police made fundamental errors in their policing operation and, years later, were proved to have failed in their duty of care to football supporters.

Just before kick-off, to avoid problems outside of the ground, a large exit and two other gates were opened allowing supporters to enter the ground via a narrow tunnel. Shamefully this action had been approved when the pens on the terrace into which these supporters now arrived were already overcrowded and so crushing at the perimeter fence was inevitable.

Again, 96 people died but in this single, terrible tragedy. Many of the dead were, as at Ibrox in 1971, just teenagers. A further 766 were injured in one of the worst disasters in football history.

The match was abandoned after just six minutes and, as bodies were laid out on the pitch in bright sunshine, the warning from that Islington Gazette reporter at Highbury almost fifteen years earlier that perimeter fencing at football grounds could cause a 'major hazard' was remembered much too late as shadows gathered over football once again.

One minute to go at Anfield

Liverpool did eventually beat Forest again to face Merseyside neighbours Everton in an emotional FA Cup Final which they won 3.2. Liverpool had also not lost a match in 1989 since a 3.1 defeat at fierce rivals Manchester United and had completed an amazing 24-match unbeaten run in league and cup. They had won their last four league games at Anfield.

Arsenal, on the other hand, had lost only two in 16 matches since their cup defeat by West Ham United and had been league leaders for much of the season.

They now faced their final three league matches: the first two of which were at home. To say that George Graham's team looked as though they had bottled it right at the end was an understatement. They lost the first of these games to Derby County, 2.1, and could then only draw 2.2 with Wimbledon.

It looked as though Liverpool would clinch the title, especially as Arsenal now faced them at Anfield in the final match of the 1988-89 league season; a fixture re-scheduled because of the awful events at Hillsborough.

To say that the Anfield match on 26th May 1989 – a Friday night and also being screened live on ITV - was full of expectation would not be entirely true.

After doing their best to throw away their chances of the league title at Highbury, Arsenal now travelled to a ground where they hadn't won previously in 15 attempts.

They were three points behind Liverpool and adrift by four goals in terms of goal difference. However, they had scored more goals and so a win by two clear goals would make Arsenal champions as the respective goal differences would then be the same but with Arsenal having scored more. Liverpool, by contrast, hadn't lost by two or more goals at home for three years.

With Arsenal's full-backs Dixon and Winterburn being allowed to push forward and stop Liverpool's wingers, Liverpool were strangely lethargic with mental and physical exhaustion clearly playing its part.

The score was 0.0 at half-time after which Alan Smith headed in a free-kick from Nigel Winterburn to put Arsenal ahead in the 52nd minute. Still, it looked like an impossible task but then, incredibly, in injury time, in the very last minute of the match – the last minute of the entire First Division season – Michael Thomas, put through by Alan Smith, charged into the Liverpool area and beat goalkeeper Bruce Grobbelaar to score.

26 May 1989

Arsenal grabbed the league title at Anfield in the last minute of the season

38 seconds later, the referee blew his whistle and Arsenal were champions for a ninth time. They had waited 18 years to win it again, just as they did after winning it in 1953.

18

Years between Arsenal's title wins in 1953, 1971 and 1989

Arsenal were also the last club in the top-flight of English football to win the league while fielding all-English sides, which they did on 11 occasions that season.

George Graham had won his second title with Arsenal: the first as a player in the 1970s, the second as a manager at the end of the 1980s – a decade that, for football, was in many ways best left behind.

Arsenal hadn't defended a league title since 1934-35 – the last of their three consecutive title wins in the 1930s – and they didn't come close to it in 1989-90. They finished fourth, one point and one place behind Tottenham Hotspur again, just as in 1986-87. They were also seventeen points behind Liverpool who were perhaps spurred on more by the previous season's final day loss than Arsenal were by victory.

Because of the Heysel ban on English clubs, Arsenal could not compete in the European Cup – only the second time they had qualified for a competition that had begun in 1955.

There was trouble on the pitch for Arsenal when, on 4th November 1989, they beat Norwich City in a fractious game at Highbury. Norwich were 2.0 up at half-time – the second after a hotly disputed free kick – and then 3.2 close to the end.

David O'Leary then equalised and, right at the end of the match, Michael Thomas (again) raced into the penalty area and was apparently brought down. Lee Dixon had scored a penalty earlier and, though he missed this, his second, he managed to poke the ball into the net for the winning goal, whereupon a mass fight broke out in the goal net with most players from both sides pushing and shoving each other as tempers boiled over.

Both clubs were heavily fined by the FA as a result of failing to control (or subsequently condemn) their players.

Queens Park Rangers knocked Arsenal out of the FA Cup that season – 2.0 in a Fourth Round replay. They also went out of the League Cup in the Fourth Round – at Second Division Oldham Athletic, 3.1 with Quinn scoring Arsenal's only goal.

The Gunners might have blamed Oldham's artificial pitch at Boundary Park for the result - not being used to the unusual bounce or speed of the ball on such a surface – but they could hardly level the same complaint at QPR: their artificial pitch at Loftus Road had been replaced with traditional grass again just under two years earlier.

The early 1990s

The ending of the Cold War was synonymous with the collapse of the Soviet Union.

After Mikhail Gorbachev - the first in a series of much younger leaders compared to the past - had been installed as leader of the Soviet Union in March 1985, he promoted a much more liberal approach to politics (Glasnost) and introduced capitalist, free-market elements into the economy (Perestroika) in place of the central planning of the economy, which had been controlled by the Communist Party since the revolutions of 1917.

The main reasons for this at the time were that the Soviet Union's domestic economy was in difficulty and it was struggling to keep up with the costs of the arms race with the USA under its President, Ronald Reagan, who had come to power there four years earlier.

Politically, this meant that the Soviet Communist Party found it almost impossible to contain and control Gorbachev's reforms at home and across those countries controlled by the Union (also known as USSR - the Union of Soviet Socialist Republics).

Popular movements such as the Solidarity movement in Poland and anti-communist parties in Hungary, Czechoslovakia, Bulgaria and Romania led to their governments being overthrown; in East Germany, the Berlin Wall fell in November 1989 symbolising the collapse of the Soviet regime and communist ideology in Europe.

9 November 1989

The Berlin Wall – symbol of the Cold War and the country's division into East and West Germany after the Second World War– fell, paving the way for German reunification the following year

The Baltic states of Lithuania, Estonia and Latvia became independent of the Soviet Union before Ukraine also withdrew. On Boxing Day - December 26th, 1991 - the Soviet Union was officially dissolved, the economic and political union breaking up into fifteen separate and independent nations.

Amid a series of high-level summits between Gorbachev and Reagan the Cold War - the great and global fear of near nuclear oblivion - ended mostly peacefully.

£1.3 million

Amount paid to QPR for goalkeeper David Seaman

George Graham had long coveted David Seaman – coached by former Arsenal goalkeeping legend, Bob Wilson – and he enjoyed some element of revenge for the cup defeat by signing him from Queens Park Rangers for £1.3 million (a British record at the time for a goalkeeper) to replace John Lukic, In Graham's words:

"I still think John Lukic is one of the top three keepers in the country. I just think David Seaman is the best."

He also signed Anders Limpar, a Swedish winger, from Cremonese in Italy to replace Brian Marwood who had been dispatched to Middlesbrough.

After a disappointing season Graham, as uncompromising as ever, was having a clear-out and, in shades of the Martin Keown chapter, even central defender David O'Leary was banished to the reserves for some three months after asking for an extra week of rest following Ireland's hugely successful participation in the 1990 World Cup in Italy that summer.

As in 1988-89, Arsenal opened their 1990-91 league campaign with an away win at Wimbledon – 3.0 – and, again as in 1988-89, they went on to win the league, though much less dramatically.

They only lost one First Division match all season, away at Chelsea on 2nd February 1991 with Alan Smith scoring their only goal in a 2.1 defeat. It was a tremendous feat and they came as close as any other team in football history had done in matching Preston North End's invincible side which had played through an entire season unbeaten just over a hundred years earlier.

2 February 1991

Arsenal lost at Chelsea 2.1 – their only defeat of the 1990-91 league season

Arsenal finished seven points clear of Liverpool in the end and, thanks mainly to Adams marshalling of that famous back four, only conceded 18 league goals.

Arsenal's cause wasn't helped though by a trip to Old Trafford on 20th October 1990. They beat Manchester United 1.0 with a goal by Anders Limpar but a Nigel Winterburn tackle on United defender Denis Irwin sparked another pitch battle involving all but one of the players.

This was to be the first in a series of battles between the clubs that often spilled over into angry confrontation as the intensity of their rivalry increased over the next fifteen years.

1991

The Yugoslav Wars began in Slovenia, leading to ten years of conflict and the break-up of Yugoslavia

Manchester United were subsequently fined by the FA and docked a league point whereas Arsenal were also fined and had two points taken away following the warning of sterner penalties to come if there was a repeat of the Norwich disgrace just over a year earlier. This left Arsenal eight points behind league-leaders Liverpool at the time.

39 days after the Old Trafford 'brawl' the two teams faced each other again, this time in the League Cup fourth-round tie at Highbury. In an extraordinary match on 28th November 1990 Alan Smith scored two goals but Manchester United responded with six, including a hat-trick from Lee Sharpe.

Arsenal then had to face problems of a quite different kind off the pitch. Tony Adams was convicted of a drink-driving offence and in December 1990 was sentenced to four months in prison – later commuted to two months.

Adams had struggled with alcohol since almost the beginning of his 22-year Arsenal career under the apparent mid-1980s influence of players such as Kenny Sansom and Graham Rix. After the UEFA ban on English clubs following the Heysel disaster, midweek drinking sessions had often taken the place of midweek matches.

Paul Merson too was suffering from alcoholism and a gambling addiction. In spite of his tough stance on any misdemeanour from his players, George Graham was remarkably supportive of these two key players and tried to handle their problems within the privacy of the Highbury dressing room.

By the time the league title was assured with two matches still to play after Nottingham Forest met Liverpool again and beat them 2.1, George Graham was turning his attention to the possibility of another Arsenal Double to repeat his 1970-71 achievement as a player.

They had struggled in the Fourth Round of the FA Cup. After three draws, Lee Dixon and Paul Merson scored Arsenal's goals in a 2.1 win over old adversaries Leeds United and they had then raced through to the Semi-finals where they faced Tottenham Hotspur.

This was the first time the two sides had met in an FA Cup Semi-final.

Having beaten Spurs at this stage of the League Cup before they must have felt optimistic about making the Final against Nottingham Forest (who, for once, did not have to get past Liverpool in their own Semi-final; beating West Ham United 4.0 instead).

Both league games between the two teams that season had finished in 0.0 draws. However, in a match played in front of just short of 78,000 at Wembley Stadium on 14th April 1991, Paul Gascoigne scored a spectacular goal from a free-kick after just five minutes, before Gary Lineker put Tottenham 2.0 up just five minutes later.

Alan Smith replied for Arsenal on the stroke of half-time but Lineker scored his second just twelve minutes from time to seal a 3.1 win for Tottenham. The battle of the North London Double winners had been won by Tottenham and Arsenal would have to wait for another opportunity to achieve league and cup immortality.

As after their previous title-winning season in 1988-89, Arsenal again finished fourth in the league in 1991-92, although their attacking options had been added to with the signing of Ian Wright.

Arsenal were a part of Ian Wright's life almost from the beginning, with him being born in Woolwich in November 1963. After working as a plasterer, he had played for Crystal Palace for six years where he had become their record post-Second World War goal-scorer.

£2.5 million

Amount paid to bring Ian Wright to Arsenal

He signed for Arsenal in September 1991 for £2.5 million which was an Arsenal club record fee at the time.

Wright scored on his debut – a 1.1 draw at Leicester City in the Second Round of the League Cup on 25th September 1991. He did even better three days later when making his league debut at Southampton, scoring a hat-trick in a 4.0 win; David Rocastle scored the other goal.

Just as in 1987-88 Arsenal failed to win any of their first three league games in 1991-92 and lost eight league matches in total – a far cry from that single league defeat of the previous season. After losing at Liverpool on 29th January 1992 – 2.0, with trainee midfielder Ray Parlour making his debut and conceding a penalty – Arsenal went unbeaten in the final 17 league matches of the season – but the damage had already been done earlier in the season.

From Benfica to Wrexham

However, with the UEFA ban on English clubs competing in European competition now lifted, Arsenal got to play in the European Cup – the first club from England to do so after the ban - for only the second time.

They comfortably beat Vienna of Austria 6.2 on aggregate in the First Round but then faced the mighty Benfica from Portugal, winners of the European Cup in 1961 through beating Barcelona and then beating the other Spanish giants - Real Madrid - the following year to retain the trophy.

In the event, the first leg – played at Benfica's 'Stadium of Light' ground in front of 80,000 passionate fans – went pretty well for Arsenal. The match finished 1.1 with striker Kevin Campbell, who had joined Arsenal as a schoolboy in 1985, scoring their vital away goal.

Depressingly, the return leg at Highbury on 6th November 1991 became synonymous with a change of tactics from George Graham. Defender Colin Pates scored for Arsenal after 19 minutes but Isaias equalized for Benfica after 35 minutes to take the game into extra-time in which they scored twice more to put Arsenal out, on aggregate 4.2.

While George Graham was impressed with Benfica as an attacking force, he was concerned with his own team being far too open at the back while trying to chase victory – a weakness the experienced Portuguese exploited far too easily.

Programme Notes

A home European Cup defeat to Benfica signalled a changed in tactics from George Graham to a counter-attacking style reminiscent of Herbert Chapman

Another shock FA Cup defeat – this time at Fourth Division Wrexham's Racecourse Ground in the Third Round on 4th January 1992 did not improve Graham's mood.

Alan Smith scored for Arsenal to put them ahead just before half-time but two goals in two minutes within the last eight minutes of the match from the captain, and former Manchester United player, Mickey Thomas, and then the winner from striker Steve Watkin put Arsenal out.

Graham's resolve to rethink his defensive match tactics in future had become all the more urgent.

Changes were afoot across Europe at this time. A period sometimes known as the 'Autumn of Nations' had begun in 1989 where civilians in Eastern and Central Europe began to challenge communist rule.

Churchill's Iron Curtain was gradually being drawn back and peoples' revolutions were leading to freedom for millions. First, the Berlin Wall, separating communist East Berlin from the West, began to be dismantled in 1989 with the full reunification of Germany as a single country in 1990.

The Soviet Union was similarly pulled apart and failed to be the controlling force it had been for 45 post-war years by the end of

1991.

In football, the organized fan violence of the 1980s and the tragic loss of life in shabby, unsafe stadiums began to be seen as the old football offering. The new was represented by all-seater stadiums, replica football shirts and huge financial investment from television broadcasters who had been captivated by that night at Anfield in May 1989. Arsenal's night.

Football may have gone through a stale and often sickening period but it still had the capacity to surprise and even be beautiful again.

THE MODERN ERA (1992 -)

The establishment of a breakaway or super-league had been mentioned during the 1980s as a possible antidote to arrest football's 1980s decline.

In October 1990 Greg Dyke, then Managing Director of London Weekend Television (LWT) – one of the operating companies within ITV who held the television rights to show football matches at the time - held talks with what were known in the media as the 'big five' clubs. The five were Arsenal, Everton, Liverpool, Manchester United and Tottenham Hotspur.

Dyke believed that if only the largest clubs were featured on television and that television money was shared out among members of an elite few rather than all the other clubs in the Football League (as was the case at the time where First Division clubs effectively subsidised the rest) then those clubs would naturally stand to each earn a larger share of television rights money.

Unsurprisingly the clubs were favourable to the idea and saw it as a way of financing a breakaway from the Football League. Arsenal's David Dein met representatives of the FA who, though not always on the best of terms with the Football League, were also favourable to the idea in principle.

The following month a new television company – BSkyB - was formed by a merger between Sky Television and British Satellite Broadcasting. BSkyB was seen by many as representing the future of television, providing as it did television in a digital form via satellite as opposed to the old analogue system of television that, apart from the introduction of colour broadcasts, hadn't radically changed since that first televised broadcast of Arsenal v Arsenal Reserves back in 1937.

To be successful though, BSkyB needed subscribers – people who would buy their satellite dishes and subscriptions to their TV channels. Rupert Murdoch oversaw both BSkyB and a series of influential newspapers in one of the fastest-growing media empires at the time.

Murdoch also saw the huge value of sport, which he described as a 'battering ram' in building a television audience of fans who would be prepared to pay to watch their favourite clubs play. He had enjoyed some success already with the television rights to English Test Cricket. Football, with its much greater audience, was a logical next step for him.

Matters came to a head the following year when the broadcast rights for the first five years of the new Premier League came up for auction. ITV eventually bid £262 million for live matches but was outbid by BSkyB who bid £304 million as part of a deal with the BBC which would give the latter a healthy highlights package.

There is much discussion as to whether ITV's original bid was leaked to Murdoch, who was encouraged to bid higher, by one of the big five, namely Alan Sugar, Chairman of Tottenham Hotspur and supplier of satellite dishes to BSkyB.

In the end, a legal review of the process judged that there was no case to answer and the Premier League, supported by BSkyB money from the outset, was formed on 20th February 1992.

20 February 1992

The Premier League in England was formed

The old Football League Second Division was renamed Division One, the Third Division became Division Two and the old Fourth Division became Division Three.

The three-up, three-down system of promotion and relegation, established in 1974; three points for a win in 1981 and introduction of the Play-Offs to decide league promotions in 1987 had all been seen as major innovations but this structural change exceeded all of them.

There are many who say that football sold out on that day to the money men of television; others argue that football was dead on its feet after years of seemingly terminal illness.

Whichever is true, the reality is that football was re-packaged and re-presented in a far more modern up-market format – learning from Murdoch's experience of sports broadcasting in the USA and beyond – and using new technology to both give football fans far more comprehensive coverage but a product they could now interact with from home via their remote control satellite television handsets.

Arsenal played their first Premier League match on 15th August 1992, at Highbury against Norwich City.

Steve Bould scored Arsenal's first ever Premier League goal after 28 minutes and Kevin Campbell added a second nine minutes later to give Arsenal a 2.0 half-time lead. However, Norwich replied with four second half goals to win 4.2.

23 August 1992

Arsenal's first Premier League win came at Anfield

Arsenal's first Premier League win came at the unlikely venue of Liverpool's Anfield on 23rd August 1992.

Remembering that dramatic 1989 win, they won 2.0 with goals from Limpar after 53 minutes and a second from Wright ten minutes from time.

Arsenal did not really build on this early boost; their game had become less beautiful following the manner of the previous season's cup defeats to Wrexham and Benfica.

Graham modified the offside rule, as Chapman had done in the 1930s, by now using defenders as a single unit, moving up and down the pitch together. The image of one or other of the Arsenal defenders with their arms raised to signal that an opposition forward had been caught yet again by their offside net became synonymous with how Arsenal began to play the game.

Relying on speed on the break and the deadly accuracy of the likes of Ian Wright up-front, Arsenal's game plan changed subtly to one of 'what we have, we hold.'

There was nothing especially new in this approach but, like the Chapman-influenced Arsenal teams of the late 1920s and early 1930s, it was considered to be boring to watch and even their own fans delight at singing '1.0 to the Arsenal' over and over again began to wear thin.

George Graham was undeterred:

"I would rather win a game 1.0 than 5.2"

The Highbury Board backed Graham's approach to the hilt – at least initially - with Chairman Peter Hill-Wood remembering his father Denis's famous declaration that:

"Every fan you ask will say he wants to see lively, open football. But what the fan really wants to see is his team win."

This often boring, win-at-all-costs strategy was in direct contrast to a newly-found optimism in the country at large. After some of the dark days of the 1980s, there was a move to try to re-capture some of the freshness and devil-may-care attitudes of the 1960s.

This was accompanied by a newly-found pride in everything British as the football world began to look forward to England's hosting of the UEFA European Championship (EURO) tournament in 1996.

This trend largely replicated and was influenced by the pop culture of the late 1960s with Oasis, Blur and Pulp engaging in the Britpop music trend and celebrity entertainers forging a new 'Cool Britannia' movement and energy that the incoming Labour Government of Tony Blair did its best to harness in 1997.

If Arsenal's footballers, fuelled by huge wages now being paid for their services, were keen to embrace this celebration of celebrity, the club itself was beginning to look out-of-touch and even old-fashioned.

Arsenal appeared to go backwards in the league in the next two seasons, finishing tenth in 1992-93, a huge 28 points behind champions Manchester United, and then fourth in 1993-94 but still 21 points behind United again.

It should be remembered though that as in the 1980s when both Liverpool and Everton were the dominant clubs in the land, this was the beginning of Manchester United's long league domination under Alex Ferguson and most other clubs as well as Arsenal were finding it hard to keep pace.

1993: Year of the Cups

The new 'steal a goal and lock the match up with a well-drilled defence' strategy did pay dividends in the cup competitions though. In 1992-93 Arsenal became the first club to win the FA Cup and League Cup in the same season and both in Finals against Sheffield Wednesday. Never before or since have the same two sides contested both FA Cup and League Cup Finals in the same season.

In the League Cup (now sponsored by Coca-Cola) Arsenal beat Millwall again before dispatching Midlands clubs Derby County and Nottingham Forest. In between the Derby and Forest matches they travelled to Third Division (though fourth-tier) Scarborough FC's McCain Stadium where a Nigel Winterburn goal saw them through.

Scarborough were one of the oldest football clubs in England at the time having been formed in 1879 - seven years before Dial Square. They eventually went out of business and disappeared as a football club in June 2007.

Arsenal beat another London club – Crystal Palace – 5.1 on aggregate over the two-legged Semi-final to face Sheffield Wednesday at Wembley on 18th April 1993.

American John Harkes gave Wednesday a shock lead after just eight minutes before Paul Merson equalized 12 minutes later. The winning goal came after 68 minutes from Northern Irish midfielder Steve Morrow who had largely filled in for the injured Paul Davis that season.

It was Morrow's first goal for the club but his celebrations at the end were short-lived after Tony Adams attempted to hoist him on his shoulders but fell awkwardly, breaking Morrow's arm. Morrow subsequently missed the second Cup Final between these two teams.

The FA Cup Final took place on 15th May 1993. Arsenal's progress had been quite straightforward after requiring another replay to get past Leeds United in the Fourth Round. They beat Nottingham Forest 2.0 (after also beating them 2.0 in that League Cup tie earlier in the season) and the team they had lost the Final to in 1978 – Ipswich Town – 4.2 to arrive at the Semi-final where they faced Tottenham again.

A goal from Tony Adams earned them a 1.0 win and a certain amount of revenge for their defeat to Tottenham in the Semi-final two years earlier.

The Final was another close affair with Ian Wright (playing with a broken toe) heading Arsenal ahead after 20 minutes, only for David Hirst to cancel it out with a goal for Wednesday after 61 minutes.

The game finished 1.1 after extra-time and went to a replay – the first since 1990 when Ian Wright had taken the football world by storm in Crystal Palace's battle with Manchester United.

The replay was also David O'Leary's last game for the club and took place – also at Wembley – five days later on 20th May 1993. Kick-off was delayed for half-an-hour because of an accident on the M1 which temporarily halted thousands of fans heading down to London from Sheffield.

It was the first time in 70 years that the start time of a Wembley match had been delayed, with the last occasion being the 1923 FA Cup Final between Bolton Wanderers and West Ham United.

Wright again put Arsenal ahead, this time after 34 minutes but Wednesday equalised once more in the second half through Chris Waddle. The game also finished 1.1 and so extra-time was played again.

Arsenal won their second cup of the season one minute from the end of the match, with a headed goal from Andy Linighan following a corner from Paul Merson.

Linighan had played at the centre of defence in place of Steve Bould (he had played a covering role for regulars Adams and Bould throughout the season) and was playing with a broken nose after Mark Bright of Sheffield Wednesday had earlier elbowed him in the face (poetic justice was done when he out-jumped Bright for his late winning goal).

This was George Graham's fifth trophy in seven years, after the longest FA Cup Final in football history.

5/7

Five domestic trophies in seven years for George Graham's Arsenal

It would also prove to be the last to go to a replay: in 1999 the FA decided that all subsequent FA Cup Finals would go to extra-time and penalties if required so that there would now always be a winner on Cup Final day itself.

Arsenal won both major English cup competitions exactly ten years after being losing Semi-finalists in each.

UEFA European Cup Winners' Cup

Winning the FA Cup meant that Arsenal qualified to play in the 1993-94 European Cup Winners' Cup competition for the first time since losing the Final to Valencia in 1980.

The first match took place on 15th September 1993 in a First Round tie away to OB Odense of Denmark. Goals from Wright and Merson gave Arsenal a 2.1 win and their progress through the competition was steady, though it did include an astonishing away win against Standard Liège of Belgium on 3rd November 1993 in the Second Round.

Having beaten them 3.0 at Highbury they won the second leg in Belgium 7.0, to go through to the next round 10.0 on aggregate. This was Arsenal's biggest away win in all European competitions.

In stark contrast they edged past Italian giants Torino in the next round 1.0 on aggregate; a Tony Adams goal at Highbury being the only goal over both legs.

Similarly, they progressed narrowly – 2.1 – in the Semi-final against Paris Saint Germain of France with a Kevin Campbell goal at Highbury on 12th April 1994 giving them another 1.0 win after the first leg had finished 1.1.

And so, on 4th May 1994, Arsenal faced another Italian team – Parma, managed by future England manager Sven-Göran Eriksson – in the Final.

It was played at the Parken Stadion in Copenhagen, back in Denmark where Arsenal's latest European campaign had begun.

Alan Smith scored after 20 minutes to give Arsenal another 1.0

victory and the Cup Winners' Cup was finally theirs – their first European trophy since George Graham had played in the Arsenal team that won the Inter-Cities Fairs Cup 24 years earlier.

As had happened so often after a successful season, Arsenal came fourth again in the league. They lost seven league games in total including their first of the season – away at Coventry City on 14th August, 1993 – where Mick Quinn scored the Premier League's first hat-trick of the new season.

They also went out of both cup competitions in the Fourth Round – to Aston Villa in the League Cup and Bolton Wanderers in the FA Cup.

In 1994-95 Arsenal played in their first UEFA Super Cup match, set up to decide the best club side in Europe. In those days it took place between winners of the UEFA European Cup – re-branded as the UEFA Champions League since 1992 in another move towards a modern era for club football, dependent as it was on TV money – and the UEFA European Cup Winners' Cup.

Arsenal thus faced AC Milan of Italy in the first leg at Highbury in a match which ended 0.0. In the San Siro stadium in Milan a week later on 8th February 1995 they lost 2.0 to give AC Milan the trophy.

Also in 1994-95, as holders, Arsenal made it to the European Cup Winners' Cup Final again, with Ian Wright scoring in every round apart from the Final itself.

They only just made it past Sampdoria of Italy in the Semi-final though. Wright and two from Bould secured a 3.2 first leg victory at Highbury on 6th April 1995 but they lost by the same margin in the second leg in Italy (Swedish international Stefan Schwarz scoring a crucial late goal) and only progressed to the Final by 3.2 on penalties.

Memories of that famous other Italian win in the Semi-final against Juventus fifteen years earlier would have been conjured up by older Arsenal fans but, unfortunately, the Final would also end in defeat.

This time on 10th May 1995 they faced Real Zaragoza of Spain in the Parc des Princes stadium in Paris. Real opened the scoring in the second half but Arsenal equalised through Welsh striker John Hartson, who had joined as a 19-year old from Luton Town in January of that year for £2.5 million (a record British transfer fee for a teenager at that time).

The match moved into extra time and it looked as though – in shades of Valencia, 1980 – penalties would once again be required to decide the outcome. However, right at the end of the match the former Tottenham player, Nayim, launched a speculative lob from fully 40 yards out. Misjudging it, the ball went over David Seaman's head and into the net to clinch a 2.1 win for the Spanish side. Whether or not Nayim had meant to score was open to discussion; the result was not.

Did you know?

eBay, the online auction website, was launched (as AuctionWeb) on 3rd September 1995 with a broken laser pointer being one of the first items sold

Arsenal had done no better in the domestic cup competitions either. On 7th January 1995 they drew away to George Graham's old club, Millwall, of Division One in the Third Round of the FA Cup in what was to be Alan Smith's last appearance for the club.

The match was played at the New Den (now, simply, 'The Den') ground in South Bermondsey where Millwall were playing in their second season having moved from the Old Den in 1993.

It was the first new all-seater stadium to be completed after the Taylor Report - which reported on the likely causes of the Hillsborough disaster and had recommended a move to either modify or build all-seater stadia in the future – and the first new professional football stadium to be built in London since 1937 (a year after the major stadium changes at Highbury).

11 days later Arsenal lost the replay at home, 2.0. In between these matches they had gone out of the League Cup in the Fourth Round at Liverpool, 1.0.

Programme Notes:

Some Millwall moments - Arsenal's earliest rivals:

1886: Dial Square's first match took place in Millwall

1887: Royal Arsenal's first defeat was at Millwall

1888: Royal Arsenal's first match at the Manor Ground was against Millwall

1893: Record home attendance at the Invicta Ground of 12,000 came in FA Cup tie against Millwall

1995: Lost in the FA Cup to Millwall, formerly managed by George Graham and hastening his departure from Arsenal

In the Premier League that season they plummeted to 12th place.

The end of George Graham

There is, though, a background story to accompany the team's fall from grace and it centres on that of their manager.

The criticism of George Graham's teams grinding out results with dull, unadventurous football had continued, in spite of his winning six major trophies during his almost nine years as Arsenal's manager in a sustained period of success not seen since the 1930s.

He relied hugely on the pace of Ian Wright on the break and yet was criticized for not really finding a good enough strike partner for him. Contract negotiations were notoriously tough and his 'there is no money available for new players' stance meant that Arsenal probably missed out on top signings such as Roy Keane. In short, Manchester United rather than Arsenal were looking much more likely to be the team to dominate the 1990s rather than Arsenal; the great championship-winning side of 1991 had become stagnant. In Alan Smith's words:

> *"Playing under George Graham just wasn't enjoyable anymore. He'd said everything he could say to us. Everything was so stale."*

Unfortunately for Graham, he hadn't said everything to the players, the Arsenal Board, or the fans. It transpired that both he and former coach Steve Burtenshaw had received 'unsolicited gifts' from Norwegian agent, Rune Hauge, during the transfer to Arsenal in 1992 of two of Hauge's clients: John Jensen (to supposedly replace David Rocastle who had moved to Leeds United) and Pål Lydersen – neither of whom were successful at Highbury.

Jensen had scored one of Denmark's goals in their shock win in the

EURO '92 Final but he rarely if ever reached such heights in North London. The payments, or 'bungs,' included £35,000 to Burtenshaw for the Jensen transfer but were much more lucrative for Graham: £140,000 for the Lyderson element and £285,000 for the Jensen 'sweetener.' He had deposited the funds in an offshore bank and not disclosed them to the taxman.

Graham was subsequently sacked by Arsenal on 13th February 1995 for 'bringing the club into disrepute.'

13 February 1995

George Graham sacked for 'bringing the game into disrepute'

Whilst it is hard to accept Graham's argument that he hadn't asked for extra payments for himself, it is almost impossible to deny that he deliberately hid them from the authorities in order to avoid paying tax.

He may not have been the only football manager accepting bungs at this time but he was the one who was found out and, of course, the press had a field day.

John Major's Conservative government of the time had been embroiled in a series of sleaze scandals involving ministers David Mellor, Alan Clark, Neil Hamilton and Jonathan Aitken over sexual affairs, 'cash for questions' and secret arms deals.

In financial circles also, stories of insider trading were rife and it was another individual, Nick Leeson, who was hung out to dry for unauthorised trading that eventually brought down Barings Bank.

George Graham's own misdemeanours fitted perfectly with the ongoing social, political and financial embarrassments of the time which would help lead to such a landslide General Election victory for the 'New Labour' Party in 1997.

Graham made the case that he had told Arsenal Chairman Peter Hill-Wood about the issue in September of 1994, but perhaps the Arsenal Board were happy to let Graham go when they did - especially after the Millwall defeat and the torrent of criticism over the team's playing style?

In an interesting reverse of the 1919 situation when Henry Norris had argued against the sleaze and possible match-fixing of others, the Arsenal Directors would have had no desire to be the guilty party and so it may have been in Hill-Wood's best interests all round to deny all knowledge, sack Graham as soon as they found out, and avoid any threat of points deductions or even relegation.

Perhaps they considered these possible FA sanctions and panicked? The FA did eventually ban Graham from football for a year in a sentence that they felt befitted the severity of the case and would simultaneously be a warning to others.

To not be in the Premier League and in receipt of such huge television income in the modern era would have been unthinkable. One Director who had done very well out of Graham's successes and the club's rising share price – David Dein – certainly did not fight to keep him, finding Graham a tough opponent to his own, increasingly ambitious, plans to commercialize the club further or possibly as he was already courting a new and quite different individual as Arsenal manager.

For Arsenal's players, the reaction was one of stunned bemusement after nine years of strict discipline imposed by their manager. Alan Smith again commented:

"I was amazed. For years he'd always been the upholder of the badge."

Another Scot, former Manchester United player Stewart Houston, had been Graham's assistant since 1990 and was installed as caretaker and the run to the European Cup Winners' Cup Final that year was undoubtedly down to his coaching prowess and bringing of new energy into the squad.

George Graham served his ban and then took over at Arsenal's historic foes – Leeds United - before, in the autumn of 1998, becoming manager of their greatest rivals: Tottenham Hotspur.

Bruce Rioch

In June 1995 Arsenal turned to Bruce Rioch as a permanent replacement for George Graham. Rioch had really made his name as a player with Derby County where he won a League Championship medal in 1975.

Born in Aldershot, he nevertheless played for Scotland 24 times as his father had been born there. In fact, Rioch became the first Scotland captain to have been born in England.

For three years previously he had been the manager of Bolton Wanderers, leading them to the Premier League via promotion first from Division Two and then from Division One after a 4.3 Play-Off win in the spring of 1995.

He had also turned Bolton into a giant-killing cup team with memorable wins over Liverpool (and also a League Cup Final defeat) as well as that FA Cup victory over Arsenal themselves just over a year earlier.

On joining Arsenal, Rioch was quoted as saying:

"I've got to make them a great football team, which means not just winning a cup or trophy but making people remember."

David Dein was now pretty much in charge of Arsenal's transfer dealings, rather than the manager, and was almost completely single-minded in his approach. He was far more decisive than Rioch and for that reason found him much easier opposition than George Graham had been when discussing new players.

Although Dennis Bergkamp was officially Rioch's first signing in June 1995, it was really Dein who had been monitoring this situation and had stepped in to make the deal, paying an estimated £7.5 million transfer fee to smash the record fees of £2.5 million previously paid for Ian Wright and John Hartson.

£7.5 million

Amount paid for Dennis Bergkamp – three times higher than Arsenal's previous transfer record fees

The previous parsimony and tight control over players' fees and wages under George Graham were well and truly demolished in that single transaction.

Bergkamp himself was actually a Tottenham Hotspur fan who had previously idolised Glenn Hoddle as a young football fan growing up in the Netherlands' capital of Amsterdam.

He had progressed through the Ajax youth system, starring for the first team where he won the UEFA Cup and European Cup Winners' Cup as well as numerous Eredivisie league titles.

A rising star of the Dutch national team with fantastic, natural technique, he had moved to Internazionale of Milan two years earlier where he had helped them to a further UEFA Cup trophy. However, numerous changes of management and style along with fatigue after the 1994 World Cup tournament in the USA meant that his experience in Italy was generally unhappy.

Bergkamp supposedly asked his agent to inquire about a move to North London – to Tottenham – but Chairman Alan Sugar might have been unlikely to sanction such a big money move. He probably saw foreigners coming to England just for the high wages and would have doubted their ability to adapt to the tough English league system.

Dein had been monitoring this situation closely and swooped to provide Arsenal fans with a true statement of the club's intent.

This intent was amplified the following month when England captain and star midfielder from the 1990 World Cup, David Platt, arrived from another Italian club – Sampdoria - for £4.75 million.

Rioch now had two well-known World Cup stars in his new squad. The team formation was consequently changed to a 3-5-2 to accommodate a central midfield pairing of Bergkamp and Platt.

If Rioch got on particularly well with Platt, it was suggested that he was less successful with some of the other senior players. Ian Wright, who was the top scorer for the club for six consecutive seasons from 1991-92 to 1996-97 had scored 30, 35 and 30 goals in the previous three seasons and yet was often forced to play out on the left wing. He only scored 22 in 1995-96.

John Hartson had been one of George Graham's last signings but barely played at all after he left, with Bergkamp preferred as an attacking option.

The 1995-96 season started off well enough, with Arsenal unbeaten in the first eight games and playing more expansive football than under Graham before losing, as in 1991, away to Chelsea 1.0 on 30th September 1995.

19

Points behind Manchester United in Bruce Rioch's only season as Arsenal manager

Arsenal eventually finished fifth in the Premier League which did qualify them for the following season's UEFA Cup but, perhaps more pertinently, they finished 19 points behind champions Manchester United.

Another early defeat in the FA Cup occurred at Sheffield United's Bramall Lane. They fared better in the League Cup including wins over the other Sheffield club – Wednesday – and old cup rivals Newcastle United. In the Semi-final they faced their great 1930s rivals Aston Villa once again.

The teams drew 2.2 at Highbury with Bergkamp scoring both of Arsenal's goals and Dwight Yorke getting a brace for Villa. This also proved to be the last match played by John Jensen for the club before a move back to Denmark with Brondby.

The second leg at Villa Park finished goalless after extra time and so Villa progressed on the away goals rule and went on to beat Arsenal's old League Cup nemesis of 28 years earlier, Leeds United, 3.0 in the Final.

Arsenal's last game of the season was in the Premier League against Rioch's old club, Bolton Wanderers, at Highbury on 5th May 1996. Both of his big pre-season signings, Bergkamp and Platt, scored for Arsenal but, with perfect symmetry, it proved to be his last as manager and Rioch was sacked in August 1996.

Officially it was reported that, after spending such huge sums on glamour signings to bring success to the club, a fifth place finish was simply not good enough. Unofficially there were reports of a row with David Dein which had brought matters to a head after just 61 weeks. Captain Tony Adams later remarked:

> *"Bruce...could quite easily have been where Arsène Wenger is today"*

but few people would remember Rioch or his one-season reign.

Stewart Houston, who had stayed on as assistant to Rioch, again took temporary charge as caretaker manager before leaving to manage Queens Park Rangers.

Pat Rice - famous full-back from the 1971 Double team - then took over briefly as caretaker before, in September 1996, Frenchman Arsène Wenger became the new Arsenal manager.

The role of David Dein

As we have seen, Dein was the thrusting entrepreneur on the Arsenal Board. In the 1988-89 season, he had pushed through a re-development of the Clock End when a roof was added and 48 executive boxes installed in spite of the earlier concerns that local families would not benefit. Seating eventually replaced the only remaining standing area four years later.

The Taylor Report's stipulations meant that the North Bank would also have to be modified or replaced. Dein persuaded the Arsenal Board that the only way of raising money for this project was, as West Ham United had done before them, to launch a Bond Scheme.

£1000 - £1,500

Price of bonds before fans could apply for season tickets to sit in the new North Bank

Bonds were offered to fans for between £1,000 and £1,500 which would last for 150 years and enable them to buy annual season tickets – at discounted prices for the first 10 years.

There were initial protests from Islington Council who turned down Dein's original plans for a new stand on the basis of its linking with the rest of the stadium not satisfying the listed status of the East and West stands. This meant that both stands were considered to be of special architectural or historic interest to the nation and could not be demolished, extended, or altered without special permission. The Council commented, smugly:

"David Dein will have to reduce the size of his ego"

The fans felt even more bitter as, again, it felt as though the 'ordinary fan in the street' was being priced out of watching Arsenal play at Highbury.

The Independent Arsenal Independent Supporters Association (AISA) was formed in the summer of 1991 to protest against the development but, largely thanks to Dein's determined ambition, the new stand was built anyway.

The old North Bank was demolished at the end of the 1991-92 season and the new two-tier North Bank Stand opened in August 1993. This was the final part of Highbury stadium to be re-developed.

2 May 1992

The last match to be played in front of the old North Bank

In the last ever match before the old North Bank on 2nd May 1992, Arsenal had beaten Southampton 5.1 with Ian Wright securing a hat-trick with literally the last kick of the match to clinch the Golden Boot award for leading league scorer in what was his first season with the club. He had enjoyed a running battle for supremacy with Gary Lineker of Tottenham so the achievement was appreciated by Arsenal fans all the more.

The movement away from the ordinary but passionate football fans of the Dial Square club built by Danskin and Humble can – and is – condemned by many.

Dein may also have been one of the engineers of a changing football landscape – even though Sky and not ITV were the largest funders and beneficiaries – but it is hard to criticize him for being obsessed by Arsenal's need to commercialize further and build a proper football merchandising operation in the modern era.

Here was a club that had regularly fallen on hard times, financially - almost since it had been formed The money coming into the game was huge in the 1990s but, as a legacy of Thatcherism, market competition was greater than ever before and football clubs now represented big business interests. Their thirst for money as much as glory on the field was seemingly unbounded and certainly unparalleled in football history.

Dein also understood that English football needed to change. Via the FA he was representing England at UEFA and FIFA and could see that players needed to be more professional and technically gifted.

It was this view that compelled him to seal the Bergkamp deal and to also recommend that a foreigner, who he had been tracking for some eight years via a mutual friend, take over as Arsenal manager for the first time.

Arsène Wenger

Arsène Wenger was born in Alsace-Lorraine – a region of Northen France, dominated by Strasbourg, its capital - which had first been created by the German Empire in 1871 after their victory in the Franco-Prussian War.

The area had effectively swapped hands between (been 'ceded' to) Germany and France since then and had returned to France after the Second World War. Born into a multilingual environment the young Wenger easily learned German and English as well as his native French.

He spent much of his time in travelling over the border to watch leading German football teams and admired the fast-flowing attacking style of Borussia Mönchengladbach, especially on the counter-attack.

Günter Netzer was their inspirational midfield general whose creativity and superb passing could slice open defences. He saw also the value in having a player like Netzer as the manager's eyes and ears on the pitch.

Unsurprisingly Wenger also learned a lot from the technical proficiency of the German players and he fused this with his own desire for creativity and freedom of expression.

Very like the 'Total Football' of his Dutch neighbours, the 'Push-and-run' style of Arthur Rowe's Tottenham in the early 1950s and even the fluid, flexible style of the 'Mighty Magyars' from Hungary, Wenger believed that there should be:

"...in every single position a player who could really play both sides of the game: attacking and defending"

6: Image of Arsène Wenger

These principles were underpinned by a scientific approach to football coaching that few in European football understood at the time.

For Wenger, diet and nutrition were absolutely key elements, as was isometrics where muscle strengthening and body tuning were encouraged but without necessarily leading to greater body bulk in his players. Wenger's own 'Holy Trinity' was made up of proper recuperation after matches, diet and suitable treatment for injuries.

Wenger's ideas on style and physiology were not just abstract theories or training ground routines to practice; he also had an unlimited thirst for learning – hence his nickname among some of "Le Professeur" - and an obsessive desire to win by playing entertaining, attacking football. In an early managerial post at Nancy in France, he would often be physically sick if his team lost.

Wenger made his name at Monaco in the South of France where he won the French league title in 1988 and French Cup in 1991. His side also reached a European Cup Winners' Cup Final in 1992, which they lost to Werder Bremen of Germany 2.0.

However, three days before that, another football stadium disaster had occurred, this time in a French Cup Semi-final between SC Bastia and Olympique de Marseille. Holders Monaco had already won through to the Final again but it was a match that would not be played.

On that fateful Semi-final day of 5th May 1992, the Bastia and Marseille teams met in Bastia on the island of Corsica at the Armand Césari Stadium where a temporary terrace had been erected without the proper construction rules being followed and in a hurry to take advantage of the high capacity expected for the tie.

The stand quickly became unstable during the match and collapsed. 18 football fans were killed with many more becoming trapped. In the end, some 2,300 people were injured as a result of what became known as the Armand Cesari Stadium disaster.

2,300

People injured in the Armand Cesari Stadium disaster

Wenger's French team were still deeply affected in their European Final against Werder Bremen and Wenger was quoted as saying:

"We never played that day. We simply couldn't. It's as if the game never really started."

Monaco also reached a Champions League Semi-final two years later which they lost to Milan who would go on to win the trophy that season.

Wenger's sides were regularly involved in a titanic struggle with the Olympique de Marseille team. Marseille usually got the upper hand in this local, south coast rivalry and went on to achieve the greater national success in league and cup competitions. However, their President Bernard Tapie was later investigated for criminal acts such as match-fixing.

Glenn Hoddle was recruited by Monaco from Tottenham - in the Gunter Netzer role Wenger had been so impressed by - as was a 17-year old French player called Thierry Henry.

Wenger was definitely on the Tottenham radar at this time. Agent Dennis Roach had helped him to secure Hoddle and friendly matches were arranged between the two teams. Irving Scholar, now Chairman of Tottenham, and felt to be more outward-looking than most of the Arsenal Directors (with the exception of Dein) at the time, also had a house in Monaco and so could monitor Wenger's approach closely.

However, he chose Terry Venables (courted by Arsenal in the last days of Don Howe's management) to replace former manager David Pleat instead.

Perhaps disillusioned by Tapie's behaviour and needing a change, Wenger then spent two seasons with Nagoya Grampus Eight (now, Nagoya Grampus) of the Japanese Professional Football League, known simply as the J League.

He guided them to second place in his first season - after being bottom of the league when he had first joined - and also the Emperor's Cup and Super Cup before being released early to join Arsenal in September 1996.

As fiercely determined as ever, there are those who also say that his time in Japan calmed him somewhat which was probably just as well coming into a mid-1990s Arsenal side of big personalities, very much stuck in its ways and in a tough English Premier League dominated at the time by Alex Ferguson's Manchester United.

There had been no real experience of non-British managers in English football in 1996. When Dr Jozef Vengloš of Slovakia (then Czechoslovakia) had joined Aston Villa six years earlier, after the 1990 World Cup, he had become the first manager born outside Britain or Ireland to take charge of a top tier club in England. His stay was short and unsuccessful: in his one season in charge, Villa finished just two places above the relegation zone.

So, it was a big risk for Arsenal – a particularly English institution - to appoint their first foreign manager, yet Chairman Peter Hill-Wood was confident that they had appointed the right person for the job at the time:

"I believe Arsène Wenger is going to be a great success and drag football in this country into the 20th century. There is no doubt in my mind we are blinkered and backward as a sporting nation. Look at the British results in Europe, they were not good, including ours. We keep telling ourselves we have the best league in Europe, but it is not true. We need to catch up with the Continentals and we think Arsène is the man to help us."

There has been speculation ever since Wenger's appointment that he was the intended choice of Hill-Wood – and certainly Dein - back in 1995 when they failed to back Graham, and that Rioch was no more than a stop-gap.

Certainly, Glenn Hoddle – newly installed as England national team manager after Terry Venables' stint had finished after that summer's EURO '96 – was full of praise for his old manager, the style of play he favoured and the tools he would bring to his new armoury.

Wenger himself quickly assessed the team and wider aspects of the club. He saw the issue with the houses packed around Avenell Road and the rest of the Highbury site making redevelopment of the ground almost impossible.

He saw a training ground with poor facilities, bumpy pitches and run-down buildings (which miraculously caught fire and had to be completely rebuilt soon after he arrived) that had to be shared with the students of University College, London who owned it and had the first choice on Wednesday and Friday afternoons.

He saw in pre-match preparation players eating completely the wrong kind of food at completely the wrong time, and he saw players who were drunk in training.

On the pitch, as with Hoddle and Netzer before him, Wenger spotted, in his first season, that he could convert Dennis Bergkamp into this kind of role, with his passes described by later teammate Thierry Henry as 'caviar' in terms of curve timing and pace, and into a counter-attacking style of play that Herbert Chapman would have been proud of.

Another French teammate, Patrick Vieira, would later wax lyrical over Bergkamp's vision:

"Dennis thought about things other players couldn't even imagine."

Bergkamp would become the latest creative midfielder in the great Arsenal traditions of Alex James, Jimmy Logie and Liam Brady.

12 October 1996

Arsène Wenger's first match in charge of Arsenal

Wenger's first match in charge of Arsenal came on 12th October 1996, away at Blackburn Rovers – somewhat ironically given the club's record away defeat took place at Ewood Park in 1909 (7.0)

There was no repeat of such a hammering almost exactly 87 years later. Ian Wright scored the first goal of the Wenger reign after just three minutes and then added a second to give Wenger and Arsenal a winning, 2.0 start.

Arsenal topped the league table for a while before going on to finish a creditable third in the Premier League that season behind Kevin Keegan's Newcastle United who had been involved in a titanic struggle with eventual champions Manchester United.

Arsenal finished seven points behind United and the Wenger-Ferguson rivalry would define his and Arsenal's early years under his control.

After a home defeat to Leeds United in the Fourth Round of the FA Cup John Hartson left for West Ham United. Perhaps Wenger was making an early statement of intent as to the standards and ambition he expected from his players:

"I believe that the... great players are guided by how football should be played, and not by how football should serve them."

Ironically Arsenal had already been knocked out of the UEFA Cup – which Bruce Rioch's team had striven so hard to qualify for - before Wenger took charge, and by the team he used to watch so regularly: Borussia Mönchengladbach of Germany.

They lost both legs of the First Round 3.2 and Wenger is alleged to have suggested some tweaks to caretaker Pat Rice before the second match and before he officially took over, which club captain Tony Adams took exception to:

"I said to him that he had put our entire season in jeopardy by doing what he had done."

Wenger certainly listened to the opinions of his senior players after that inauspicious start and, after the disciplinarians of Graham and Rioch, preferred to keep things simple with one-to-one tactical training and a desire to fully understand each and every one of his players. He was keen for his players to express themselves rather than just stopping opponents as they had done under Graham.

He was interested only in their quality and potential. With his upbringing in Alsace-Lorraine, nationality was entirely irrelevant to him. Like Graham though, he stood by his players and tried to gradually improve them through coaching and learning to improve and be better than they already were.

Did you know?

The first Harry Potter novel - Harry Potter and the Philosopher's Stone - was released on 30th June 1997

He soon won Tony Adams around to his cause such that his career – and possibly even his life – was extended by his conversion to Wenger's ideas and methods:

"Wenger is a physiologist and brought a philosophy of good nutrition and how best to look after your bodies to the club."

In 1997 Wenger began to make some key signings to add to his squad. He was clearly looking for a long-term replacement for the ageing Wright who had been the scorer of so many of Arsenal's goals in the 1990s and had presumably not seen John Hartson as the answer.

17-year old striker Nicolas Anelka, whose family were originally from the Caribbean island of Martinique, had experienced extreme poverty and racism in Paris. He arrived from Paris Saint-Germain for £500,000 in February 1997.

Emmanuel Petit who had scored the vital, winning penalty in Monaco's ill-fated French Cup Semi-final match in 1992 arrived for £2.5 million and was converted by Wenger from central midfield to a holding midfield role. Midfielder Gilles Grimandi also arrived from Wenger's former club.

Fellow French midfielder Patrick Vieira had arrived at Highbury for £3.5 million just before (but almost certainly in anticipation of) Wenger's arrival – again possibly due to David Dein's influence.

Vieira, like Dennis Bergkamp, had also had a relatively unhappy time in Italy at the other Milan club – AC Milan – but he and Emmanuel Petit would prove to be a powerful midfield partnership for Arsenal.

Vieira would also forge a particularly intense rivalry with Manchester United captain Roy Keane and go on to replace Tony Adams as club captain when Adams retired in May 2002.

Experienced defensive midfielder Rémi Garde had arrived from Strasbourg, close to where Wenger had grown up, on the same day as Vieira, to add to the French signings.

Programme Notes:

Rémi Garde became the first foreigner to captain Arsenal

Garde would make history on 28th October 1998 by becoming the first foreigner to captain Arsenal: this in a third- round League Cup tie at Derby County's Pride Park which Arsenal won 2.1.

If Hill-Wood and his fellow directors had been concerned about Wenger spearheading a purely French invasion, they would have been relieved to see speedy winger Marc Overmars arriving from Ajax of Amsterdam for £5.5 million.

Overmars would fit perfectly into Wenger's rapid counter-attacking style, especially when linking up with fellow Dutchman and former Ajax player Dennis Bergkamp.

Wenger was bringing in the players he felt the club needed while trying to persuade others – especially the famous Arsenal Back Four - to stay and play their parts in the revolution which was to begin in earnest in the 1997-98 season.

The Second Double

Ian Wright scored Arsenal's first goal of the 1997-98 season in a 1.1 draw away at Leeds United on 9th August 1997.

Just over a month later, on 13th September 1997, he broke Cliff Bastin's goalscoring record of 178 goals for Arsenal with a hat-trick in a 4.1 win over Bolton Wanderers after Bolton had taken the lead.

13 September 1997

Ian Wright broke Cliff Bastin's goalscoring record

Ray Parlour scored the other goal in this historic match. Few supporters expected Bastin's record ever to be broken in the modern era, even though Wright had been averaging around two goals per match since his arrival six years earlier.

He was the ultimate goal machine and his image was used by the sports clothing firm Nike in posters in the mid-1990s (often also showing the Manchester United goalkeeper Peter Schmeichel) with the slogan:

"Behind every great goalkeeper, there's a ball from Ian

Wright."

He would go on to score 185 goals for the club but, soon after taking the record, he suffered a hamstring injury which ruled him out for much of the season, allowing Anelka to make his mark for the club.

Arsenal were unbeaten in their first six Premier League games and their first defeat of the season came in Greece on 16th September 1997 where they lost 1.0 to PAOK Salonika in the First Round of the UEFA Cup.

A Bergkamp goal earned them a 1.1 draw in the return leg two weeks later but the 2.1 aggregate loss saw them exit European competition at the first hurdle for the second successive season.

They progressed much further in the League Cup with straightforward wins over Birmingham City, Coventry City and West Ham United before facing another London rival, Chelsea, in the two-legged Semi-final.

Arsenal won the first leg at Highbury 2.1 with goals from Overmars and Stephen Hughes (who had started his football career at Arsenal). Chelsea won the second leg 3.1 though, with Bergkamp's goal not enough to prevent Chelsea heading to Wembley 4.3 on aggregate.

Champions Manchester United were looking to make it a hat-trick of consecutive Premier League titles that season and proved to be Arsenal's main rivals in the league.

At one point the men from Old Trafford were 11 points ahead of Arsenal but, just as United themselves had done two years earlier against Newcastle United who were at one point 12 points clear, Arsenal began to rein them in.

After Marc Overmars scored in a shock 3.1 home defeat to

Blackburn Rovers on 13th December 1997 Arsenal went 18 matches unbeaten including 10 successive victories between 11th March and 3rd May 1998.

10

Successive Arsenal victories in the spring of 1998

They only lost that one League Cup match at Chelsea in the following 29 league and cup matches in a strange echo of the 1990-91 season when their only league defeat had been at Stamford Bridge.

One of those consecutive league wins came in effectively the title decider at Old Trafford on 14th March 1998 when Overmars scored the only goal 11 minutes from time to seal a 1.0 win against Manchester United.

They secured the title itself on 3rd May 1998 with a 4.0 home win against Everton. Slaven Bilic's own goal after just six minutes was followed by two from Overmars and one, just a minute from the end, by reformed character Tony Adams in a very public show of self-redemption and repayment of the faith that Wenger had shown in him.

For his part, Wenger became the first foreigner to win the league title in English football – by just a single point from Manchester United in the end.

If Arsenal's passage in the League Cup had been straightforward, it was anything but in the FA Cup. They struggled to get past Port Vale of Division One in the Third Round, only progressing 4.3 on penalties after a replay.

Having won at Middlesbrough in the Fourth Round they again

drew 0.0 at Highbury against Crystal Palace before winning the replay 2.1.

Programme Notes:

Since being elected to the Football League at the same time in 1893 there have been some key moments between Newcastle United and Arsenal:

1893: First Football League game was at home to Newcastle

1904: First match in the First Division was at Newcastle

1906: Lost first FA Cup Semi-final to Newcastle

1919: Newcastle were Arsenal's first opponents in the First Division at Highbury

1932: FA Cup Final (lost)

1952: FA Cup Final (lost)

1998: FA Cup Final (won)

2005: Arsenal's first match of their final league season at Highbury was against Newcastle

Dennis Bergkamp scored the only goal of the Quarter-final match against West Ham United who were far harder to beat than they had been in the League Cup; the match again ending in a 1.1 draw.

The replay on 17th March 1998 also finished 1.1 with Anelka scoring just before half-time for Arsenal and the striker he replaced – John Hartson – dramatically sending the match into extra time six minutes from the end. No further goals were scored and Arsenal again won 4.3 on penalties.

After three replays during their Cup run, Arsenal beat Wolverhampton Wanderers 1.0 at the first attempt in the Semi-final at Villa Park. Their only goal came after just 12 minutes and was scored by striker Christopher Wreh, cousin of former FIFA World Player of the Year George Weah.

Wreh had also followed Wenger from Monaco and had previously been most famous for outrunning a lion in a Liberian game show the previous summer.

Arsenal faced old Cup rivals Newcastle United in the Final on 16th May 1998. Losing to the team from the North-East in 1932 and again in 1952, it proved to be third time lucky for Arsenal this time with goals in each half from Marc Overmars and then Nicolas Anelka securing a 2.0 win.

It also confirmed a second Double of League and Cup for Arsenal, seventeen years after they had first achieved it and in Arsène Wenger's first full season as manager.

Wenger himself refused to take much credit for the building of this second Double-winning team citing the foundation of the 'old guard' as the key factor in their success:

"I think I added something to this team and we were successful. But Adams, Bould, Keown, Winterburn, Seaman, Dixon - they were already here. I added the

offensive force but Bergkamp was already here when I arrived as well."

Towards a hat-trick of Doubles

Over the next seven seasons, Arsenal never finished below second in the Premier League and never worse than Semi-finalists in the FA Cup in six of those as they tried to repeat their 1997-98 (and 1970-71) Double feats.

Following the 1998 World Cup Finals in France in which Patrick Vieira and Emmanuel Petit had both featured in the winning team (Petit scored the third French goal in the Final) expectations at Highbury were high, especially with such a high contingent of French players managed and coached by a French manager.

However, in 1998-99 the league position of the previous season was reversed as Arsenal finished in second place in the Premier League, one point behind champions Manchester United. Arsenal only lost four league matches that season compared to six when winning the title a year earlier.

United would become the first English side to complete a Treble that season of Premier League, FA Cup and Champions League with a memorable late win against Bayern Munich of Germany. They became the first English side to win this trophy since Liverpool in 1984 and only the fourth team in Europe at the time to complete such a Treble.

16 September 1998

Arsenal played their first match in the re-branded UEFA Champions League

As Champions of England Arsenal also played in the Group Stage of the Champions League for the first time since it had been rebranded from the European Cup and for the first time in Europe's premier club competition since that ill-fated loss to Benfica almost seven years earlier.

Organised on a mini-league basis where only the Group winners and the two best runners-up would qualify for the knockout phase, they played their first Champions League match away at RC Lens (Racing Club de Lens) in northern France on 16th September 1998.

The match finished 1.1 with Marc Overmars opening the scoring (and thus Arsenal's first ever Champions League goal) only for RC Lens to equalize in the last minute.

With an eye on likely crowd attendances for their home matches in the Champions League and consequent commercial opportunities, the FA agreed that Arsenal could play those games at Wembley Stadium rather than Highbury.

There were even rumours that David Dein was keen to buy Wembley Stadium outright and move the club to a new London venue for the second time in their history.

Their first home Champions League at Wembley came on 30th September 1998 against Panathinaikos of Greece. Arsenal won 2.1 with goals from both central defenders –Adams and Keown – in front of a huge crowd of 73,455.

Although they would also beat Panathinaikos in the way leg, it wasn't enough to take them out of the Group Stage of the competition and into the knockout rounds.

A shock 1.0 defeat in the home game against RC Lens (in front of their largest recorded attendance for a 'home match' of 73,707) and then a 3.1 loss away at Dynamo Kiev did the damage.

On 11th November 1998 Arsenal had also gone out of the League Cup in rather more emphatic style: 5.0 at home to Chelsea. This was (and remains to date) Arsenal's worst home defeat under Arsène Wenger.

73,707

Record attendance at Wembley Stadium for an Arsenal 'home' match in the Champions League

Arsenal did defend their title stoutly throughout the season, losing only one of their first seven league matches – at Sheffield Wednesday.

Arsenal beat Leeds United on 20th December 1998, 3.1 with goals from Bergkamp, Vieira and Petit, with a single reply from Jimmy Floyd Hasselbaink of Leeds. In their remaining 26 Premier League and FA Cup matches of that season, they lost only two more games – once in the league and once in the FA Cup.

The league loss came. after 18 unbeaten league games, in the return match at Elland Road, Leeds on 11th May 1999. Having won 3.1 away at Tottenham with goals from Emmanuel Petit, Nicolas Anelka and Nigerian striker, Nwankwo Kanu, who had signed just three months earlier, Arsenal were in pole position to win the title again.

Manchester United had drawn 2.2 with their own fierce local rivals – Liverpool - and, if Arsenal had beaten Leeds, they would have retained their title. Even a draw may have been sufficient, with goal differences between the two clubs so close (though United had scored significantly more goals).

The match was heading for a 0.0 draw before, just four minutes from the end, their scorer at Highbury in December, Jimmy Floyd Hasselbaink, scored for Leeds United to win the game 1.0.

Even then, and having matched their previous season's points total of 78, Arsenal would still have taken the title had, ironically, Tottenham held on for a win in United's final league game of the season at Old Trafford. After going 1.0 up Tottenham lost 2.1 and United had secured the first part of their Treble success.

The cup match that Arsenal lost was also against Manchester United in the FA Cup Semi-final replay on 14th April 1999. The two sides had drawn 0.0 in the original tie at Villa Park three days earlier and returned to Birmingham for a pulsating match.

David Beckham had put United into the lead after 17 minutes, only for Dennis Bergkamp to equalise in the second half. United captain Roy Keane who supposedly admitted that he had:

"a lot of hatred for Arsenal"

was sent-off and Bergkamp had an opportunity from the penalty spot in the very last minute of normal time to send Arsenal back to Wembley to face Newcastle United in a repeat of the previous year's FA Cup Final.

United goalkeeper Peter Schmeichel saved the penalty and Ryan Giggs then scored a wonder goal after a mazy run from near the halfway line just 11 minutes from the end of extra-time to give the 10 men of Manchester United a 2.1 victory.

Wenger commented later:

"'I can still hear the shouts of that team, having won... They couldn't believe it because they were down to 10 men. And I think that put them in a state of euphoria. In the same way, they won the title – just."

Had Bergkamp scored that late penalty and Hasselbaink not scored that late winner at Leeds, Arsenal might have repeated their

Double triumph in successive seasons – a feat no English club has ever achieved.

In the event, they would finish as runners-up to Manchester United in the Premier League in each of the following two seasons as well – making it three seasons of near misses in a row.

Thierry Henry

In the summer of 1999 Nicolas Anelka had seemingly become increasingly unhappy and disillusioned with life in England – earning him the occasional nickname of 'The Incredible Sulk.' In particular, he blamed his isolation within the Arsenal team on Dennis Bergkamp and Marc Overmars talking to each other in their native Dutch.

Anelka moved to Real Madrid in Spain for £23.5 million, earning Arsenal a handsome profit on the £500,000 they had originally paid for his services.

A new striker and another member of the victorious French World Cup winning side of 1998 joined Arsenal that August.

£10.5 million

Amount paid by Arsenal to Juventus for Thierry Henry

Thierry Henry had starred as a winger in that tournament and also when under Wenger's tutelage at Monaco. Now 21 years old, he too had experienced an unhappy time in Italian football and signed from Turin giants Juventus for £10.5 million – Arsenal's first eight figure signing.

As with Bergkamp before him, Wenger saw a greater striking

potential in Henry as a centre-forward and Bergkamp would quickly become his chief supply line.

Brazilian defender Sylvinho was also signed that June from Corinthians. Tottenham Hotspur had made numerous approaches for the player but he chose Arsenal ahead of them and became the first Brazilian player to play for the club, eventually replacing Nigel Winterburn at left back. Sylvinho would be followed by compatriot Edu from the same Corinthians club three years later.

Henry was the club's top goalscorer in his first season in North London, scoring 26 goals in all competitions. He would repeat the achievement in each of the next six seasons and so become the only Arsenal player to be the top scorer in seven consecutive seasons, beating Ian Wright's previous record of six.

Programme Notes:

Arsenal's record goal-scorers in consecutive seasons:

Thierry Henry: (7) 2000 - 2006

Ian Wright: (6) 1992 - 1997

Ted Drake: (6) 1935 – 1940

Doug Lishman: (5) 1951-1955

If some fans had presumed that Cliff Bastin's scoring record would never be beaten in the modern era and had been proved wrong when Ian Wright broke the record, most would never have dreamed that it would be beaten again so quickly.

However, they were proved wrong again as Thierry Henry did

break it in a Champions League tie away at Sparta Prague – capital city of the Czech Republic – on 18th October 2005, when he scored his 185th and 186th goals in a 2.0 win. He suggested that:

> *"It's funny, when I arrived here and for two, three or four years, people were saying that I wasn't a natural-born killer. I'm still not but I think I can score goals."*

Henry went on to score 228 goals in 377 appearances for Arsenal and his phenomenal performance makes him one of the club's and the Premier League's finest strikers of all time. In a crumb of comfort for Ian Wright, he did score more hat-tricks for Arsenal: eleven to Thierry Henry's nine.

The new millennium begins

Many events and festivities were held across the world, leading up to New Year's Eve on 31st December 1999 to mark the passing of the second and the beginning of the new, third millennium.

Going out in the Fourth Rounds of both League Cup and FA Cup, as they had done ten years earlier, Arsenal's only significant achievement of 2000 was to reach the Final of the UEFA Cup once again.

2 March 2000

Arsenal beat a Spanish club for the first time

After their first ever victory over a Spanish team – Deportivo La Coruna – 5.1 on 2nd March 2000, Arsenal went on a run of twelve consecutive wins from 16th March 2000, including Premier League and UEFA Cup matches.

They beat Wenger's old German rivals from the ill-fated 1992 Final with Monaco, Werder Bremen, and their French conquerors from the previous season RC Lens to reach the UEFA Cup Final on 17th May 2000.

The Final took place at the same Parken Stadion in Copenhagen where Arsenal had beaten Parma to win the European Cup Winners' Cup six years earlier. Their opponents in the Final were Galatasaray of Turkey.

The game was overshadowed somewhat by the violence that had occurred in Istanbul before Galatasaray's Semi-final first leg against Leeds United in which two Leeds fans had been stabbed to death.

The match was a dull affair. Neither side scored in either normal or extra-time and the Turks won (the first European trophy to be won by a team from Turkey) 4.1 on penalties with only Ray Parlour converting his spot kick for Arsenal.

26 June 2000

The human genome - DNA, the blueprint for human beings - was mapped for the first time

As two years previously, Arsène Wenger spent much of the summer looking to reinforce his squad especially as Marc Overmars had left for Barcelona, for a then record Arsenal transfer fee of £25 million.

As with Anelka before him, Arsenal made huge profits on their stars heading for Spain's La Liga.

In his place, Wenger recruited fellow Frenchman Robert Pires from his old rivals from the South of France - Olympique de Marseille - for £6 million allegedly in the face of opposition from

Real Madrid and Juventus.

Pires played mainly on the left wing and, like Bergkamp, would provide plenty of ammunition for Thierry Henry to convert into goals. They also bought another French winger – Sylvain Wiltord - for £13 million, then a club record transfer fee, who had starred in that summer's EURO 2000 tournament for France.

In the Premier League, on the way to becoming runners-up to Manchester United again, they also suffered one of their worst defeats at Old Trafford in their history. On 25th February 2001 they lost 6.1 in a repeat of the scoreline almost fifty years earlier.

Dwight Yorke scored after just three minutes on his way to a 22-minute first half hat-trick. Although Thierry Henry equalised for Arsenal thirteen minutes later, Wenger's determination to attack left his team horribly exposed at the back as United went 5.1 up by half-time.

It was a particularly difficult afternoon for Latvian central defender Igors Stepanovs as Wenger looked to find a defensive replacement for Tony Adams in his final season at the club. It was also confirmation, if any was needed, that United would retain their title and suggested a gulf in class which was reflected in their finishing ten points clear at the end of the season.

Arsenal sought consolation in the other cup competitions once again, getting to the Quarter-final stage of the Champions League where they went out to Valencia of Spain.

Arsenal did make steady progress in the FA Cup, beating two clubs from the north west of England – Carlisle United and Blackburn Rovers – and two from West London – Queens Park Rangers and Chelsea – before meeting their old adversaries Tottenham Hotspur in yet another major cup Semi-final.

This match took place at Old Trafford on 8th April 2001 but the outcome of Arsenal's return to the scene of their battering by Manchester United less than two months earlier was a much happier one, winning 2.1 with goals from Vieira and Pires in front of a crowd of 63,541.

2001

The first FA Cup Final to be played in Wales

They faced Liverpool in the Final at the Millennium Stadium in Cardiff (currently known as the Principality Stadium). First opened for the 1999 Rugby World Cup Finals, the Welsh national rugby team had played its 'home matches' at Wembley Stadium while their own new national stadium was being built. A new Wembley Stadium had now been planned on the site of the original Empire Stadium which was demolished between 2002 and 2003 and so the Welsh returned the favour of hosting FA Cup Finals at their ground between 2001 and 2006.

The 2001 FA Cup Final was thus the first to be held in Wales and the first to be held outside of Wembley (not including replays) since, in a quirk of fate, Herbert Chapman's Huddersfield Town had beaten Preston North End at Stamford Bridge in 1922 – almost eighty years earlier.

The attendance for this historic occasion on 12th May 2001 was 74,200 and they saw Swedish winger Freddie Ljungberg, who had signed for the club three years earlier, put Arsenal into the lead just 18 minutes from the end.

It looked as though Arsenal were heading for victory but two goals in five minutes from Liverpool and England striker Michael Owen – the second with just two minutes of the match left – gave Liverpool the victory.

For the team from Liverpool, it was third-time lucky and revenge which had been a long time coming after their FA Cup Final defeats to Arsenal in 1950 and 1971.

Programme Notes

Since being elected to the Football league at the same time in 1893, there have also been some key cup games between Arsenal and Liverpool:

1950: FA Cup Final (won)

1971: FA Cup Final (won)

1978: League Cup Semi-final (lost)

1980: FA Cup Semi-final (won)

1987: League Cup Final (won)

2001: FA Cup Final (lost)

Sol Campbell

Worried by the mauling central defender Igors Stepanovs had received at the hands of their fierce rivals from Manchester United; alarmed at how the team had caved in so late in the FA Cup Final against Liverpool and having to deal with the retirement of Tony Adams, Wenger did not need to look far for a possible solution in the centre of his defence.

After more than 300 appearances in nine seasons for Tottenham

Hotspur, 'Sol' Campbell appeared to publicly state a desire to 'actually win something' and play Champions League football in particular.

So, following the path forged by goalkeeper Pat Jennings almost 24 years earlier, he made the switch to Arsenal on 3rd July 2001 on a contract that made him the highest paid player in British football history at the time. Moreover, he had moved on a free transfer so Tottenham received no fee for one of their most prized assets.

This was allowed to happen due to what became known as the 'Bosman Ruling' of 1995. Remembering George Eastham's challenge to the retain and transfer system 35 years earlier, a Belgian footballer - Jean-Marc Bosman - had wanted to move to Dunkerque in France from Belgian club RFC Liège where his contract had expired and his wages had been reduced as he was no longer playing for the first team,

Dunkerque would not meet the transfer fee demanded by RFC Liège and so they refused to let the player leave. Bosman took his case to the European Court of Justice in Luxembourg, citing a restraint of his ability to practice his trade.

The Court ruled in December 1995 that this did amount to a restriction of freedom for workers within the European Union and in contravention of the European Community Treaty. As with the Eastham ruling in England, this decision affected football transfers across Europe.

In the light of this ruling six years earlier, Tottenham had previously offered Campbell a contract that would have made him the club's highest-paid player in their history and he had seemingly reaffirmed his allegiance to Tottenham, even allegedly stating that he would never play for Arsenal.

Like all players and managers before him who had made the journey in either direction down the Seven Sisters Road, it was a brave move that tested the character of the individuals involved. Given the background in this particular case, there were major protests, outbursts of loathing and taunts of 'Judas' that such a player should join Arsenal and supposedly because he felt their rivals had more chance of success.

He had been the rock at the heart of the Spurs defence and his leaving the club left it with a cavernous gap. Citing David Dein's influence once again, Campbell remarked:

"David Dein made me feel protected. He was going to help and promised to be there for me. Come to us, he said, and you will be part of our family. We will protect you."

After a stuttering start to their 2001-02 Premier League programme, Arsenal faced Real Mallorca of Spain in their first Champions League group match of the season on 11th September 2001. They lost 1.0 to a 12th-minute penalty but that date will be forever marked by devastating acts of terrorism in the USA.

Four attacks coordinated by the Islamic terrorist group Al-Qaeda took place on United States landmarks including the World Trade Center in New York and the US Defence HQ in Arlington, Virginia.

The events, known collectively as '9/11,' caused almost 3,000 deaths and more than 6,000 injuries and precipitated an international 'War on Terror' including military action in Iraq and Afghanistan that would colour much of the rest of the decade.

In the Premier League Arsenal lost at home to Newcastle United just before Christmas but then did not lose at home again in the league that season.

Moreover, they were unbeaten away for the whole of the season.

Their last away defeat in the Premier League had come on the last day of the 2000-01 season on 19th May 2001 in a 3.2 defeat at The Dell, then home to Southampton. Saints hero Matt Le Tissier scored a spectacular winner one minute from the end of what would be their final match at the ground before moving to St Mary's Stadium.

Programme Notes:

Arsenal were unbeaten away in the league for the whole of the 2001-02 season

However, Arsenal did not then lose a league match away until 19th October 2002 when a young Wayne Rooney – five days before his 17th birthday – became the Premier League's then youngest-ever scorer when he struck the winner for Everton at Goodison Park in the final minute to secure a 2.1 win. Arsenal had gone 23 away games without losing a match.

55

Consecutive matches in which Arsenal scored

Freddie Ljungberg had given Arsenal the lead after just eight minutes in that match and this was part of another record.

Since and including the Southampton game at the end of the 2000-01 season Arsenal would score in 55 consecutive matches – therefore including every league game of the 2001-02 campaign – in a sequence that only ended at Old Trafford on 7th December, 2002 when Juan Sebastián Verón and Paul Scholes scored for Manchester United and they finally managed to shut Arsenal out at the other end.

Arsenal won their final 13 Premier League games of the 2001-02 season and the first league game of 2002-03 - a 2.0 home win over Birmingham City - before drawing 2.2 away at West Ham United's Upton Park. The winning sequence was over after another record: 14 consecutive Premier League wins.

14

Consecutive Premier League wins for Arsenal

Although Manchester United would stop Arsenal's record-breaking scoring run the following season it was at Old Trafford in 2001-02 that Arsenal sealed the Premier League title after those three consecutive years of coming second to Manchester United (this time it was Liverpool who came second, seven points behind Arsenal).

A single second-half goal by Sylvain Wiltord on 8th May 2002 gave Arsenal a 1.0 victory before, in another piece of football symmetry from their last title-winning Double season of 1997-98 they put four goals past Everton in their final league game.

After the long-unbeaten and scoring records, Wenger first contemplated his team going an entire season unbeaten but he would have to wait a while longer. Another record was in his midst – a third Double of League and FA Cup wins.

Having beaten last season's victors Liverpool in the Fourth Round, previous FA Cup Final opponents Newcastle United in a Quarter-final replay and Middlesbrough in the Semi-final at Old Trafford, they faced London rivals Chelsea at the Millennium Stadium in the Final on 4th May, 2002 – four days before they would clinch the title back at Old Trafford.

Ray Parlour scored twenty minutes from the end and another goal ten minutes later from Ljungberg – in his second, consecutive Final – gave Arsenal a 2.0 win.

Ljungberg became the first player to score in consecutive Cup Finals since Bobbie Smith had done so for their great North London rivals, Tottenham Hotspur, in 1961 and 1962.

Smith had helped Tottenham to their first and only Double in 1960-61. 41 years later Arsenal secured their third and Wenger's second. Only their greatest rivals over the previous decade – Manchester United – have won the Double more than once, also sealing their third with their 1998-99 success after Arsenal had run them so close.

Three consecutive FA Cup Final appearances - again.

In August 2002 Wenger signed another Brazilian player – defensive midfielder Gilberto Silva - who was the son of a blacksmith and came from the same kind of poverty-stricken background as Humble and McLintock.

Silva had impressed at the 2002 World Cup in Japan and South Korea and would partner Patrick Vieira in midfield, replacing Emmanuel Petit who had also departed for Barcelona with Marc Overmars.

As we have seen, Arsenal's record-breaking unbeaten away and scoring sequences were both ended in the autumn of 2002 at Everton and Manchester United respectively and they would finish five points behind Manchester United in the league again (and runners-up to United for the fourth time in the previous five seasons). Arsenal's hopes of retaining their title ended on 4th March 2003 at Highbury in a match against their title-slayers from 1998-99: Leeds United.

The match finished 3.2 to Leeds who thus ensured their Premier League survival. Thierry Henry and Dennis Bergkamp (who had each scored their 100th goals for Arsenal in January 2003) scored for Arsenal but Mark Viduka won it for Leeds with a fine strike just one minute from the end.

Programme Notes

Some moments when Arsenal's path has crossed that of Leeds United:

1966: Lowest attendance at Highbury came in a league match against Leeds

1968: League Cup Final (Arsenal's first) (lost)

1972: FA Cup Final (lost)

1978: Highest League Cup victory came against Leeds

1999: Leeds ended Arsenal's Premier League hopes

2003: Leeds ended Arsenal's Premier League hopes

Arsenal got an element of revenge over Manchester United and ended any Double hopes they may have had in a Fifth Round FA Cup tie at Old Trafford on 15th February 2003 with a 2.0 win thanks to goals by Edu and Wiltord.

United manager Alex Ferguson is supposed to have been so annoyed with his side's performance that he kicked a boot at David Beckham's head in the dressing room after the match.

Arsenal then beat the previous year's FA Cup finalists Chelsea on 25th March 2003 at Stamford Bridge, in a replayed Quarter-final match, 3.1, with an own goal from John Terry and one each from Wiltord and Cameroonian defender Lauren (who was in his third season for the club).

2003

US, UK and other forces invaded Iraq, leading to the overthrow of dictator Saddam Hussein

Arsenal next faced the team they had beaten in the 1936 Final: Sheffield United.

The Semi-final was held at Old Trafford on 13th April 2003 and settled by a single goal from the cup hero of the previous two seasons Freddie Ljungberg, giving Arsenal a 1.0 victory and a third consecutive appearance in the FA Cup Final to match their record of 1978-80.

No other team in FA Cup history has ever appeared in three consecutive Finals in more than one sequence. Arsenal were the first team to achieve this in the twenty-first century as they had been in the twentieth.

The Final against Southampton at the Millennium Stadium on 17th May 2003 was another drab affair, played in poor weather conditions. Arsenal's performance wasn't much better than against Ipswich Town in 1978 but this time the score went in their favour, 1.0, with a first half winner from Robert Pires.

Although they had got so close yet again to another Double, more records were set in train that season:

After losing 2.0 at Blackburn Rovers on 15th March 2003 Arsenal would not lose again away in the Premier League for 27 matches beating their own club record of 23 away matches unbeaten from 2001-02.

After the home defeat by Leeds to Viduka's goal, they would go unbeaten in the Premier League for a record 49 games, including the whole of the 2003-04 season.

Another young central midfielder – Cesc Fabregas – joined the Arsenal Academy in September 2003 having been born in Barcelona and been part of their famous La Masia Academy as a youth.

He made his debut as Arsenal's youngest ever first-team player at 16 years and 177 days in a League Cup (now Carling Cup) Third Round tie against Rotherham United on 28th October 2003 at Highbury, in which Arsenal scraped through 9.8 on penalties after extra-time.

35 days later on 2nd December 2003 he became their youngest ever scorer in the next round of the League Cup – a competition Wenger has frequently used to give peripheral squad and youth players match experience.

The match again took place at Highbury with Wolverhampton Wanderers the visitors: Arsenal won much more easily – 5.1. Fabregas got his goal two minutes from the end.

The 'Invincibles'

No team since Preston North End in that first Football League season in the nineteenth Century had been undefeated throughout. Wenger clearly felt that he was building teams that would stand a good chance of achieving the accolade in the twenty-first century as, no doubt, did Alex Ferguson at Manchester United.

Moving Kolo Touré - a player who had arrived from the Ivory Coast two years previously – back to the centre of defence to partner Sol Campbell proved to be another masterstroke of Wenger's strategic thinking as Arsenal kicked off their 2003-04 Premier League season on 16th August 2003 with a 2.1 home win against Everton; Henry and Pires scoring their goals.

They concluded it on 15th May 2004 with another 2.1 win at Highbury, this time against Leicester City with Henry scoring again and Patrick Vieira completing the victory and the record of going unbeaten throughout the entire league season. Preston's record had been equalled after 115 years.

However, there were some key moments in the season when the record looked to be in jeopardy. At Old Trafford (where else?) on 21st September 2003 Arsenal probably came the closest to being beaten all season.

In a bruising encounter against Manchester United in which Patrick Vieira was sent off, players from both sides were subsequently fined by the FA for their behaviour at the end of the match, in a flashback to the fighting in the same fixture almost thirteen years earlier.

One minute from time – just as between the same sides in the FA Cup Semi-final replay of 1999 - the referee had awarded a penalty. This time it was to Manchester United and Arsenal's record hung by the width of their posts and crossbar.

German goalkeeper Jens Lehmann, aged 33, had joined Arsenal from Borussia Dortmund in July 2003 to replace David Seaman in goal. He undoubtedly brought intensity and outward aggression to the team and tried to put United striker Ruud van Nistelrooy off by persistently moving along his goal-line.

It seemed to work as van Nistelrooy's shot hit the crossbar and rebounded to safety. A melee of relieved Arsenal players, with Martin Keown to the fore, surrounded the Dutch striker as the game finished 0.0, taunting him after the match which became known as the 'Battle of Old Trafford.'

On Good Friday (9th April) 2004 Arsenal found themselves in worse trouble, being 2.1 down at half-time to similarly historic rivals, Liverpool. Thankfully for them and the record Henry added two goals to his first half strike to complete his hat-trick and Pires scored another as they ran out 4.2 winners.

Having lost in the Semi-final of the League Cup to Middlesbrough, it was Manchester United who ended Arsenal's Double hopes yet again, with a 1.0 win in the FA Cup Semi-final at Villa Park on 3rd April 2004; Paul Scholes scoring the only goal of the match.

Three days later London rivals Chelsea similarly knocked them out at the Quarter-final stage of the Champions League on aggregate after a 2.1 win at Highbury, and after Jose Antonio Reyes – who had arrived from Sevilla in Spain during that season's January transfer window - had put Arsenal into the lead right on half-time.

The defeat was not only galling for Arsenal fans in that they lost to their London rivals but that they were hoping for great things in Europe that season to match their domestic dominance.

On 25th November 2003, in a Champions League group match, they had pulled off one of their greatest ever European victories away from home in beating the mighty Internazionale in Milan's San Siro stadium 5.1. Three of Arsenal's goals came in the last five minutes of the match as Inter collapsed to their first ever home defeat to an English team.

25 November 2003

Arsenal beat Inter Milan at the San Siro: the first English club ever to do so

Arsenal picked themselves up and avoided three defeats in six days with their Good Friday Premier League win over Liverpool and did not lose again, clinching the title at Tottenham's White Hart Lane – just as they had done 33 years earlier – on 25th April 2004 with a 2.2 draw. Their goals came from Patrick Vieira and Robert Pires that day as the Frenchmen played their part in creating English football history.

In 2003-04, eleven years after winning both trophies, Arsenal had got to the Semi-finals of the FA Cup and League Cup; they got to the Quarter-finals of the Champions League and went through the season unbeaten in the league to win the Premier League title:

Played 38 Won 26 Lost 0

Another historic FA Cup win

Arsenal continued the 2004-05 season where they had left off in their 'Invincibles' year. They won their first five Premier League matches and equalled Nottingham Forest's 26-year old record of 42 games without defeat by beating Middlesbrough at Highbury on 22nd August 2004.

The unbeaten sequence ended in the second 'Battle of Manchester' on 24th October 2004 where Arsenal lost another tough encounter 2.0 to Manchester United.

This time Ruud van Nistelrooy did convert a hotly-disputed second-half penalty – won by Wayne Rooney - and Rooney himself added a second in the final minute.

After winning 1.0 at United's rivals Manchester City on 25th September 2004 via a goal from boyhood fan left-back Ashley Cole, the defeat at Old Trafford also marked the end of Arsenal's long unbeaten away run in the league after 27 matches.

Programme Notes:

Manchester United have ended some of Arsenal's key match sequences on three occasions:

22 matches unbeaten (1987)

55 consecutive matches in which they scored (2002)

49 matches unbeaten (including 27 away games in the league) (2004)

Arsenal did respond by beating Tottenham at White Hart Lane 5.4 on 13th November 2004 in the highest-scoring North London derby match in history.

Henry, Lauren, Vieira, Ljungberg and Pires scored one goal each for Arsenal and four separate players got the goals for Tottenham in what was the Premier League's first ever match that featured nine separate goal-scorers.

The title got away from Arsenal again and they took their frustration out on Everton who yet again appeared at Highbury at the end of the league season and were promptly thrashed 7.0 on 11th May 2005.

The goals came from Dutch striker Robin van Persie - in his first season after signing from Feyenoord of Rotterdam in the Netherlands – two from Pires and further goals from Vieira (his last league goal for the club), Edu, Bergkamp and combative midfielder Mathieu Flamini – also in his first season at Arsenal.

Flamini was in the hard man mould of Peter Storey and would leave three years later for Inter Milan before returning to the club for a second stint in 2013.

Manchester United also knocked Arsenal out of the League Cup that season with a 1.0 win in the Fifth Round but lost a third critical encounter in the FA Cup Final at the Millennium Stadium in Cardiff on 21st May 2005.

2005

Arsenal became the first team to win the FA Cup on penalties

The match finished 0.0 after extra-time – the first goalless draw in an FA Cup Final since 1912 – and went to penalties. Arsenal won 5.4 and became the first team to win the FA Cup on penalties, with Patrick Vieira scoring the winning goal with the last kick of the match and his last for Arsenal as he left for Juventus - just as Liam Brady had done after the 1980 Final.

Changes on and off the pitch

In June 2003, Russian businessman and billionaire Roman Abramovich had bought control of Chelsea Football Club, pouring money into the club and its infrastructure in a bid to challenge

Manchester United and Arsenal on the domestic stage and major football brands such as Real Madrid and Barcelona in Europe.

Chelsea had finished as runners-up to Arsenal's Invincibles and had now replaced their manager Claudio Ranieri with the Portuguese José Mourinho, who had just won the Champions League – much coveted by Abramovich – with Porto.

Along with the money from TV broadcasting, Abramovich paid off Chelsea's debts and poured money into the club, transforming them and seemingly brandishing an open cheque book with which Mourinho could buy the best players available.

This development alone introduced Chelsea as serious Premier League contenders and effectively broke the stranglehold of Arsenal and Manchester United, either one of whom had won the league title in each of the previous nine seasons.

In 2004-05 Mourinho's Chelsea made the breakthrough, winning the title, with Arsenal coming second – again – and Manchester United relegated to third place for the second season running. Arsenal now had serious competition from their old London rivals as well as from Manchester.

The Premier League itself was moving even further away from the Football League in terms of money flooding into the game after sponsorship deals with Carling, Barclaycard and Barclays.

The Football League sought their own sponsorship deals and money from broadcasters and reorganised themselves in 2004 such that the 2004-05 season was sponsored by Coca-Cola and the three leagues re-branded from First, Second and Third Division to Championship, League One and League Two respectively. However, the big money in football in England resided in the Premier League.

Harold Wilson had talked about the 'white heat' of technology in the late 1960s when he had been Prime Minister and it was continuing to change fans' behaviour, building on the personal computer boom first seen in the 1980s and underpinning the rise of the internet in the following decade.

The 2000s and 2010s saw the huge further expansion of Internet-based applications that had first come to prominence in the 1990s, with World Wide Web pages proliferating and mobile 'phone web applications coming to the fore.

Not only were people around the world better connected with parallel developments in faster broadband connections and WiFi 'hotspots' they were also able to communicate interactively through 'social media' networks such as Facebook, Twitter and LinkedIn which sat on this vast telecommunications infrastructure.

David Dein was acutely aware of both the huge commercial possibilities offered by global fan audiences, connected by the internet and international broadcast deals, as well as the restrictions imposed by Arsenal's Highbury ground.

Champions League matches at Wembley Stadium had attracted crowds well in excess of 70,000 – proving the potential of the local fanbase – and yielded receipts of around £1 million per match – hence Dein's initial interest in buying Wembley before the FA took it over and redeveloped it.

Given the huge new spending power now present at Stamford Bridge, as well as far greater gate receipts earned by Manchester United at the expanded and much larger Old Trafford, it was clear that something needed to be done to avoid Arsenal falling too far behind their major rivals.

Against much opposition from local residents and businesses and the same AISA supporters' group which had opposed the North Bank Bond Scheme more than ten years earlier, the club bought a parcel of land at Ashburton Grove in the Holloway district of

Islington where, after agreeing to pay huge sums to help regenerate the area outside of football, Islington Council approved the club's plans for a new 60,000 capacity stadium to be built.

Location was not the main concern, as it had been for Henry Norris in 1913, but the profitability of the club and its ability to compete was at the heart of the issue just as it had been then.

Though he could see the enormous benefit in moving from an ageing 38,000 capacity stadium to a modern, all-seater 60,000 new build, fit for purpose for twenty-first-century football, Dein was also concerned that Wenger would not have sufficient funds to buy players and be able to compete on the pitch in the meantime.

Huge profits from the sales of star players such as Anelka, Overmars and Petit helped to fund the new stadium development and the extra 22,000 fans would yield an extra £1 million pounds just in gate receipts for each home match; but that was only once everything was up and running.

How would their best players be replaced while so much of the club's funds available for investment would have to go into the Ashburton Grove project (the estimated budget for the whole stadium project was estimated at £390 million)? Chelsea and Manchester United would not stand still on the field while Arsenal tried to catch up off of it.

Each of Arsenal's league title wins under Wenger – in 1998, 2002 and 2004 had come after summers where no major international football tournament had taken place and it was no coincidence that so many of the Arsenal team's squad were international players performing on the world's stages and would thus be jaded and take time to adjust to the rigours of yet another English football season.

Dein worried that the squad was simply not big enough to compete in English and European campaigns and saw this as a reason why they had so far failed to win the biggest and richest European prize of all: the UEFA Champions League.

He was most concerned that the man he had done so much to bring to Arsenal - Arsène Wenger – needed money for players now and would leave the club if he felt he was growing too old to challenge for the trophy because of the lack of funds available for transfers.

Single-minded as ever, Dein later went on to seek funding from Stan Kroenke, proprietor of the Colorado Rapids soccer team in Denver, USA. Though Kroenke was positive – and subsequently would invest in Arsenal – the Arsenal Board did not favour Kroenke or the way Dein had handled negotiations directly, with the result that he left the club in 2007. Wenger, in particular, was shocked by his departure, stating that:

> *"It is a huge disappointment because we worked very closely together, David has contributed highly to the success of the club in the last 10 years and even before that as well. Red and white are the colours of his heart."*

So close to the pinnacle

In the late summer of 2005 Arsenal set off on another season which would be their last at Highbury. In commemoration of this, the team wore redcurrant shirts in each of their home games in the 2005-06 season just as they had done 120 years earlier when Royal Arsenal had worn those same coloured shirts donated to them by Nottingham Forest.

In another quirk of fate, Arsenal's first league match in their final season at this famous old stadium was against Newcastle United who had been their opponents in their very first league match as Woolwich Arsenal, just under 111 years earlier.

On that day in 1893, they had drawn 2.2 but two late goals on 14th August 2005 from Henry and van Persie secured a 2.0 victory.

Arsenal struggled in the Premier League losing 11 matches in total – their worst total since the ill-fated George Graham season of 1994-95 – and eventually finished fourth. Manchester United recovered to a runners-up position but, again, there was no stopping Chelsea who finished eight points ahead of United and scoring 91 goals to follow their record-breaking 95 of the previous season.

28 August 2005

Hurricane 'Katrina' made landfall in New Orleans, USA, causing the deaths of over 1,200 people and more than $108 billion in damages – one of the world's costliest natural disasters

Lancashire clubs did for Arsenal in both domestic cups. Bolton Wanderers beat them in the Fourth Round of the FA Cup at the Reebok Stadium while Wigan Athletic prevailed in the Semi-final of the League Cup.

Arsenal had beaten Liverpool at Anfield 6.3 on route to this stage of the competition - which was the first time Liverpool had conceded six goals at home in some 80 years – but had lost the first leg at Wigan's JJB Stadium 1.0 and, though they won 2.1 at Highbury two weeks later, with goals from Henry and then van Persie in extra-time, Jason Roberts' goal one minute from the end saw Wigan through to the Final on the away goals rule.

Given Dein's and others' worries over the squad's ability to compete in Europe whilst facing such a hectic domestic schedule, going out of both cups in the January probably helped their progress in the Champions League.

Having qualified from the Group stage which included matches against their old Dutch adversaries from 1970 and 1971 - Ajax of Amsterdam – they faced the daunting prospect of playing Real Madrid who had dominated the European Cup when it began, winning in each of its first five seasons, and who were winners of the Champions League as recently as 2002. To add to this, no English team had ever won at their Santiago Bernabeu stadium.

As so many times before, Arsenal changed the course of football history when, on 21st February 2006, a Thierry Henry goal just after half-time gave them a 1.0 victory in the first leg of their Round of 16 tie. This was Real's first home defeat in 18 Champions League matches stretching back to October 2002.

21 February 2006

Arsenal beat Real Madrid at their Santiago Bernabeu Stadium

A 0.0 draw back at Highbury meant they would play old Italian rivals Juventus in the Quarter-final. A 2.0 win at Highbury and another 0.0 draw in the second leg saw them face another Spanish side – Villarreal – in the Semi-final.

On 19th April 2006 Arsenal beat Villarreal 1.0 in the first leg with a goal by Kolo Touré just before half-time. This was the last ever goal to be scored under the floodlights at Highbury and was followed a week later by yet another 0.0 draw in the second leg at the Estadio El Madrigal in Spain.

Arsenal had made it through to the Champions League Final for the first time in their history, and the first club from London to do so.

The Final took place at the Stade De France in Paris on 17th May 2006. Arsenal's opponents were Barcelona. Like Arsenal, Barcelona went into the Final unbeaten in that season's competition but, unlike Arsenal, they had won the trophy once before, in 1992.

Arsenal goalkeeper Jens Lehmann was sent off early in the match but, just as Touré had done in the Semi-final, his central defensive partner Sol Campbell put the 10 men of Arsenal into the lead in the 37th minute.

They held on to that lead until just under a quarter of an hour from the end when Samuel Eto'o equalised before another defender – Brazilian Juliano Belletti (who later joined Chelsea) – scored the winner four minutes later.

A 2.1 defeat was no disgrace to an emerging Barcelona team who would go on to dominate this competition, beating Manchester United in the 2009 and 2011 Finals and Juventus in 2015 but it was not the conclusion that Arsenal were hoping for at the end of their time at Highbury.

Like English counterparts Leeds United 31 years earlier, Arsenal had lost in Paris in the Final of the ultimate European football club competition and would have to rebuild and start all over again.

Arsenal's final league game at Highbury had taken place ten days earlier on 7th May, 2006 when they had beaten League Cup conquerors Wigan Athletic 4.2 with goals by Pires and a hat-trick from Thierry Henry, who finished as the Premier League's top goalscorer for the third consecutive season, equalling Alan Shearer's record from 1994-97.

Programme Notes:

Thierry Henry scored Arsenal's last goal at Highbury

Henry's penalty in the 76th minute was the last league goal to be scored in the famous old stadium (in the 2010th Highbury match) and it was perhaps quite fitting that Thierry Henry should score it after effectively replacing Ian Wright who had scored the last goal in front of the stadium's old North Bank.

Not only that, the win secured Champions League qualification for the following season. Arsenal had to better the result of bitter rivals Tottenham to beat them to the fourth qualifying place. Tottenham eventually lost 2.1 at West Ham United after a supposed bout of food poisoning prior to their match.

On 26th July 2006 the famous clock was removed from Highbury's South Stand and moved to their new stadium where it faces the new 'Clock End Bridge.' A 25-ton crane and four people took nine hours to move and re-install it at its new home.

Still, there was much sadness on leaving Highbury given the nature of their arrival 93 years earlier and their bullish determination to overcome such opposition to their move – then as now. As old favourite Liam Brady put it:

> *"Leaving the stadium was heartbreaking, and it was therefore important to stay in Islington. We didn't change our home, just our house."*

The Emirates

The original – and official – name for the new ground was 'Ashburton Grove' but Emirates Airline agreed to pay an estimated £100 million for the stadium's 'naming rights' which would also go on to include shirt sponsorship.

This contract was subsequently renewed and extended in November 2012. The stadium is therefore often referred to as

'Emirates Stadium' or, more usually: 'The Emirates.'

Programme Notes:

Arsenal's Home Grounds:

1886: Plumstead Common

1887-88: Sportsman Ground

1888-90: Manor Ground

1890-93: Invicta Ground

1893-1913: Manor Ground

1913-2006: Highbury

(1998-2000 Wembley Stadium for Champions League matches)

2006 – Emirates Stadium

Fittingly, the first match to take place at the new stadium was a testimonial game for one of Arsenal's greatest players: the now retired Dennis Bergkamp. The Champions League Final defeat in Paris had marked his last game as a first-team player for Arsenal.

In this first match of a new era for the club on 22nd July 2006 an Arsenal team faced a team from Bergkamp's first and home club, Ajax.

Klaas-Jan Huntelaar scored the first-ever goal at the new stadium for the visitors before an Arsenal team containing other greats such as Ian Wright, Emmanuel Petit, Patrick Vieira and Marc Overmars rallied to win 2.1. Dutch and Ajax stars from the 1970s and 1980s Johan Cruyff and Marco van Basten came on for Ajax later in the game to provide a fitting tribute to the past and exciting, expectant introduction to the future.

If football royalty had been present at the first Emirates game, then the actual Royal Family also gave their seal of approval. Just as 74 years earlier, when the Prince of Wales had opened Highbury's West Stand, so Prince Philip, the Duke of Edinburgh, officially opened the new stadium, on 26th October 2006.

As in 1920 when that first international match had taken place at Highbury between England and Wales, the Emirates hosted 'friendly' internationals with the first taking place on 3rd September 2006: another local derby between Brazil and Argentina which Brazil won 3.0

Given the magnificent re-development of Highbury in the 1930s, it was perhaps appropriate that one of their great rivals from that era – Aston Villa – should be their opponents in their first competitive match at The Emirates. The Premier League match on 19th August 2006 ended in a 1.1 draw with Gilberto Silva rescuing a point for Arsenal just six minutes from the end.

Seven years of drought

Arsenal never finished outside of the top four in the Premier League in each of the following seven seasons but neither did they finish in the top two places either, unlike between 1998 and 2005 when they had never finished below second place.

Arsenal fans began to wonder more and more whether the golden years under Arsène Wenger had passed with the break-up of the Invincibles team and the European failure in Paris.

Certainly, Wenger favoured the development of youth and younger players such as Theo Walcott, who had arrived from Southampton, which he feared would be put in jeopardy by continually bringing in more experienced players.

There is no doubt also that The Emirates development cost Arsenal at least two to three seasons in terms of lack of money which might otherwise have been available for players in the various transfer windows.

Ashley Cole had left for Chelsea in part exchange for Frenchman William Gallas who had played his part in Chelsea's defence in their two title-winning campaigns.

The huge Togo striker Emmanuel Adebayor was another arrival from Monaco, while Thierry Henry left for Barcelona for an estimated £16 million at the end of the 2006-07 season.

Some people blamed the club's demise on having too many international players in their ranks and Arsenal did become the first club in European football history to field a team containing 11 different nationalities during the same Champions League game – a 2.1 win over Hamburg on 13th September 2006.

In short, though, Arsenal were nearly very successful but these years were relatively stagnant compared to what had gone before under Wenger. In 2006-07 they did get to another League Cup (Carling Cup) Final and yet again they beat Tottenham in the Semi-final.

The first leg took place on 24th January 2007 at White Hart Lane and Arsenal were two goals down at half-time, including an own goal by Julio Baptista. The Brazilian forward had arrived from Real Madrid just before the season began, with José Antonio Reyes heading back to Spain as part of the deal. Baptista made up for his error by scoring two goals in the second half as Arsenal secured a 2.2 draw.

In the second leg at The Emirates Arsenal won 3.1 after extra-time with an own goal from Tottenham this time, one from Adebayor and another from young French striker Jérémie Aliadière.

Arsenal faced Chelsea in a major Cup Final once more on 25th February 2007 and scored through Theo Walcott after just 12 minutes but an equaliser by Chelsea's Didier Drogba, eight minutes later, and then a second just six minutes from the end gave Chelsea a 2.1 win.

A stormy match including three red cards and seven yellows, which didn't end until the 103rd minute, such was the additional time added, it was also the last League Cup Final to take place in Cardiff with Wembley Stadium ready to host the FA Cup Final later that season – its first since 2000 – which Chelsea also won.

Over the next ten days, Arsenal's season collapsed with a 1.0 defeat at Blackburn Rovers in an FA Cup Fifth Round replay, and then an exit from the Champions League to PSV Eindhoven from the Netherlands after a 1.1 draw at home saw them knocked out 2.1 on aggregate.

It was a similar story the following season with Arsenal, incredibly, coming up against Tottenham in the Semi-final of the League Cup again.

The first leg took place at The Emirates and finished 1.1 thanks to a late equalising goal by Theo Walcott. However, with such a good record in Semi-finals against their neighbours, and Tottenham not having beaten them since November 1999, Arsenal must have been confident when heading to White Hart Lane for the second leg on 22nd January 2008.

It didn't work out that way with Tottenham winning 5.1, Adebayor scoring a late consolation goal for Arsenal.

In the Premier League Arsenal had gone on another 22-match unbeaten run which ended in a 2.1 defeat on 9th December 2007 at Middlesbrough; Arsenal's goal coming from Czech midfielder Tomáš Rosický who had joined in May 2006 from Borussia Dortmund.

Programme Notes:

Arsenal v Tottenham Hotspur in Cup Semi-finals:

1968: League Cup (won)

1987: League Cup (won)

1991: FA Cup (lost)

1993: FA Cup (won)

2001: FA Cup (won)

2007: League Cup (won)

2008: League Cup (lost)

They then went on another unbeaten league run of 14 matches and were definitely title contenders before losing a crucial game away at Chelsea (yet again!) on 23rd March 2008, 2.1. French right-back Bacary Sagna put Arsenal into the lead before Didier Drogba again scored two late goals to give Chelsea the win.

Just under a month earlier Arsenal's Brazilian-born Croatian striker Eduardo da Silva, who had joined from Dinamo Zagreb before the start of the season, had his leg broken in a rash tackle at Birmingham City's St Andrew's Ground on 23rd February 2008.

Wenger became increasingly outraged at what he thought were unfairly physical tactics by opponents to stop his young, free-flowing side.

After losing 4.0 at Old Trafford to Manchester United – who would once again become Premier League Champions that season – in the Fifth Round of the FA Cup, Arsenal did at least make history in Europe by becoming the first English team to beat AC Milan in their San Siro Stadium (just as when beating Internazionale there five years earlier).

The Champions League match on 4th March 2008 finished 2.0 to Arsenal with goals from Cesc Fabregas and Emmanuel Adebayor coming in the last six minutes of the match.

However, in the Quarter-final they went out to Liverpool. After a 1.1 draw at The Emirates, they lost the second leg at Anfield 4.2, Adebayor scoring one of Arsenal's goals and the other coming from French midfielder Abou Diaby who had arrived from Auxerre.

In 2007-08 a global financial crisis had thrown many of the world's markets into crisis and whole economies into recession. Initiated by a loans crisis in the housing market in the USA it was made worse by banks and other financial institutions taking on far too much risk – in a costly reminder of the 1930s.

As politicians and economists looked to make cuts and savings to deal with the crisis, in the equally high-risk world of football Manchester City Football Club was purchased in August 2008 by the Abu Dhabi United Group. As at Chelsea, the club's debts were paid off and money thrown at the club, nominally to pay enormous transfer fees for what were seen at the time as some of the best players in the world.

Arsène Wenger was hugely unimpressed by the development, just as he had been when Roman Abramovich had taken over at

Stamford Bridge.

Wenger was in many ways a purist football coach, trying to create a unique 'identity' for the way Arsenal played football. The very idea that enormous wealth should buy success more quickly than a well-coached, carefully constructed team was against his deepest principles. The reality, though, was that Arsenal were competing on an increasingly less level playing pitch.

Programme Notes:

Some Chelsea moments:

1907: First London derby

1928: First two teams to wear numbers on the backs of their shirts

1950: FA Cup Semi-final (won)

1952: FA Cup Semi-final (won)

1991: Arsenal's only league defeat of the 1990-91 season came at Stamford Bridge

1998: League Cup Semi-final (lost)

2002: FA Cup Final (won)

2004: Chelsea knocked Arsenal out of the Champions League in the Quarter-finals

2007: League Cup Final (lost)

2009: FA Cup Semi-final (lost)

2017: FA Cup Final (won)

On 13th September 2008, midfielder Jack Wilshire made his competitive debut in a 4.0 win at Ewood Park, home of Blackburn Rovers. A late substitute for Robin van Persie, he became Arsenal's youngest-ever league debutant at the age of just 16 years and 256 days, beating the previous record held by Fabregas. However, despite a promising future, the 2008-09 was very much more of the same for Arsenal.

They went out in the Fifth Round of the League Cup, 2.0 at Turf Moor, home of Blackburn's big rivals, Burnley, and old foes deprived them of further trophies – even in Europe.

Chelsea beat them 2.1 in the Semi-final of the FA Cup on 18th April 2009 at Wembley. Theo Walcott had again put Arsenal ahead early in the first half but Didier Drogba again scored a late second-half winner.

They struggled to fourth in the Premier League, eventually coming 18 points behind champions Manchester United. There were some exciting matches though including two 4.4 draws – at Tottenham on 29th October 2008 and at Liverpool on 21st April 2009.

The latter match was part of a sequence of five away league matches in which Arsenal scored three or more goals, ending with a 3.0 win at Portsmouth's Fratton Park on 2nd May 2009.

5

Consecutive away league victories in which Arsenal scored three or more goals

Incredibly the great 1930s Arsenal had achieved a similar sequence in the 1932-33 season, also ending with a win at Portsmouth – 3.1 on 3rd December 1932.

Arsenal had progressed well in the Champions League after beating AS Roma 7.6 on penalties in their Stadio Olimpico and then Villarreal again in the Quarter-final. Manchester United ended Arsenal's European ambitions, though, by winning the Semi-final first leg in Manchester 1.0, and then winning 3.1 at The Emirates on 5th May 2009.

Ironically, United produced a ruthless display of counter-attacking in Arsenal's own back yard and were 3.0 up before Robin van Persie scored a late penalty for the home side.

Arsenal had never before lost a Semi-final in European competition and Manchester United marched on to a final against Arsenal's 2006 victors, Barcelona, in an attempt to make history by becoming the first team to retain the Champions League trophy in the modern era, after their victory over Chelsea the previous season. They failed at the final hurdle, also in Rome, losing 2.0.

2009

Barack Obama became the 44th and first black president of the USA

The 2009-10 season started off well with a 6.1 win at Everton on 15th August 2009. Their goals that day came from Gallas, fellow centre-back Belgian Thomas Vermaelen who had arrived from Ajax, and young Brazilian midfielder Denilson. Denilson would be a regular in midfield until Jack Wilshire emerged in the first team the following season.

A 4.2 home win against Portsmouth and back-to-back wins against Celtic in the qualifying round of the Champions League gave Arsenal fans much hope but a 2.1 defeat at Manchester United including another Wayne Rooney goal stopped them in their tracks before Manchester City also beat them, 4.2, at their City of Manchester Stadium – now known through naming rights by another airline Etihad Airways as 'Etihad Stadium' or 'The Etihad.'

One of Arsenal's scorers at Old Trafford was former Russian Footballer of the Year Andrei Arshavin who had joined for a then record fee of £15 million.

£15 million

Amount Arsenal paid for Russian Andrei Arshavin

He had scored from fully thirty yards in that game and had also scored in the home leg against Celtic as well as all four goals in that previous season's draw at Liverpool. However, Arshavin could not help Arsenal to maintain a consistent league challenge as they finished in third place, eleven points behind champions Chelsea.

Programme Notes:

In October 2009 Arsène Wenger became Arsenal's longest-serving manager

In October 2009, Arsène Wenger glided past George Allison to become Arsenal's longest-serving manager but the stagnation at the club continued.

Manchester City beat Arsenal at The Etihad again - 3.0 in the League Cup Fifth Round – while Stoke City got some revenge for those successive Semi-final defeats in the early 1970s by beating them 3.1 in the Fourth Round of the FA Cup with Denilson scoring Arsenal's single goal.

Meanwhile, in the Champions League, Arsenal made it to the Quarter-final stage again before coming up against Spanish nemesis Barcelona again. After a 2.2 draw at The Emirates, they headed for the Nou Camp on 6th April 2010 where Danish striker Nicklas Bendtner – who had joined the club as a 16-year-old – scored first before the prolific Lionel Messi responded with four goals of his own.

18 December 2010

The 'Arab Spring' began with popular protests in Tunisia, leading to uprisings in Syria, Libya, Egypt and demonstrations across the Arab world

The 2010-11 season again started well with Arsenal unbeaten in their first seven matches in all competitions. However, things drifted away to leave them in fourth place, twelve points behind champions Manchester United and, perhaps more alarmingly, now also behind Manchester City who finished third.

United also put them out of the FA Cup in a Sixth Round match at Old Trafford: 2.0 again and including a goal from Wayne Rooney (again!). This match came on 12th March 2011, just four days after they had gone out of the Champions League to Barcelona at the Nou Camp again.

Arsenal had won the first leg of this Round of 16 tie at Highbury: 2.1 with goals from van Persie and Arshavin but Messi again scored in Spain – just two this time – although Bendtner - Arsenal's scorer there in the previous season - missed a golden opportunity to score for Arsenal at the end of the match to make the score 4.4 on aggregate, which would have put Arsenal through on the away goals rule.

Unlike Michael Thomas in 1989, there was to be no fairytale ending for Arsenal this time.

The gloom was temporarily lifted in the League Cup. They comprehensively beat Tottenham in the Third Round at White Hart Lane with a 4.1 win thanks to goals from Arshavin, two from

French attacking midfielder Samir Nasri, now in his third season with the club, and young striker Henri Lansbury who had been on the club's books since the age of eight.

They scored another four goals at Newcastle's St James's Park before dispatching their vanquishers from five seasons previously – Wigan Athletic – and then Ipswich Town in the Semi-finals to face Birmingham City in the Final at Wembley on 27th February 2011.

Birmingham City would be relegated from the Premier League that season but still they had enough on the day to hold off Arsenal, appearing in their first major Final since that defeat to Chelsea in the same competition four years earlier.

Arsenal's performance was again lacklustre. The match finished 2.1 to Birmingham with Robin van Persie scoring for Arsenal but even the nature of the winning goal rather summed up Arsenal's performance and reputation as the 'nearly men.'

A mix-up in the penalty area between regular Polish goalkeeper for the past two seasons, Wojciech Szczęsny, and French central defender Laurent Koscielny, who was playing in his first season at the club, led to Birmingham's Obafemi Martins taking advantage to score the winning goal.

A mini exodus of Arsenal players to Manchester began after this with Samir Nasri and French defender Gaël Clichy heading for Manchester City, to be followed later by Bacary Sagna.

Robin van Persie, now club captain after Cesc Fabregas had returned to Barcelona, would remain with Arsenal for one more season before leaving for Manchester United, upset over Arsenal's apparent lack of ambition in the transfer market.

Going somewhat against the Arsène Wenger grain they had bought established, experienced players such as the Spanish midfielder Mikel Arteta from Everton and giant German international central defender Per Mertesacker from Wenger's old rivals Werder Bremen.

Welsh midfielder Aaron Ramsey who had signed from Cardiff City three years earlier but then suffered a broken leg was also beginning to make an impact.

It wasn't a great season though. After the high expectation and then disappointment over losing the League Cup Final the previous season, even the most optimistic fan struggled to remain optimistic of success and, again, things just seemed to drift away from an inconsistent Arsenal team.

AC Milan got their revenge and knocked them out of the Champions League 4.3 on aggregate in the Round of 16; this after Arsenal had lost the first leg 4.0 at the San Siro and won the second leg 3.0 at The Emirates. Sunderland put them out of the FA Cup in the Fifth Round.

Manchester City knocked Arsenal out of the League Cup at The Emirates with a Sergio Aguero winner coming seven minutes from time.

Manchester United were rather more decisive, beating an under-strength Arsenal 8.2 at Old Trafford in the Premier League on 28th August 2011. Walcott and van Persie scored for a shell-shocked Arsenal while (naturally!) a Wayne Rooney hat-trick featured in United's goals.

This wasn't just a huge defeat to Arsenal – in so many ways even worse than the 6.1 drubbing in 2001 – it represented the domination of both Manchester clubs that season. Arsenal would scramble to third place but a full 19 points behind both clubs who were tied on 89 points with City becoming Champions on goal difference.

It was almost 60 years since Arsenal had won the title from Preston on goal average but that measure of success must have seemed even longer ago in the summer of 2012.

Another French striker arrived from the South of France in June 2012 - Olivier Giroud – and, later that summer, Spanish midfielder Santi Cazorla joined from Málaga.

As usual, things looked promising as Wenger stuck to his passing, footballing instincts. After beating Coventry City in the League Cup (now the Capital One Cup) at the Emirates they beat Reading on 30th October 2012 in an astonishing 7.5 victory at their Madejski Stadium in the next round.

12

Goals in a League Cup match for the first time

This was the first time that twelve goals had ever been scored in a League Cup match.

Unfortunately, Arsenal tiptoed out of the competition in the next round at League Two Bradford City 3.2 on penalties, after a 1.1 draw in which Vermaelen had equalised with just two minutes of normal time remaining.

They were going well in the FA Cup until Blackburn Rovers beat them 1.0 in North London in the Fifth Round. Similarly, in the Champions League, they got to the Round of 16 again when they went out to Bayern Munich from Germany.

The damage was done at Highbury when Bayern won 3.1. Ironically Arsenal's goal was scored by Lukas Podolski, a German striker playing in his first season for Arsenal and who had previously played for Munich.

In yet another incredible performance away from home in Europe on 13th March 2013, Arsenal won the second leg in the Allianz Arena 2.0 with goals from Giroud and Koscielny but still went out on the away goals rule after scoring just two away goals to the Germans' three.

Programme Notes

Arsenal were the first English team to beat Bayern Munich in the Allianz Arena

Arsenal did though become the first English club to win in the Allianz Arena and the first English club to beat Bayern at home since Norwich City won at their old Olympic Stadium in the UEFA Cup almost twenty years earlier.

In the Premier League Arsenal went backwards, eventually finishing fourth – 16 points behind champions Manchester United and with more recent rivals Manchester City and Chelsea also ahead of them.

Arsenal did though set in train another record of 12 consecutive away wins in all competitions by a club in English football's top tier. After Per Mertesacker scored in a 2.1 loss at Tottenham on 3rd March 2013 they then won in Munich and every subsequent away game until a 1.1 draw on 6th October 2014 at West Bromwich Albion halted the sequence.

Two more FA Cups

On 17th August 2013 Arsenal opened their 2013-14 Premier League campaign with a 3.1 loss at home to Aston Villa again after Giroud had scored after just six minutes of the season.

Either forced by bitter fan reaction to that defeat, funds required for Emirates development lessening or Arsène Wenger himself recognising that a ninth consecutive season without a trophy – whether with a young, free-flowing team or not – would be unacceptable, he went into the market with serious intent and serious funds toward the end of the transfer window.

The result was the purchase of German international midfielder Mesut Özil from Real Madrid. The fee was estimated at £42.5 million, making him not only Arsenal's record signing but also the most expensive German footballer of all time.

£42.5 million

Mesut Özil became the most expensive German player of all time when signing for Arsenal

If it signalled a new approach or just a statement of Arsenal's real intent to win things again it would take time to work in the league.

Manchester City won the Premier League title again while Arsenal could only reach fourth place. After Alex Ferguson's retirement, Manchester United struggled to seventh place while a resurgent Liverpool were runners-up.

Liverpool beat Arsenal at Anfield 5.1 in the Premier League and Manchester City scored six against them in a 6.3 victory at the Etihad giving rise to a general criticism of Arsenal that they now rarely succeeded away at their biggest rivals.

On 21st August 2005 Arsenal had played their 500th match with Arsène Wenger as their manager, losing at Chelsea 1.0.

On 22nd March 2014 came Wenger's 1000th match in charge – incredibly, away at Chelsea again. This time they lost 6.0 and those two statistics probably best sum up how great the difference between the two London clubs had become.

500, 1000

In both his 500th and 1000th matches as Arsenal manager, Arsène Wenger's teams faced Chelsea – and lost both times.

Arsenal became the first English team to win in Borussia Dortmund's Westfalenstadion with a 1.0 win on 6th November 2013, courtesy of an Aaron Ramsey strike, but they went out in the Round of 16 to fellow Germans Bayern Munich once again.

Arsenal did though get to another FA Cup Final. Having beaten Tottenham 2.0 at the Emirates in the Third Round on 4th January 2014 with goals from Cazorla and Rosicky they cruised past Coventry City, both Merseyside clubs and then Wigan on penalties in the Semi-final to face unfancied Hull City at Wembley on 17th May 2014.

Hull may have been underdogs but they shocked Arsenal by going two goals ahead in the first eight minutes before Arsenal rallied through Cazorla and Koscielny, after which an Aaron Ramsey winner in extra-time gave them a 3.2 victory.

Finally: the trophy drought had been broken.

2014

Russia annexed the Crimea region of Ukraine after a military invasion

The following season Arsenal went all the way to Wembley again. This time they had managed to get past Manchester United in the

Sixth Round with a 2.1 win thanks to goals from new Spanish defender, Nacho Monreal, and striker Danny Welbeck who they had signed from United.

Former Dutch national manager Louis Van Gaal, now in charge at Old Trafford, had deemed Welbeck to not be up to the standard required of the Red Devils. Wayne Rooney, of course, scored for United.

After that result, they got past Reading in the Semi-final after extra-time with two goals from Chilean striker Alexis Sanchez, who had joined just before the 2014-15 season began after shining in the 2014 World Cup in Brazil.

They faced Aston Villa for the eleventh time in the FA Cup but the first time in the Final which took place at Wembley on 30th May 2015. This time the result was far more emphatic with Arsenal winning 4.0 through goals by Walcott, Mertesacker, Giroud and Sanchez.

Curiously, after losing to Arsenal in the 2014 Final, Hull City were relegated to the Championship the following season; similarly, their beaten opponents in 2015 – Aston Villa – were also relegated to the Championship the following season.

After successful spells at Inter Milan in Italy and then Real Madrid in Spain, José Mourinho had returned to Chelsea and managed them to the Premier League title once again while Manchester City were runners-up and Arsenal third, twelve points adrift of the champions.

Wenger also saw his 'new' team knocked out by his 'old' team – AS Monaco – in the Round of 16 of the Champions League once again. Frustratingly they won 2.0 in Monaco in the second leg on 17th March 2015 with goals from Giroud and Ramsey but had already lost the first leg 3.1 at home and so, once more, went out on the away goals rule.

Unlike in 1980 and 2005, Arsenal were unable to make it a third sequence of three consecutive FA Cup Finals in 2016. They did make it to the Quarter-final stage but lost at home 2.1 to Watford with Danny Welbeck scoring two minutes from the end, but it wasn't enough. They didn't have enough to get past the Round of 16 in the Champions League either, eventually losing to Barcelona again, 5.1 on aggregate.

In the Premier League, one of the most exciting campaigns in recent football history saw Leicester City crowned champions after narrowly avoiding relegation in their previous season.

The real battle for Arsenal was, again, for Champions League qualification and this time their main competitors were Tottenham Hotspur who were in the title race until a late defeat at Chelsea ended their chances.

Both league matches between Arsenal and Tottenham ended in draws, though Arsenal did knock Tottenham out of the League Cup again at White Hart Lane in the Third Round before succumbing to Sheffield Wednesday at Hillsborough 3.0 in the next.

Arsenal looked very strong in the league around the turn of the year and did eventually finish as runners-up for the first time since 2005, but fell away just as Leicester City – and indeed Tottenham – were finding consistency.

It was another season of what might have been and the disappointment of knowing that their recent FA Cup victories had not been the springboard to either Premier League or Champions League success.

23 June 2016

The British people voted to leave the European Union

As the British people voted on 23rd June 2016 to leave the European Union which they had been a key part of and helped to build and develop over the previous 43 years, and the England national football team were dumped out of Europe's EURO 2016 by Iceland four days later, questions over Europe's future and the likely effects on English professional football raged.

For all his early domestic success, Arsène Wenger's lack of achievement with Arsenal on the wider, European and international stages was bringing him almost continual criticism from some elements of the Arsenal fanbase.

Arsenal had been runners-up in the Premier League twice in the previous 12 seasons and many fans, critics and football observers cited the lack of a real and sustained challenge for the League Title itself as evidence that new managerial and coaching blood was now required.

Backwards and forwards

Arsenal's new Premier League campaign could hardly have got off to a worse start. On 14th August 2016, they faced Liverpool at the Emirates and, having got themselves in front through a Theo Walcott goal after half-an-hour, found themselves 3.1 down before eventually losing 4.3.

However, Arsenal then went unbeaten in the Premier League until, 15 matches later, they lost, 2.1, at Everton on 13th December 2016. Arsenal had also been knocked out of the League Cup (now the EFL Cup) by then – 59,000 fans saw them again lose at The

Emirates, this time, 2.0 to Southampton on 30th November 2016.

After the Everton defeat, Arsenal lost their very next match - also in the North West – to Manchester City and also, 2.1. After recovering over the Christmas period the team struggled to an uncharacteristic five league defeats during the spring before facing derby rivals Tottenham Hotspur on 30th April 2017.

30 April 2017

Arsenal lost the final North London derby at White Hart Lane, 2.0

Second-half goals from Dele Alli and a penalty from Harry Kane ensured that Spurs would win the last North London derby game between the two clubs at White Hart Lane before they moved out for building work to be completed on a brand new stadium next door.

A week later, Arsenal faced Manchester United at the Emirates. It was the first time in almost exactly 40 years that the two sides had faced each other in a top flight league match when both had been outside of the top four places. In the event, two second-half goals in quick succession from Swiss midfielder, Granit Xhaka – who had been signed from Borussia Mönchengladbach for a fee thought to be in excess of £30 million – and United old boy, Danny Welbeck gave Arsenal a 2.0 win.

The result also ended an unbeaten run of 25 Premier League matches by United (they hadn't lost since a 4.0 drubbing across London at Chelsea's Stamford Bridge on 23rd October 2016) in a reverse of those occasions in 1987, 2002 and 2004 when it had been United ending Arsenal's long unbeaten sequences.

In spite of Arsenal winning this and their four remaining Premier League matches, the result against Spurs meant that Tottenham would finish above Arsenal in the league for the first time since 1995, going on to be runners-up to Chelsea.

If this was hard to take for loyal Arsenal fans, the club eventually finished fifth in the Premier League - outside of the top four places in the Premier League for the first time since 1996 – and failed to qualify for the UEFA Champions League. They qualified for the group stages of the UEFA Europa League instead; seen as very much a secondary competition, this only served to intensify the pressure on Arsène Wenger and calls for change.

Arsenal had made it through to the knockout stage of that season's tournament but failed at the Round of 16 stage yet again. On 15th February 2017, they faced the German might of Bayern Munich (just as they had at this stage in 2013 and 2014) once more at the Allianz Arena. Alexis Sanchez cancelled out an early Bayern goal to make the score 1.1 at half-time. Bayern then scored four second-half goals after Laurent Koscielny, who was captaining the Arsenal side, went off injured and his team promptly collapsed to a 5.1 defeat.

In the return leg on 7th March 2017, Theo Walcott again put Arsenal ahead before Laurent Koscielny went off again (this time sent off) – and Arsenal capitulated again, losing by the same scoreline as the first leg – 1.5 – and crashing out on aggregate 10.2.

Arsenal did have some success – once again in the FA Cup where they won the trophy for the third time in four seasons. Arsenal had faced Manchester City in the Semi-final at Wembley on 23rd April 2017 and were trailing to a Sergio Aguero goal before Spanish defender, Nacho Monreal, equalized for the Gunners just nineteen minutes from the end.

In extra-time – during which City's Kelechi Iheanacho became the first-ever fourth substitute to be introduced in a senior English club match – Arsenal went ahead through Sanchez to complete their comeback, holding on for a 2.1 victory and, unlike 110 years earlier, progressing to the Final itself.

That Final took place on 27th May 2017 and was the 136th to be contested, though only the sixth to be competed for by two London clubs - in a repeat of the 2002 Final. Sanchez put Arsenal ahead after just five minutes; a lead they held until Diego Costa equalized for the new League Champions just a quarter-of-an-hour from the end.

27 May 2017

Arsenal won the FA Cup for a record 13th time

Aaron Ramsey was the Arsenal hero – just as he had been in the FA Cup Final three years earlier – with a second Arsenal goal just three minutes later. Arsenal then held on to win the trophy for a record 13th time and make Arsène Wenger the most successful manager in the competition's history with seven wins.

Where next?

After 131 years of football history, it is easy to see how Arsenal have been one of England's most pioneering football clubs, just as those working men in the Dial Square foundry would have insisted upon.

Theirs is a rich history in terms of football records and success on the pitch though it has often been a double-edged sword off of it.

Struggles for financial survival which have been the downfall of so many other clubs that were formed back in the Victorian Age have finally given way to huge global riches - against a background of human conflict, hardship and disaster.

And yet, despite the creation of some of the finest teams in English football history, they have, as yet, been unable to match on the European stage the football success enjoyed by some of their nearest rivals.

Arsenal have grown relentlessly and irresistibly to become one of the world's foremost football brands and yet, in spite of qualifying for the Champions League in 19 consecutive seasons and not forgetting some astonishing, historic wins away from home, they remain some way behind the likes of international clubs such as Real Madrid, Barcelona and Bayern Munich.

Discipline and controversy have never been distant cousins of Arsenal football club – even in the Modern Era. In the seven years between 1996 and 2003, over 50 red cards were shown to Arsenal players. Injuries – especially to key midfield players – also seem to have recurred on an uncannily regular basis and undermined the kind of squad required to take on European as well as English competition.

After 21 years at the helm of this club that was quintessentially English but always with a strong Scottish seam running through it, the Frenchman, Arsène Wenger, still has to prove whether, despite being loaded towards the start of his reign (though none of his Arsenal teams has ever finished outside of the Top 5 in the Premier League), his undoubted domestic football successes will be matched by international success that can then be sustained.

Whether or not that does happen, it is still a far cry from those days in Kent - the Garden of England - when Arsenal's poverty-stricken founding fathers could be beaten up on the suspicion of being French spies.

The End

Follow the latest Arsenal news and opinion every day by visiting our Arsenal club page on The Football Ground website:

http://www.thefootballground.com/clubs/uk-ireland/england/arsenal-football-club

HONOURS TIMELINE

1886

Club formed as Dial Square

1893-94

First season in Football League, Second Division

1903-94

Promoted from Second Division as runners-up

1905-06

Losing FA Cup Semi-finalists

1906-07

Losing FA Cup Semi-finalists

1912-13

Relegated back to Second Division

Move to Highbury

1919-20

'Promoted' to First Division

1925-26

Runners-up in First Division

1926-27

Losing FA Cup finalists

1927-28

Losing FA Cup Semi-finalists

1929-30

Won FA Cup

1930-31

Won First Division title

1931-32

Runners-up in First Division

Losing FA Cup finalists

1932-33

Won First Division title

1933-34

Won First Division title

1934-35

Won First Division title

1935-36

Won FA Cup

1937-38

Won First Division title

1947-48

Won First Division title

1949-50

Won FA Cup

1951-52

Losing FA Cup finalists

1952-53

Won First Division title

1967-68

Losing League Cup finalists

1968-69

Losing League Cup finalists

1969-70

Won European Inter-Cities Fairs Cup

1970-71

Won First Division title

Won FA Cup

(First Double)

1971-72

Losing FA Cup finalists

1972-73

Runners-up in First Division

Losing FA Cup Semi-finalists

1977-78

Losing FA Cup finalists

Losing League Cup Semi-finalists

1978-79

Won FA Cup

1979-80

Losing FA Cup finalists

Losing European Cup Winners' Cup finalists

1982-83

Losing FA Cup Semi-finalists

Losing League Cup Semi-finalists

1986-87

Won League Cup

1987-88

Losing League Cup finalists

1988-89

Won First Division title

1990-91

Won First Division title

Losing FA Cup Semi-finalists

1992-93

Won FA Cup

Won League Cup

1993-94

Won European Cup Winners' Cup

1994-95

Losing European Cup Winners' Cup finalists

Losing European Super Cup finalists

1997-98

Won Premier League title

Won FA Cup

(Second Double)

Losing League Cup Semi-finalists

1998-99

Runners-up in Premier League

Losing FA Cup Semi-finalists

1999-2000

Runners-up in Premier League

Losing UEFA Cup finalists

2000-01

Runners-up in Premier League

Losing FA Cup finalists

2001-02

Won Premier League title

Won FA Cup

(Third Double)

2002-03

Runners-up in Premier League

Won FA Cup

2003-04

Won Premier League

(Invincibles)

Losing FA Cup Semi-finalists

Losing League Cup Semi-finalists

2004-05

Runners-up in Premier League

Won FA Cup

2005-06

Losing League Cup Semi-finalists

Losing Champions League finalists

2006-07

Losing League Cup finalists

2007-08

Losing League Cup Semi-finalists

2008-09

Losing FA Cup Semi-finalists

Losing Champions League Semi-finalists

2010-11

Losing League Cup finalists

2013-14

Won FA Cup

2014-15

Won FA Cup

2015-16

Runners-up in Premier League

2016-17

Won FA Cup

Keep up-to-date with Arsenal's successes by visiting our Arsenal Honours page on The Football Ground's website:

http://www.thefootballground.com/clubs/uk-ireland/england/arsenal-football-club/arsenal-honours

BIBLIOGRAPHY

Books

The Rivals Game, Douglas Beattie, Know The Score Books, 2011

Football Fables, Iain Macintosh, A & C Black, 2008.

Football Oddities, Tony Matthews, The History Press, 2005

Rebels for the Cause, Jon Spurling, Mainstream Publishing Company, 2004

Arsènal: The making of a modern superclub, Alex Fynn & Kevin Whitcher, Vision Sports Publishing, 2011.

Fever Pitch, Nick Hornby, Indigo, 1996

Stillness and Speed, Dennis Bergkamp with David Winner, Simon & Schuster, 2013

Arsène Wenger, Xavier Rivoire, Aurum Press, 2008

Thierry Henry: Lonely at the Top, Philippe Auclair, Pan Books,

2013

Football Club Origins and Nicknames, Michael Heatley, Ian Allan Publishing, 2008

A History of Football in 100 Objects, Gavin Mortimer, Serpent's Tail, 2012

Arsenal On This Day, Paul Donnelley, Pitch Publishing, 2009

Red Letter Days: Fourteen dramatic events that shook Arsenal, Jon Spurling, Pitch Publishing, 2014

Invincible, Amy Lawrence, Penguin, 2015

Highbury: The story of Arsenal in N5, Jon Spurling, Orion, 2006

The Life & Times of Herbert Chapman, Patrick Barclay, Weidenfeld & Nicolson, 2014

The Real Arsenal, Brian Glanville, JR Books, 2009

Woolwich Arsenal FC: 1893-1915, Tony Attwood, Andy Kelly and Mark Andrews, Hamilton House, 2012

Newsbrands

Numerous national and international sources including, in particular, *The Islington Gazette, London Star and North London Press.* These were sourced in the main from cuttings collections at The Islington Local History Centre.

Web

Numerous online sources including:

The official website of *Arsenal Football Club* at
www.arsenal.com/history

The History of Arsenal at
http://www.blog.woolwicharsenal.co.uk/

11v11 at http://www.11v11.com/teams/arsenal/

ABOUT THE AUTHOR

Mark Rasdall is a writer and football historian with a background in content production and online search. He is an Associate of the Chartered Institute of Library and Information Professionals, and a Member of both the Historical Society and the Association of Football Statisticians.

He has been obsessed with football since watching England win the 1966 World Cup on the family's black and white television with his father and grandfather who generally didn't 'get on' and for whom only football was a shared and happy experience.

As a child he learned a lot about Geography, Mathematics and History just from following football: Geography because he wanted to know where clubs like Newport County or Port Vale were located as they didn't appear to be on the coast of Great Britain; Maths through hours spent in calculating goal average and working out prospective points totals from games remaining, and History because he always wanted to know where people and places had come from.

To this end, he has set up a company called The Football Ground, a wholly-owned subsidiary of Burwell Web Communications, which specialises in creating and curating football content. He hopes to help children and young adults who love football to learn so much more from it, as he once did.

This is a Burwell Web Communications production.

www.burweb.co.uk

Forthcoming books in the *First Football Histories* series:

The Chelsea Story

The Tottenham Hotspur Story

Please join our mailing list for news on our latest book releases at http://www.thefootballground.com/books/mailing

Thank you for your time in reading this book

If you enjoyed it, please leave feedback on amazon.

You can also contact us directly on info@thefootballground.com

Follow us on Facebook for our latest developments and productions in the field of football history:

http://www.facebook.com/Thefootballground

Printed in Great Britain
by Amazon

16692540R00214